KILLING FOR LIFE

The

Apocalyptic

Narrative

of

Pro-Life

Politics

CAROL MASON

Cornell University Press

Ithaca and London

First published 2002 by Cornell University Press
First printing, Cornell Paperbacks, 2002

Printed in the United States of America

Library of Congress Cataloging-in-Publication Data

Mason, Carol, 1964-
   Killing for life : the apocalyptic narrative of pro-life politics / Carol Mason.
      p. cm.
Includes bibliographical references and index.
   ISBN 0-8014-3920-5 (cloth : alk. paper)—ISBN 0-8014-8819-2 (pbk.: alk. paper)
   1. Pro-life movement —United States. 2. Radicalism—United States. 3. Political violence—United States. 4. Millenialism—United States. I. Title.
   HQ767.5.U5 M365 2002
   363.46'0973—dc21

                                    2002005744

Cornell University Press strives to use environmentally responsible suppliers and materials to the fullest extent possible in the publishing of its books. Such materials include vegetable-based, low-VOC inks and acid-free papers that are recycled, totally chlorine-free, or partly composed of nonwood fibers. For further information, visit our website at www.cornellpress.cornell.edu.

Cloth printing   10 9 8 7 6 5 4 3 2 1
Paperback printing   10 9 8 7 6 5 4 3 2 1

Contents

Acknowledgments

I began pondering the intellectual problem of killing for life while at the University of Minnesota, where my work on narrative was supported by a Shevlin Fellowship. Stephanie Athey, Polly Carl, Maria Damon, Kurt Gegenhuber, Betty Joseph, Maureen Konkle, John Mowitt, Roberta Poletes, Paula Rabinowitz, David Roediger, Marty Roth, and Steve Waksman helped solidify my inquiry by reading and arguing with me.

Later, with the support of a Frieda L. Miller Fellowship from the Bunting Institute at Radcliffe College, I conducted archival research and presented ideas at Harvard University, Political Research Associates, Hampshire College, and the Center for Millennial Studies at Boston University. I thank Jean Hardisty, Marlene Gerber Fried, and the Bunting fellows for their influence and support. In particular I owe terrific debts of gratitude to Chip Berlet for his generosity, expertise, and encouragement, to Lee Quinby for her enormous support, and to Sally Bermanzohn for her camaraderie and feedback. The Radcliffe Research Partnership Program allowed me to work with Jacqueline Soohen, whose aid and lasting insights were indispensable.

Most of this book was revised in Geneva, New York, where Leslie Horowitz, Richard Salter, Elizabeth Stark, Virginia Tilley, and Sherrie Tucker helped me debate particular issues and develop an appropriate voice. My editor at Cornell University Press, Catherine Rice, also was instrumental in this process. Student assistants Peter Starr and Gillian Dineen helped to secure permissions; Ben Chan and Matthew Gosney also provided important sources and insights. Christine Marie Rolland de Denus provided computer help, bibliographic assistance, and high adventure throughout the Finger Lakes region when work got to be too much. Susan Henking, Eric Patterson, and the department of English at Hobart and William Smith Colleges were enormously supportive of this project. My sister and my mom too provided moral support, often when I least expected and most needed it. I thank them all.

Earlier versions of some chapters have appeared in journals and edited volumes. I thank the editors and publishers for allowing me to reprint material and ideas from the following: "From Protest to Retribution: The Guerrilla Politics of Pro-Life Violence," *New Political Science* 22, 1 (2000):

11–29, reprinted in *Violence and Politics: Globalization's Paradox*, ed. S. Bermanzohn, K. Worcester, and M. Unger (New York: Routledge, 2001), 127–45; "Minority Unborn," in *Fetal Subjects, Feminist Positions*, ed. Lynn Morgan and Meredith Michaels (Philadelphia: University of Pennsylvania Press, 1999), 159–74; and "Cracked Babies and the Partial Birth of a Nation: Millennialism and Fetal Citizenship," *Cultural Studies* 14, 1 (2000): 35–60. I am especially grateful to *Cultural Studies* editor Cindy Patton for her review.

Listening intently to those who champion the unborn is always educational. I have learned much from Philip Benham and countless other "prolifers" during protests, church meetings, and rallies across America. I have also benefited from connecting with people who do not share my political views but care about clarity and integrity in writing. The Emerging Writers Group of Brooklyn, especially David and Cheryl Pace, were thoughtful readers of my more experimental writings on abortion politics. I thank them all for sharing their stories and their prayers.

Working with those who devote their professional or activist lives to securing reproductive freedom is educational and inspiring. I thank Ann Bower, Vicki Breitbart, Rosemary Candelario, Elizabeth Dickinson, Marylou Greenberg, Miranda Kennedy, Lynn Paltrow, Vivian Saldana, Alexander Sanger, Tracie Stein, Debra Sweet, Erika Tullberg, and Peter Wilderotter for their challenges to my perspective or approach and for their devotion to the cause.

I dedicate this book to the memory of clinic workers Leanne Nichols and Shannon Lowney, whose murders made a scholar stop and think about her responsibility as a researcher and writer.

Killing for Life

Introduction

The Productive Power of Apocalyptic Narrative

In an exposé titled *Soldiers in the Army of God*, men discuss the future of America, hoping for a revelation that can lead to the end of pro-life violence as well as to the end of abortion. One says passionately, "If the American people woke up and realized that they had to choose between legalized abortion and legalized homosexuality and legalized all-the-rest-of-the-desecration—or civil war that could cause the rivers to run red with blood, hey, you know what? We'll see legalized abortion go like that." He snaps his fingers. "We'll see legalized homosexuality go like that." Another snap. "Because American people are not willing to die for homosexuals. They're not willing to die to keep their babies slaughtered." In awe, a second man breaks in to say, "Whoa. You just did it. You just showed what's going on here, the dynamic here, Neal, so clear."[1]

For those who are not engaged by current pro-life discussions, how-ever, Neal Horsley's speech likely is clear as mud. What does homosexual-ity have to do with abortion? When did pro-lifers start talking about civil war instead of civil disobedience? And rivers running red with blood? Is this a fantasy or a fear?

Chances are, even if we are not members of the most "violent wing of the anti-abortion movement," this last element of Horsley's exuber-ance may be familiar.[2] Rivers running red with blood and other crimson tides are a kind of apocalyptic imagery that is as old as the Bible and as current as any blockbuster now playing in a theater near you. Horsley's speech is essentially apocalyptic not because it evokes doomsday visions but because it expects revelation. Apocalypse means revelation, and Horsley anticipates just that in terms of America's waking up. As sol-diers in the Army of God, Horsley and his cohort not only await that revelation but seek to spur it on, to reveal what they consider to be the horrors, the evil, and the truth of abortion. Understanding how abor-tion came to epitomize horror, evil, and truth involves recognizing that some pro-life writings since the 1960s narrate the fight for life as Amer-ica's Armageddon.

Anti-abortion letters, manuals, and mission statements written by Catholics and Protestants alike, by individuals defending the unborn by vi-olent insurrection and through institutions respected as moderate lobby-ing organizations that defend a right to life by legal means—all kinds of pro-life writing since the 1960s—indicate an increase in apocalypticism. In such writings, abortion is an apocalypse, a revelation of just how immoral America has become. It represents, even more than slavery in the United States or genocide in Nazi Germany, the ultimate of human atrocities and signals the end of humane society. For people such as Horsley and for many others who might listen to him and call him crazy, we are living in a fatalistic era, and abortion is a sign of the end times of our national hu-manity, if not of mortal life itself. This apocalyptic narrative is what gives ideological coherence to the vast variety of individuals and institutions that describe themselves as pro-life.[3]

As the abortion debate became the abortion wars that have resulted in the brutal murders of doctors and clinic employees, people began to ques-tion the term *pro-life*. Pro-choice groups suggested that lethal protest of abortion was the epitome of anti-abortion hypocrisy. "Pro-life, your name's a lie," they chanted, "you don't care if doctors die." But pro-life groups denounced the killings as they had denounced the bombings and arson that came before. Those who kill abortion providers are not "pro-life" at all, they said; those killers have no philosophical or organizational ties to the pro-life movement. The contest over what *pro-life* means and who counts as a "pro-lifer" begged what seemed to me to be the key concern, however. What does *life* mean if someone feels compelled to murder in the name of saving lives? What can *life* mean if it does not denote the opposite of death? Under what assumptions and conditions does someone decide to kill for *life*?

For Horsley, someone becomes a pro-life killer when all other avenues of protest are eliminated and passivity is unacceptable. Horsley's controversial website, known variously as the Christian Gallery and the Nuremberg Files, is an example of lawful expressions of outrage suppressed by authorities, he says.[4] The website, which lists names and addresses of persons who provide abortions and work in clinics, was shut down when a court ruled that it was in effect a hit list for would-be pro-life killers. Eventually that ruling was overturned, and the website resumed operation only to gain more notoriety when it became part of a fugitive's plan to terrorize abortion providers out of their jobs. In November 2001, prison escapee Clayton Waagner went to Horsley's home and, with Horsley at gunpoint, demanded that he post on his website directives for forty-two reproductive health care employees: to avoid being killed, Waagner instructed, they must resign their jobs. Rather than providing a safe release of pent-up frustration, the website served as an important tool in this terrorist pro-life plan.

Waagner, who claimed responsibility for sending nearly five hundred anthrax threats to clinics nationwide in the weeks after the terrorist hijackings of September 11, 2001, and the anthrax attacks on congressional and media offices, was apprehended before he killed anyone. But some pro-life terrorists remain at large, and others who have done time in jail for pro-life destruction are now free. Their collective actions—including the assassination of seven abortion providers and clinic personnel since 1993, the fire-bombings and pipe-bombings of hundreds of clinics since the 1980s, the sabotage of clinics with butyric acid, and the psychological warfare tactics of fake anthrax letters and regular death threats—have irrevocably connected the term *pro-life* with terrorism.[5] Clearly, however, not everyone who has taken a personal, political, or religious stance against abortion is a terrorist. More to the point, pro-life politics—that is, the most prevalent practices and strategies, lawful or not, among anti-abortion activists and organizations today—are not essentially destructive or repressive.

On the contrary, pro-life politics are as creative and productive as Neal Horsley's vividly imaginative speech in which he sees a new civil war in

America's future. In presuming or portraying abortion as apocalypse and envisioning that time of revelation or war, pro-life politics narrate some people as warriors against abortion and others as enemies of life. I focus on this narrative practice not to praise its inventiveness or aesthetic quality but to suggest that it makes killing for life acceptable. The apocalyptic narrative of pro-life politics is what, in effect, creates new abortion warriors, producing soldiers in the Army of God.

Killing for Life thus considers the productive power of apocalyptic narrative.[6] The first three chapters, however, barely mention narrative; instead, they provide the cultural contexts for pro-life violence, document the reality of illegal tactics and legal strategies, and introduce apocalypticism and millennialism as major themes undergirding both militant acts and litigation campaigns against abortion providers.

Chapter 1 argues that pro-life apocalypticism thrived with the onset of a paramilitary culture that flourished after the U.S. war in Vietnam ended in 1975. As America sought to regain a sense of moral goodness and to cope with returning veterans who were accused of unprincipled bloodshed in Indochina, pro-life organizations launched by New Right leaders began to turn away from right-to-life rhetoric and adopt more apocalyptic language. According to their apocalyptic narrative, if abortion is not stopped in America, God in his wrath will cease to protect us. If we do not recognize abortion as a sign of the end of American or Christian culture, we will never survive the punishment. Evangelical Christianity and the main strand of Protestant millennialism—the belief in biblical prophecy about the end of the world and the end of history—were booming in the mid- to late seventies, so apocalyptic language appealed to Christian Protestants. With the rapid spread of Protestant millennialism, two other post-Vietnam phenomena—the militia movement and a revitalization of white supremacism—were fueled by and perpetuated apocalyptic ideas of their own. Paramilitary culture and millennialism influenced anti-abortion activism, which became more militant, and pro-life writing became embellished with apocalyptic imagery and references to biblical wrath. From these cultural contexts, a new abortion warrior emerged and guerrilla tactics flourished.

Chapter 2 examines this idea of guerrilla tactics, tracing the trends in illegal, vigilante operations that resulted in sabotage and death, as well as trends in pro-life "guerrilla legislation," which seeks to sabotage abortion providers. I argue that the pro-life violence of the 1990s signaled a move away from protest and toward retribution. Pro-life litigation and legislation, especially as described in an underground manual apocalyptically titled *Firestorm: A Guerrilla Strategy for a Pro-Life America*, also indicate this trend. In fact, pro-life guerrilla warfare and pro-life guerrilla legislation function together politically, even if they are not orchestrated. Close analyses of *Firestorm* and other primary sources show that pro-life ideology accommodates retributive violence not only implicitly and in practice but explicitly and in principle. Pro-life retribution is seen as a way to restore the order of God. In this light, the phenomenon of killing for "life" is revealed not as an oxymoron but as an act of logical consistency and a political manifestation of religious retribution.

Does this trend toward retribution mean that pro-life vigilantism is bound to increase because it is logical according to a militant Christian subculture that sees the United States as fostering a conspiracy against life? Or does the retributive violence testify to the fizzling out of the pro-life movement, given that killing for life is so oxymoronic that it lays bare the hypocrisy of those few who would take up arms to defend the unborn? To avoid the apocalyptic dualism that fuels pro-life politics, I suggest looking into the past rather than trying to predict the future.

Chapter 3 extends and sharpens the discussion of pro-life legislation by interrogating existing notions of fetal protection as they have played out in two distinct yet related arenas. Viewed comparatively, court hearings and decisions concerned with (1) the incarceration of women who may give birth to "crack babies" and (2) the late-term abortion procedure labeled *partial birth abortion* advance the idea that apocalypticism, rather than the right to life, is structuring pro-life politics. For those of us writing about abortion politics in the mid-1990s, the way in which the partial birth abortion debate superseded the issue of jailing pregnant African American drug users for endangering their unborn children was a matter of moving from bad to worse. It was callous enough that hospitals should be profiling pregnant black women suspected of drug abuse and testing them without consent, but proposing to criminalize all women and doctors who were using abortion as a last resort to halt actual catastrophic pregnancies seemed merciless. I was intrigued by the relationship between the two.

Why was it that fetuses portrayed as crack babies were discussed in terms of degeneracy, abnormality, and godlessness, whereas the "partially born" were emphatically depicted as whole, intact, genetically normal, and morally innocent? I decided that in addition to the underlying racial assumptions at play in these two cases of fetal protection, there were some cultural, indeed millennialist, assumptions about purity and impurity operating. There seemed to be a link between spiritual purity or innocence and the racial purity of the unborn. The term *fetal protection*, therefore, encompasses a double meaning: protect us from the fetuses who would be born as members of degenerate races, and let us protect those fetuses who would emerge as wholly pure in the genetic sense and holy pure in the spiritual sense.

Thus, the first three chapters provide examples and backgrounds for examining abortion politics through the lens of apocalypticism. Whether seen as a major component of the paramilitary culture that emerged after Vietnam or as a de facto element of millennialism that has characterized the religious right since the 1960s, apocalypticism seemed to seep from the "extreme" of pro-life violence to the "mainstream" of fetal protection in the 1990s. But more than mere rhetoric, apocalypticism structures pro-life politics as narrative. In the second three chapters, I consider the narrative form and function of that apocalypticism not only as it articulates the fight for life as America's Armageddon but also as it narrates pro-life individuals as active Christian soldiers and pro-choice individuals as conspirators against life, the Christians' nemeses in a holy war.

To demonstrate the ubiquity of pro-life millennialism and to burst the myth that only the most violent fringes of the anti-abortion movement portray abortion in terms of apocalypse, I examine in chapter 4 the Old Testament story of Gideon as it was employed by both the leader of Operation Rescue and the authors of a pro-life novel. The biblical tale of Gideon's triumph was evident in Operation Rescue's 1999 protest in Buffalo, New York, as well as in *Gideon's Torch*, a 1995 novel written by Charles Colson and Ellen Vaughn and published by Word Publishing. Both of these renditions of the Gideon story narrate pro-life Christians as a chosen minority facing a satanic majority hell-bent on providing abortions. But this tale tells more than an age-old conflict between good and evil; by portraying pro-lifers as Christian soldiers and their political opponents as demonic enemies, the narrative conforms to the idea that abortion is the latest in a series of human atrocities, a sign of impending Armageddon. This view, circulated widely in the late 1970s and 1980s, takes the form of a historical narrative: in the nineteenth century, slavery was the moral blight of America; in the mid-twentieth century, the Holocaust perpetuated against the Jews epitomized inhumanity; in the late twentieth century, abortion signified the most atrocious of these acts, the one that surely signals the end times. Chapter 4 thus examines the narrative form of Protestant apocalypticism as it characterizes pro-life activism as extreme as Operation Rescue and pro-life writing as seemingly innocuous as *Gideon's Torch*.

In chapter 5 I consider Catholic pro-life apocalypticism while focusing on how narrative functions. To do so, I consider one of the most intriguing and obscure pro-life leaders, L. Brent Bozell, who in the 1960s deployed apocalypticism in the first anti-abortion blockades of a family planning center and a hospital. Without a sophisticated understanding of how narrative functions as an alternate temporality, it is difficult to see why and how Bozell's pro-life writing and militant protests paved the way for the apocalyptic pro-life politics that thrive today. However, by narrating himself and his cohorts as players in an apocalyptic time frame, Bozell rejected the passivity that often kept people with deep religious convictions from participating in politics. Indeed, Bozell's theories and practice of what he called a postmodern understanding of abortion influenced some of the most powerful political strategists in the nation, many of whom also deployed narrative time to mobilize citizens. Thus, narrative is not just an explanatory, descriptive story that these strategists told themselves to justify pro-life actions. Instead, narrative, Bozell's politics suggest, is transformative and productive as well as descriptive or illustrative.

In chapter 6 I examine further the transformative, productive aspect of the apocalyptic narrative endemic to pro-life politics since the 1960s and eventually focus on how pro-life writing narrates "enemies of life" as a conspiracy of blacks, Jews, foreigners, and lesbians. More than mere demonizing, this narration of "un-American" enemies seeks to interpellate them as subjects under "God's law." By *interpellate*, I mean the process in which a reader of a narrative—or a social situation—comes not only to sympathize but also to identify with what he is taking in and reacts to it in a way that gives him a new social role or even identity.[7] Although he might think he has chosen or freely accepted this new idea of himself, the process is actually structured and bound by the narrative, not him. In accusing certain people of being enemies of life, the apocalyptic pro-life narrative forces people to react in relation to—and therefore as a part of or, conversely, as a deviant resistor to—the pro-life social order. Whether renouncing or accepting the identity thrust upon him, the so-named enemy cannot help but react within the confines of the narrative that named him.

The second autobiography of Norma McCorvey, who was the Jane Roe plaintiff in the 1973 U.S. Supreme Court decision that declared laws prohibiting abortion unconstitutional, illustrates this kind of narration/interpellation nicely. An abortion clinic worker who was converted to born-again Christianity by Operation Rescue, McCorvey narrates Jane Roe as an ex-lesbian. No longer subject to man's law (*Roe v. Wade*), Jane Roe is interpellated as a new woman who is subject only to God's law, which among other things means that she renounces her lesbian relationship of more than thirty years. By narrating abortion as her own personal apocalypse, McCorvey in her autobiography gives readers more than an allegory that makes sense of her political involvement. Like the "ex-gay" and "partial birth abortion" campaigns that it references, McCorvey's autobiography is pro-life writing that seeks to narrate, articulate, and in fact produce legal subjects—people who are subject to the laws of the state or of God.

To emphasize the powerful role of narrative in pro-life politics, I have resisted writing this book as a straightforward chronology. I have also resisted organizing the discussion according to the popularly sequestered themes of race, ethnicity, class, gender, and sexuality. These issues are intermingled in nearly every chapter, however—not because they *should* be included and ever present, according to some notion of political correctness, but because throughout U.S. history, they are and have been inextricable from pro-life politics and reproductive policies.

In *Killing for Life*, I visit some of that history by examining pro-life writing from the 1960s to the present, with a special emphasis on documents from the 1990s, when anti-abortion violence peaked. It may not be surprising that, on the cusp of the new millennium, apocalypticism has surged in America. But it was eye opening for me to realize that a variety of pro-life institutions has deployed the narrative of abortion as apocalypse in a persistent yet uncoordinated fashion since at least 1979. For someone like me, who happens to believe in reproductive freedom—which includes the freedom to become pregnant, give birth, avoid pregnancy, or terminate pregnancy, and does not preclude a personal prohibition of abortion—this book is an indictment of pro-life ideology, certainly.[8] For all of us who now live in an era of grand-scale terrorism, I hope this examination of writings by or about pro-life terrorists and other abortion warriors provides a keen demonstration of the material effects of narrative practice and the power of apocalyptic language in American society.

1

New Abortion Warrior

From Right-to-Life Rhetoric to Paramilitary
Pro-Life Culture

The first issues of *Human Life Review* appeared two years after the U.S. Supreme Court set national guidelines for limits on abortion, practically abolishing restrictions throughout the states in the decision of *Roe v. Wade.* To contest the new legal status of abortion, *Human Life Review* authors stressed the human quality of prenatal life, sometimes readily conceding a difference between abortion and "the murder of a full member of society, whose life intermeshes with the lives of many others."[1] According to even those striving to establish the personhood of the fetus, abortion was not necessarily murder. Not in 1975.

Much has transpired since the midseventies, however, when the United States was reeling from Watergate and accusing servicemen returning from Vietnam of being baby killers. Since then, the term *baby killer* has become the political currency of pro-life groups and individuals. Now almost all pro-life organizations portray abortion unequivocally as murder. A concern about killing babies in the sense of aborting pregnancy seems to have supplanted the concern about killing babies as part of the immense military operation that had constituted U.S. intervention in Vietnam. In the United States, both abortion and Vietnam have come to represent profoundly psychological and symbolic realms—not just political conflicts. But rarely do we connect the two.

In a pro-life novel by Paul de Parrie, a doctor makes the link between abortion and Vietnam explicit. He is concerned because "women suffering from the now familiar Post-traumatic Stress Disorder often seen in Vietnam War vets inundated his practice. [The doctor's] persistent investigative work confirmed that 'Vietnam' for these women was an abortion table."[2] This observation, uttered by a fictional narrator, has of course no basis in fact. As studies have repeatedly shown, women who abort pregnancies are not damaged mentally or physically by the experience.[3] But something remarkable happens as post-traumatic stress disorder is transferred from the psychological and symbolic realm of Vietnam to that of abortion. Implicitly, the bloodshed, confusion, denial, guilt, and shame associated with being a baby killer is transferred from men to women.

In this chapter I consider such transference to be a matter not only of pro-life fiction. By situating abortion politics in the cultural contexts of post-Vietnam America, I find that de Parrie is not the first to displace men's baby killing in Vietnam with women's baby killing in the womb. John O'Keefe, an early and influential pro-life activist, made this transference explicit when he initiated a new kind of opposition to abortion. From the direct action techniques of activists such as John O'Keefe sprang a new tradition of not only opposing abortion but declaring war on it. Nurtured by the paramilitary culture that flourished in the United States after the Vietnam War, by the apocalyptic rhetoric of New Right politicians who inspired Christian voters, and by the revitalization of white supremacist organizing, a new type of abortion warrior emerged.

Abortion and Vietnam

Barry Goldwater, whose 1960 book *The Conscience of a Conservative* inspired untold numbers of right-wing politicians, claimed that "extremism in the defense of liberty is no vice, and . . . moderation in the pursuit of justice is no virtue."[4] This extremism was widely interpreted to signify Goldwater's willingness to use bombs, including nuclear warheads, in

Vietnam should ground troops prove ineffective. The conservatism that this declaration and *The Conscience of a Conservative* came to represent in the latter half of the twentieth century is exactly the stuff that could have saved the United States from losing the war in Vietnam. Or so says the New Warrior, the man of paramilitary culture who since the midseventies has populated pulp fiction, action adventure movies, paintball games, gun shows, and National Rifle Association rallies.

According to James William Gibson, author of *Warrior Dreams: Paramilitary Culture in Post-Vietnam America*, the New Warrior blames the federal government for the "self-imposed restraint" that supposedly prevented U.S. soldiers from winning the war in Vietnam. Gibson states that "Conservative politicians, syndicated columnists, and military intellectuals had offered versions of the 'self-imposed restraint' argument for years, both during and after the Vietnam War. By the late 1970s and early 1980s, it was not an esoteric doctrine, but a widely accepted explanation."[5] As a revitalization of the national myth of regeneration through violence, the New Warrior is exemplified in *Rambo: First Blood*, the movie about a Vietnam veteran, John Rambo, who battles local law enforcement as well as his own memories of being traumatized in a war that the federal government would not let him win.[6]

Part of the appeal of the paramilitary culture that has grown in the United States since the fall of Saigon is its promise of a new pursuit of justice in which to exercise extremism. And so we also have, according to Gibson, a New War culture, which focuses on the plight and regeneration of men after their ordeals during the Vietnam era. New War culture assumes a revisionist history of the conflict in Vietnam—a revision that supplants the massive military destruction of Indochina caused by imperialist, U.S. intervention with the personal devastation experienced by individual American soldiers. New War culture is thus a "cult of the warrior" that tries to make extremism reasonable and bring it into the mainstream. Manifestations of New War culture include conspiracy-minded militia groups organized to oppose the New World Order; macho pulp stories such as those published in *Soldier of Fortune* magazine; men's movement events such as the rallies of the Promise Keepers; and televised paramilitary games such as Combat Missions and Boot Camp.

For the new abortion warrior, New War activity is located in the courts, at the clinics, and in the womb. The stated reasons for opposing abortion and the ways of protesting it have changed since the 1960s. Strategies and rationales have become more warlike in the sense that they have adopted paramilitary and apocalyptic language. This shift is true of all sorts of anti-abortion efforts, from national membership and lobbying organizations (who are considered to be mainstream or moderate), to protest groups such as Operation Rescue (whose name evokes a military maneuver), to individual vigilantes in the Army of God, who bomb abortion facilities and terrorize abortion providers (and who are considered to be extremists). Recognizing that all these anti-abortion efforts are somehow related to the paramilitary New War culture does not mean that we need equate them with each other. When national pro-life groups or local churches denounce anti-abortion violence, they surely mean what they say. Even so, the mainstream and the extremist efforts to thwart reproductive freedom are related—both culturally and ideologically. Writings from all types of pro-life organizations and individuals reveal a shift to an apocalyptic style, often loaded with military metaphors.

As derived from Gibson's theories of the New Warrior, the new abortion warrior personifies the paramilitary and apocalyptic mentality that became prevalent among all sorts of anti-abortion efforts beginning in the late 1970s. Certainly there was strident opposition to abortion before then, just as there were war heroes before the New Warrior. War heroes—idealized by such figures as John Wayne, whose jingoism never challenged the U.S. government and whose killings never achieved much gore, gave way to the new warriors such as John Rambo, whose distrust of the federal government and penchant for explosive bloodletting indicate a more apocalyptic mentality. The new abortion warrior is an embodiment of the apocalyptic attitudes, images, and language that came to characterize anti-abortion legislation as well as the anti-abortion violence and other manifestations of paramilitary culture that have emerged since Vietnam. An account of an early pro-life activist provides evidence of the beginnings of this emergence.

The displacement of baby killing in Vietnam with baby killing in the womb is illustrated by a biographical account of an early pro-life leader, John O'Keefe, who was so distraught by his brother's death in Vietnam that he took up the anti-abortion cause.[7] Going against the grain of his Catholicism and his family, O'Keefe became a conscientious objector after he began feeling sadness and sympathy, instead of anger, at the Vietnamese soldier who supposedly killed his brother, Roy. Unlike those who were organizing against the war because they saw the destruction of Vietnamese land, villages, and people that was perpetuated by the imperialist United States, O'Keefe wanted to stop the war because of "the killing being done *in* Vietnam, like the killing that resulted in Roy's death."[8] According to one account, O'Keefe was far less (if at all) concerned with the killing that his brother contributed to as a "war hero" and "platoon leader in one of the U.S. Army's most elite combat organizations, the 28th Mobile Strike Force of the Fifth Special Forces Group."[9] Instead, O'Keefe denounced the killing supposedly perpetuated by his friend Suzanne when she terminated a pregnancy.

A nurse who "discussed her abortion in a straightforward way with O'Keefe and seemed convinced that she had made the right decision," Suzanne was one of the women who took advantage of the state-by-state liberalization of abortion laws during the 1960s, before the U.S. Supreme Court in 1973 reformed them by issuing *Roe v. Wade*. Unashamed and apparently exuberant about this newfound freedom, Suzanne talked with O'Keefe for "a full hour [and] could not drop the subject." This puzzled and troubled O'Keefe, who had never questioned the Catholic stance against abortion. "Soon," according to one author,

> the story of her abortion clicked with O'Keefe's emerging beliefs on death and pacifism. He became convinced that she was a mother, her child was dead, and she had no way to grieve for the child. She never said those things, but O'Keefe believed she was in denial and that she had been talking about the subject with him as a substitute for mourning her baby. O'Keefe equated her with the Vietnamese soldier who had killed his brother: they were both badly scarred by death and killing.[10]

O'Keefe's logic paints both Suzanne and the Vietnamese soldier as pathological enemies to be fought. Just as the Vietnamese soldier killed Roy O'Keefe, Suzanne killed her child, according to O'Keefe. Just as the Vietnamese soldier and Suzanne are equated, so too are the U.S. soldier and the unborn child. Instead of U.S. veterans suffering from the trauma of a war that included mass killings of civilians, it is American women like Suzanne who must be psychologically "scarred" and "in denial." The displacement is complete. O'Keefe went on to adopt civil disobedience and direct action as a way to protest abortion; he was in this regard the "father of rescue" of the unborn.[11]

O'Keefe's biography suggests that pro-life politics were part of the remasculinization of America after Vietnam.[12] It is not only veterans who were said to have suffered a crisis of masculinity as a result of the fighting in Vietnam; indeed, the entire country experienced a reformulation of what it means to be a good American male. The "sensitive" man of the

1970s and 1980s, exemplified in films such as *Kramer vs. Kramer* and in the poetry of Robert Bly, preceded the "kinder, gentler America" of the 1990s. Killing babies was redefined as having an abortion—an act men cannot commit (unless they are abortionists, who therefore are not real men, according to abortion warrior logic). Real men found a new war with which to revive their American manhood. Forget the swamps and jungles of Indochina. As de Parrie's pro-life novel proclaims, the womb is the new "battlefield of flesh."[13]

On this symbolic battleground, pro-life politics replay the dilemma of Rambo when he is asked to return to Vietnam on a rescue mission. In asking "Do we get to win this time?" Rambo wants to know if self-imposed restraint by the federal government will continue to thwart real American manpower.[14] Likewise, the new abortion warrior is tired of federal regulations, and most of all the license of *Roe v. Wade*, that prevent pro-life victory. The new war is about stopping baby killers. The new hope is that this time, the government will cease imposing restraint on the new warriors, will recognize that the extremism of categorically banning abortion is no vice. The new pursuit of justice is that of promoting prenatal life.

Defending prenatal life was never an objective for Barry Goldwater, that early champion of extremism and the 1964 Republican presidential candidate. But his ghostwritten and highly influential *Conscience of a Conservative* articulated elements of a spirituality-centered politics that became essential for pro-life strategists of the 1970s, 1980s, and 1990s. The resurgence of the right after Goldwater's resounding defeat in 1964 and the antiwar protests of the 1960s resulted from these spirituality-based politics, which emphasized culture over economics. As a result, we must take into account the cultural "New War" context of the political rise of the New Right, those men and women motivated by Goldwater's defeat.[15]

Beginning in the 1970s, the institutions and ideology of the New Right had a huge impact on the policies that restrict reproductive freedom in the United States.[16] It was only at the end of the 1970s, however, that New Right leaders launched on a national scale a pro-life politics worthy of a new abortion warrior. About this time, pro-life politics stopped merely defending prenatal life and went on the offense, becoming more aggressively conservative and reflecting the language and spiritual nuances in *Conscience of a Conservative*. Defending the unborn gave way to promoting American life according to conservative principles. Like the abortion warrior, the New Right created pro-life politics as a new war that should not be hampered by self-imposed restraint.

New Right

In 1979, New Right leaders including Paul Weyrich and Richard Viguerie founded two important organizations. Under their guidance, Paul and Judie Brown broke away from the National Right to Life Committee and converted a political action committee devoted to a human life amendment into a group called the American Life Lobby, now the American Life League (ALL).[17] In addition, Weyrich and Viguerie joined with other New Right leaders to convince evangelist Jerry Falwell to adopt abortion as a primary focus for a new organization called the Moral Majority.[18] Both organizations were important electoral vehicles for the New Right in that they encouraged unprecedented numbers of Christian evangelicals to register to vote.[19] The results of the 1980 presidential election, the Reagan revolution, reflected these newly registered evangelicals. Conservatives gained elective office not by virtue of the Republican Party but by virtue of the New Right, which had been working to take back the country for conservatism ever since the defeat of Goldwater in 1964.

Despite the name of Falwell's organization, the engineers of the New Right at this time were not trying to build a majority. On the contrary, they wanted to manipulate groups that were aiming to build a majority and thereby build a minority rule for themselves. This strategy is clearly seen in their decision against becoming an official political party, as Viguerie, author of *The New Right: We're Ready to Lead*, explains:

> For a while we in the New Right thought the country needed a third party. As I have said, we came to see that this was wrong. Under a two-party system, the parties don't really lead; they follow. Their business is not to form coalitions, as in Europe, within which they can keep their own shape and identity. In America their business is to build majorities, which means, very often, putting principles on the back burner.
>
> So genuine principles have to find institutional support *outside* the parties in order to influence the parties. As long as only the liberals did this, they kept gaining relentlessly. The lack of popular support didn't matter. A well-organized minority can often defeat an unorganized majority.[20]

That well-organized minority was the New Right in 1979: conservatives who were "ready to lead"—not compete with—the two-party system.[21]

In its role as a well-organized minority, the New Right continued to gain power and increase its political influence regardless of whether the Democrats or Republicans gained the majority in any given election year. Although recruiting evangelicals such as Falwell was key to gaining power, the success of the New Right did not depend on the success of the Moral Majority. In other words, whether the majority of the American public became "moral" and pro-life, or not, did not hinder the increasing influence of the New Right, whose aim was to reestablish fully conservative political policy. Pro-life politics likewise gained power, whether or not a majority of Americans voted for officials who were for or against reproductive rights for women.

Moreover, under the calculating influence of the New Right, pro-life politics went from defense to offense. One journalist marks the change as happening in the 1990s. "In the 1980's," he observes, "the outlawing of abortion was framed in the somewhat liberal terms of saving human life, and protecting human rights. And that is why a smattering of left-leaning intellectuals also signed on as anti-abortion advocates. But in the 1990's, the conservative emphasis has changed."[22] In fact, the conservative emphasis had shifted away from a rhetoric of rights by the end of the 1970s. In the late 1970s and throughout the 1980s, the New Right stopped merely protesting abortion and began using pro-life politics to promote the conservative "genuine principles" that Viguerie mentions. It is these genuinely conservative principles that characterize pro-life politics and distinguish them from the comparatively more liberal campaign to secure the fetus's right to life by opposing abortion.

Pro-life politics, more than right-to-life efforts, use opposition to abortion to promote what Viguerie calls the genuine principles of conservatism. Right-to-life politics oppose abortion through the more liberal principles of natural or human rights. The difference between a conservative pro-life position and the liberal right-to-life position lies partially in what each implies about equality. For those who take the right-to-life stance, granting an individual fetus the liberal "right" to live, to grow, and to be born presupposes many things, not the least of which is that particular rights should be granted equally among all citizens of the United States. In the 1970s, opponents of abortion were at least nominally reaching (on behalf of the fetus) for the same principle that liberal feminists wanted—equal rights, human rights. The National Right to Life Committee (NRLC) epitomizes this approach.

In making its liberal arguments against abortion, NRLC contends that "Every unborn baby is a complete, individual, living human being from the earliest moment of his or her existence at fertilization," in order to reach the question "Should unborn children have a right to life that is protected by law?"[23] The argument ignores the fact that translation of the DNA occurs twenty-four to forty-eight hours after a sperm penetrates the egg.[24] Regardless of its inaccuracy, this framing of opposition to abortion in terms of human rights is compatible with the idea of an egalitarian society, a democracy. The right-to-life position is a fundamentally liberal construction because it assumes (even while begging the question of why we should consider individual fetuses as citizens) that the Constitution grants rights equally among citizens, who are "created equal" and created *as* equals—as *political* equals.

The conservative idea of equality does not share this liberal assumption, however. Like right-to-lifers, conservative pro-lifers may use the rhetoric that "all men are created equal" to argue against abortion. But their idea of equality does not aim for or tolerate an egalitarian society in which all citizens are granted the same rights. Conservatives see the divine creation of us "all" as just that—divine, by God.

Nowhere is this notion more candidly explained than in *Conscience of a Conservative*.[25] In this volume Goldwater states that constitutionally "we are all equal in the eyes of God but we are equal *in no other respect*" and thereby redefines equality in spiritual terms. "All men are created equal" by God, according to Goldwater, and this God-given equality must not be confused with the democratic aim of an egalitarian society. He explains that "an egalitarian society [is] an objective that does violence both to the charter of the Republic and the laws of Nature."[26] This distinction between equality and egalitarianism is part of the spirituality-based politics that the New Right infused into the organization ALL.

As established by Paul Weyrich and other New Right leaders, ALL marked a departure from and a challenge to the human rights rhetoric of the NRLC. With financial and strategic help from the New Right, including advice from Weyrich and the computer mailing services of Richard Viguerie, by 1981 the ALL newsletter had 68,000 subscribers and the organization had established working liaisons with 4,000 groups nationwide.[27] Eventually ALL was able to lift the veil of humanism that had cloaked the right-to-life argument. Instead of arguing against abortion on the basis that it kills an individual human life, ALL promoted the notion of the collective American unborn as created by God.

If one distinction that can be made between liberal right-to-life and conservative pro-life groups and their rhetoric centers around their different notions of equality, another concerns their different ideas of creation.

The liberal right-to-life stance of the NRLC continues to appeal to a large number of people because it is based on a civil or human rights rationale, not on a Christian notion of creation. That God is the creator of all things is merely a corollary to the main argument that a fetus is a human being worthy of civil or human rights. NRLC puts this idea in a nationalistic perspective in a publication titled "When Does Life Begin? Abortion and Human Rights":

> Since 1776 we have striven as a nation to expand basic human rights for all. There is much yet to be done to fully implement the principle, but even as we do so, we must also defend it against those who mistakenly believe that they can expand their own rights by trampling the human rights of others.
>
> Many Americans also believe that every human being is a precious child of God, a brother or sister, of every other human being, regardless of such differences as maturity, race, sex or dependency. In this human family, the strong have a greater obligation to protect and defend the lives and rights of vulnerable persons who cannot defend themselves.[28]

The term *human rights* reverberates throughout the prose of the NRLC. Although the right-to-life stance includes nationalistic and creationist ideas, it never strays far from its liberal humanist foundations, which secure rights for all humanity.

In contrast, ALL completely avoids "rights" talk and places godly creation at the center of its mission. On the inside cover of ALL's magazine *Celebrate Life*, nationalism and creationism interlock:

> ALL FOR GOD: ALL takes the irreversible position that every life is good because it comes from the only Author of Life. Every life is providential because it plays a unique role in the Great Plan of the Almighty.
>
> FOR LIFE: Human life is life—a gift from the true God, made in his image.
>
> FOR THE FAMILY: The family, basis for society, becomes holy through observance of all the commandments, including "Thou shalt not kill."
>
> FOR THE NATION: We hold these truths to be self-evident, that every human life is created equal, that this nation may pay with the blood of its citizens for every drop of blood drawn by the curette,

and that its survival depends upon securing for the preborn the guarantee of being born as honored citizens of a country that practices, under God, liberty and justice for all.[29]

In these four pronouncements, God is "the only Author of Life," and "every human life is created equal" by God, "made in His image." This formulation is completely compatible with—and derivative of—the classic conservative principle that, as Goldwater put it, "we are equal in the eyes of God but we are equal *in no other respect*." Thus there is no mention of equal rights in ALL's more conservative statement. With creationism as its primary and "irreversible" assumption, ALL articulates a conservative, pro-life position that rejects liberal ideas of human rights and equality.

Consider also the statement that the United States "practices, under God, liberty and justice for all." It too conforms to conservative principles that do not guarantee equality and echoes the Pledge of Allegiance's final phrase, "one nation, under God, with liberty and justice for all." The words "under God" were added to the Pledge of Allegiance in 1954 to emphasize America's pledge against "ungodly" communism. As a product of 1950s anticommunist hysteria, the phrase "under God" today carries some of that red-scare mentality, but it also resonates with the Christian notion that God's law is supreme and superior to man's law. Because of this resonance, the words "under God" completely qualify the notions of social equality or political egalitarianism that might otherwise be intended in the phrase "liberty and justice for all." It is "liberty and justice for all" according to God's law, or as Goldwater put it, the "laws of Nature," which are in essence divine, according to conservative principles. Like Goldwater, who adamantly and explicitly demanded that "an egalitarian society [is] an objective that does violence both to the charter of the Republic and the laws of Nature," ALL's pro-life position is fundamentally conservative. It places "liberty and justice for all" "*under* God," under divine scrutiny, according to the divine laws of Nature—not man's law. From this vantage point, liberty and justice are not secured by man-made federal law (which is also faulted for interfering with private business and capitalist entrepreneurs). Only God can secure liberty and justice for all.

This notion of justice "under God" is clear in ALL's speculation that "this nation may pay with the blood of its citizens for every drop of blood drawn by the curette"—a curette being a medical instrument used in some abortion procedures. With this statement, ALL is not condoning or encouraging the burning of abortion clinics or the assassination of reproductive health care providers. Instead, ALL is referring to God's wrath, which is prophesied as God's plan. This theme of apocalyptic wrath is endemic to the pro-life conservatism that ALL institutionalized, and it is examined at length in subsequent chapters. The immediate point is that, with God as both creator and judge, ALL veers away from the more liberal sentiments of the NRLC. Moreover, in dismissing the right-to-life approach, with all its references to human rights and civil rights, the American Life League marks a change. The nuance of the word *life* shifts from indicating individual, singular, autonomous, and ultimately human life of "the fetus" to indicate "American life" as a collectivity—a national body created by God, operated by conservative principles, and symbolized by "the unborn."

Bernard Nathanson too, in his autobiographical *Aborting America*, which appeared in 1979, posited the unborn as a national collectivity. In this book, Nathanson details his evolution from a founding member of the National Association to Repeal Abortion Laws (NARAL's original name) to a proponent of pro-life policies. He first identifies and recants "specious arguments" both for and against abortion and then focuses on the scientific possibility of the "alpha" (his name for fetal life) as an autonomous entity. Anticipating the Reagan administration's translation of outer space as a frontier to be colonized and defended by the strategic defense initiative known as Star Wars, Nathanson compares the inner space of the womb with extraterrestrial exploration:

> In the far reaches of space, radioastronomy is listening for bleeps from beyond in an anxious search for other humanoid beings "out there" that may be transmitting their codes to us. . . . Why not listen "in here," inside the human womb? With alpha it is just as if an intelligent race of beings is transmitting massive electrical impulses from a distant star, and we are not receiving them . . . or we are refusing to receive them.[30]

By 1984, when Nathanson narrated the pro-life film *The Silent Scream*, this logic of the cosmic unborn, whose signs we must not ignore lest our national humanity decline, has crystallized. *The Silent Scream* presents abortion as "Armageddon, the violence to end all violence" in an overtly nationalistic drama.[31]

The movement's departure from right-to-life rhetoric was evident during clinic protests, which became more strident in religiosity during the 1980s. As scholar Michael Cuneo attests, "throughout the 1980s, pro-life discourse began to take on a more explicitly religious content. Scriptural passages appeared alongside civil rights slogans on pro-life placards and broadsheets, and public prayer, which was exceptional in the movement's earlier years, became a regular feature of pro-life rallies and demonstrations."[32] Cuneo attributes this shift to the increasing prominence of evangelical Christians in the movement. This prominence is in large part a result of the New Right's role in promoting ALL and the Moral Majority, whose evangelical message on abortion is as strident as it is religious. It is also essentially apocalyptic in that both organizations suggest that America's sanction of abortion will bring down God's wrath.

The paramilitary pro-life activism that flourished in the 1980s and 1990s was perhaps a logical consequence of the apocalyptic anti-abortion language that preceded it. Massive clinic protests derived especially from the efforts of Operation Rescue, whose very name reflects the paramilitarization of pro-life politics. Clinic bombing became part of pro-life politics on a grander scale in the 1980s. The religious and the paramilitary were most obviously fused, however, in the December 25, 1984, bombing of a Pensacola, Florida, clinic. Named the Gideon Project after an Old Testament story, the bombing was conceived as a birthday present for Jesus, the bombers claimed. Almost ten years later, in 1993, the first abortion provider was assassinated by a pro-life gunman—an act clearly not in accordance with a human rights rationale.

In the midst of these apocalyptic, paramilitary protests, the *right* to life was obsolete. In the emergence of paramilitary culture, the notion of life came to represent something other than individual human life, even something other than the opposite of death.[33] Killing for life in the womb retained the extremist logic of fighting for peace in Vietnam. As paramilitary culture and evangelical groups such as ALL and the Moral Majority ushered in apocalypticism, right-to-life rhetoric lost its potency. In the context of New War culture, "taking life" was eventually transformed from the sacrilege of terminating pregnancy to the sacred act of terminating abortion providers.

New War

The phrase "taking life" is a euphemism for killing, and it has both religious and paramilitary derivations. The Christian prohibition against taking life relates to the idea that only God is the author of life, as we saw in ALL's statement. Because only God gives life (never mind the work of women in the process of gestation and the labor of birth), only God can take life. Thus, the Christian idea of taking life "rests not on the assumption that human life has overriding value, but on the conviction that it is not ours to take."[34] This religious understanding of taking life meshes with another, ancient notion that infuses the paramilitary New War culture that James William Gibson documents so well.

Taking life, according to Gibson, is an older idea of killing whose element of incorporation allows the New Warrior to absorb the power of his enemy. Incorporation or absorbing power from the enemy as he is slain is a "fantastic appropriation of another's life force." It is a "sacred act" that moves moral progress along. Thus, killing an evil man is "a means to an end, not an end in itself."[35] The source of evil is not quashed with the single killing but instead is depleted. Simultaneously, the forces of good are inflated. Gibson explains: when "the good warrior kills an evil one, he effectively transforms evil power into good power. The converse is also true: when an evil villain kills a virtuous victim, evil gains strength. Hence, no matter how secular the New War warrior may appear with his high-tech weapons and tremendous 'efficient' kills, he is essentially a religious figure."[36] In this New War context, accusing people who provide or obtain abortions of "taking life" promotes the idea that more than individual human lives are at stake. Indeed, what is at stake is a larger, more cosmic and sacred battle.

The battle against abortion, according to an underground strategy manual titled *Army of God*, "is a battle not against flesh and blood, but against the devil and all the evil he can muster among flesh and blood to fight at his side."[37] Killing an abortionist does not stop all the evil of abortion; it is only one means of disrupting it and fueling, conversely, the forces of good. According to this apocalyptic and paramilitary logic, the abortion warrior is literally a soldier in the Army of God. But this army may not be "the shadowy, ultraviolent anti-abortion group" some government officials believe it to be.[38]

The Army of God may be best understood not as a member organization but rather as a mental attitude. Mark Potok of the Southern Poverty Law Center is quoted as stating, "What's very unclear is whether the Army of God is a real organization or is essentially a state of mind, though it appears to be more the latter."[39] The manual itself supports this sentiment. It claims, with some interesting convolution, that the Army of God is "not a real army, humanly speaking. It is a real Army, and God is the General and Commander-in-Chief. The soldiers, however, do not usually communicate with one another. Very few have ever met each other. And when they do, each is usually unaware of the other's soldier status. That is why the Feds will never stop this Army. Never."[40] Here we see the element of fantasy of which Gibson speaks in the notion that the army is simultaneously real and not real.

We see as well the antigovernment response to the "Feds," a sentiment that members of pro-life groups share with members of the militia movement. Sandi DuBowski, in an article whose topic was named one of the most underreported news stories of 1997, finds not just philosophical but substantial links in both personnel and finances between pro-life organizations and militia groups.[41] Larry Pratt, for instance, an executive director of and lobbyist for Gun Owners of America, raised $150,000 for Operation Rescue after federal agents seized its bank accounts when it refused to pay a $50,000 fine for blockading clinics. Pratt later received national attention when his links with militias and white supremacist groups were exposed, forcing him to step down as cochair of Pat Buchanan's 1996 presidential campaign. DuBowski also reports that militia members in Florida, Nebraska, Maine, Virginia, Oklahoma, South Carolina, New Mexico, and Montana have linked their disdain for the federal government with their opposition to abortion in word and deed. Some have been arrested for blockading, picketing, and conspiring to bomb abortion clinics. Likewise, pro-life leaders in Indiana, Wisconsin, Oregon, Texas, Missouri, and Illinois are affiliated with militias or espouse their philosophies.

One tactic shared by some pro-life and militia groups is a refusal to pay taxes. Members of the militia movement practice tax evasion as a way of freeing themselves from what they consider to be a corrupt federal government. It is important to recognize that disdain for the federal government is not illogical, as in some cases of family farmers whose small agricultural businesses failed in the 1980s. The militia movement grew in the 1970s and 1980s as white farmers and factory workers struggled to negotiate post-industrial, multinational capitalism.[42] Thus many militias have retracted their allegiance to the federal government, with some going so far as to reject all laws except the U.S. Constitution and its first ten amendments, and to redefine U.S. citizenship according to only those documents. Also known as Christian Patriots, these militias evade taxes on principle.[43] Other less strident paramilitary organizers demand that their taxes be withheld when the government uses that money for things they do not value. Similarly, pro-lifers are sometimes encouraged to refuse to pay taxes connected to reproductive health care that may include abortion services.[44]

In 1994, when Matthew Trewhella spoke at a meeting of the U.S. Taxpayers Party in Wisconsin, he seemed to epitomize the new abortion warrior. Planned Parenthood investigators, who made Trewhella's speech public by infiltrating the meeting and videotaping it, suggest that it offers evidence of possible conspiracy or collusion among extremists. Trewhella, a member of both the Taxpayers Party and the Missionaries to the Pre-Born, instructed his audience: "My son Jeremiah, I'm teaching him to be a free man. . . . I'd take my son, I'd play with his toes, I'd say toes, toes, toes . . . and I'd go up to his fingers and say fingers, fingers, fingers, and then I'd grab his trigger finger and I'd say trigger finger, and he's sixteen months old, and if you ask him 'Jeremiah, where's your trigger finger?'— he'll go like this immediately."[45] At this point Trewhella pointed to his own trigger finger, mimicking the action of his child.

Linda Kintz provides a cultural analysis that reveals something I believe is more powerful than conspiracy. She examines Trewhella's speech as it exemplifies the New Warrior identity, especially the nature of the relationship between the warriors and their magic weapons. Kintz draws from Gibson's analyses of New War culture, in which a man's gun is not merely a phallic symbol but a functioning appendage that is as much a part of him as any limb. "In Trewhella's intimate training, the body is melded to the gun as it was in the New War games" such as paintball.[46] Speaking as a pro-life activist, Trewhella exhibits the New War understanding that the gun is a weapon that acts magically as an extension of the warrior's body. Interesting, too, is how Trewhella's instruction relies on comparing the fingers of a child to his own fingers. Right-to-life rhetoric emphasizes the human features—such as fingers and toes—of a fetus in order to oppose abortion on the grounds of human rights. But abortion warriors such as Trewhella tend to mirror paramilitary culture by emphasizing the appendages of fetuses as extensions of their own limbs, or vice versa.

Using a method similar to way the New Warrior absorbs the life force when he "takes life" from an evil adversary, the abortion warrior absorbs the fantastic evil energy of abortion, transferring to himself the supposed anguish of the taking of prenatal life. What happens to the unborn also happens to the abortion warrior. Consider the words of a convicted pro-life activist as he describes how he mentally prepared himself to bomb a reproductive health care clinic:

I put myself in the baby's place, reminding myself that I had to love that baby as myself. "My arms will be torn away from my torso tomorrow! My skull will be crushed until fragments cave inward and cut into my brain!" I imagined how terrible the physical pain would be! I thought of my right arm being dismembered, and as I thought of it, I bore in mind that my arm would not be taken off cleanly with a sharp surgical instrument under anesthesia. No, it would be brutally torn out of the shoulder socket and twisted off! It would hurt so bad! But I did not think only of the terrible physical pain. I imagined the terrible mental horror and terror of looking at my right shoulder, and my right arm is gone! And blood is gushing out of where it had been![47]

The clinic bomber incorporates into his experience the torture that a fetus supposedly experiences. The clinic bomber absorbs it, transferring the physical and mental anguish to himself as the abortionist supposedly "takes life." As the clinic bomber considers the "mental horror," his language is no longer conditional; it conveys a present certainty. What will or would happen is replaced by what is happening: his skull *will be* crushed, his arm *would be* removed, then his arm *is gone* and blood *is gushing*. The present certainty is in fact a fantasy. More than identifying with the fetus as a fellow human being, the clinic bomber has put himself "in the baby's place." This is a fantasy about being back in the womb. The fascination with absorbing the pain of the unborn—the fantasy of being aborted—can be said to be derived from deeply rooted psychological fears.

As Kintz has demonstrated with psychoanalytical theory, pro-life images of fragmented fetal bodies function in the same ways as do unconscious "imagos" of mutilation, including castration. Thus "the horror and unease set off by the figure of the aborted fetus" is disturbing regardless of one's moral or political stance on abortion. For men especially, these images call forth one's relationship with women and with birth.[48] Experts in psychoanalytical theory argue that men's fear of women can stem from boyhood glimpses at a girl's or woman's naked body, which result in a fear that her lack of a penis means it has been removed, which might mean his penis could be removed too.[49] In this formulation, women are the cause of castration anxiety. Or men's fear of women may stem from unconscious fantasies of being born, of being pushed out of the womb and through the vagina, and all the flesh-tearing gore that such an event entails.[50] This unconscious fantasy, which resembles the clinic bomber's confession, can be

most threatening for the male subject, for what is also a part of this unconscious fantasy is the horror of a maternal body that is both castrated and castrating, a much more frightening image than Freud's rather calm description of the boy's first glimpse of the little girl's lack. This fantasy of birth thus signifies not only castration, or the loss of a body part, but the destruction of the entire body itself, and it is associated with the maternal body, now felt to be actively aggressive and threatening.[51]

In this fantasy, the violent aspects of birth (which entail the tearing of the placenta, the cutting of the umbilical cord, the slicing of the perineum) are every bit as formidable as—if not more monstrous than—the "violence" of abortion. Kintz thus helps explain how pro-life images represent men's fantasy-fears of birth and of women more than they represent the hard truth of abortion.

Therefore, we need to respect the fact that from a psychoanalytical point of view, the clinic bomber may be motivated by deep-seated emotional fears. The abortion warrior can be said to be projecting his fears onto the unborn. The fear of losing one's physical penis is related to a fear of losing one's sexual potency, and to a fear of losing one's power in society. These losses and lacks may be compensated by a process of projection. The abortion warrior fears loss of power, projects those fears onto the so-called most vulnerable of all people (the unborn), and fantasizes about absorbing the evil that threatens the unborn. In this way the abortion warrior relieves his unconscious anxiety; he negates the power of his fears. From a psychoanalytical perspective, Kintz is compelling in suggesting that the emotions involved in pro-life politics deserve respect.

When we consider this process of projection in a different way, however, we move from the realm of psychoanalysis more squarely back into the realm of paramilitary politics. Projection is based not only on a lack, and it is not necessarily an act of negating anxiety. Instead, projection is "an act of thrusting or throwing forward, an act that causes an image to appear on the surface."[52] Psychological projection becomes political when it thrusts forward, like the projection of a movie onto a screen, to produce a new image or fantasy. In this regard, it is a political production, not simply a psychological negation of fantasy-fears. It has a "*positing* rather than a negating function."[53] The confession of the clinic bomber does not merely exorcise or negate his fears of losing power; it posits a new relationship between him and the fantastic experience of the unborn. The clinic bomber's fantasy is not only about returning to the womb (that hoary old psychosexual epic). It is a projected fantasy that posits the womb specifically as a battlefield. And it posits him as an abortion warrior in the Army of God.

A series of bombings in and around Atlanta, Georgia, in 1996 and 1997 demonstrated the real ramifications of political projection epitomized by the likes of Trewhella and the Army of God. The name "Army of God" now became a recognizable if not a household term, despite the fact that it "has been used for nearly two decades and in states from Oregon to Virginia" to lay claim to pro-life vandalism, burnings, shootings, and bombings.[54] Letters from the Army of God claimed responsibility for the Atlanta bombings, which were intended to harm people more than to destroy buildings. Targets of these bombs were, in early 1997, a women's clinic and a lesbian bar, and, in July 1996, the site of the summer Olympics. The three chosen targets indicate a conspiracist rationale. The bomber was assumed to be protesting abortion, homosexuality, and the multicultural, multiracial pluralism exemplified by Olympic competition. All three are characteristics of an anti-Christian New World Order, according to such conspiracism. The bombs killed no one but injured many.

Approximately a year later, in January 1998, the Army of God distributed a letter, similar to those delivered in Atlanta, in which it claimed responsibility for the first bombing of an abortion clinic that involved a fatality. An explosion at a Birmingham, Alabama, clinic killed a security guard, Robert Sanderson, and maimed a nurse, Emily Lyons. First sought as a material witness when his pickup truck was spotted leaving the scene, Eric Robert Rudolph is now considered the sole suspect in both the Atlanta and Alabama bombings. Suspicions were strengthened by forensic evidence. Nails and metal plates found among Rudolph's belongings were identical to those used in the construction of all three bombs. The letter that appeared in conjunction with these bombings warned abortion providers that they are "not immune from retaliation" and that the distribution of "the genocidal pill RU-486" would not thwart pro-life retribution. The letter closed with a promise: "Death to the New World Order."[55] Rudolph's case, still unresolved, illustrates how the abortion warrior emerges from and engages paramilitary culture.

As the manhunt for Rudolph proceeded through the dense Appalachian terrain of North Carolina, he became a folk hero. Residents of the area expressed their disdain of the federal agents in their midst.[56] Many locals delighted in Rudolph's evasion and saw the "Feds" as big city buffoons. Militia group members found less humor in the invasive presence of the Bureau of Alcohol, Tobacco, and Firearms and the FBI. Militia members flooded the Internet with commentary about the case in chat rooms and through electronic mail.

One group, the North Carolina Militia Corps, issued a warning to "corrupt law enforcement" not to "violate any member's rights." The warning did not condone the clinic bombing attributed to Rudolph, but it expressed the distrust of federal officials that is characteristic of paramilitary culture. The warning read, in part, "While we are horrified because of the event that took place in Birmingham Alabama we are appalled at the horrendous abuse of power being shown by the federal government agencies when they have not shown the courage or had the—shall we say balls—to arrest the murderers at many [of] our Nationally know[n] terrorist sites." By "murderers at many [of] our Nationally know[n] terrorist sites," the writer is referring to what he sees as "the guilty from Waco, Ruby Ridge, and Oklahoma City."[57] Militias commonly believe that federal agents are to blame for the deaths of the 85 members of the Branch Davidians in Waco, Texas, in 1993; for the deaths of the son and wife of white separatist Randy Weaver in Ruby Ridge, Idaho, in 1992; and for the deaths of 168 people in the bombing of the federal building in Oklahoma City in 1995. Pro-life leaders connect these standoffs with abortion politics as they denounce former Attorney General Janet Reno for storming the Waco compound and for authorizing the "storming of the womb compound."[58] The North Carolina Militia Corps was not the only group that feared another disastrous standoff like those that had led to the deaths in Ruby Ridge and Waco.

Former Green Beret colonel James "Bo" Gritz offered to serve as a mediator between the federal agents and Rudolph.[59] This offer reprised his brief role as negotiator during the FBI siege at Ruby Ridge and replayed the narrative setup of the film *Rambo: First Blood*, in which John Rambo's former commander in Vietnam sought to ease the fury of local and federal officials and bring in the fugitive safely. Although rebuffed by officials, Gritz wanted to keep both them and bounty hunters, who were encouraged by the posted reward of a million dollars, from killing Rudolph before giving him a chance to surrender. Gritz said, "Eric's mom recently expressed fears that her son will be shot on sight. I share her concern." "It's time to thwart those with blood money in their eye and save Eric Rudolph!"[60] By speaking for Rudolph's mother, Gritz assumed the role of surrogate father, which was also a significant element in *Rambo*.[61] Gritz, who once claimed to be the inspiration for the character of Rambo, now projected himself into the role of his father-figure commander.

Before Gritz arrived on the scene, the Rudolph family had used a lawyer to represent them. Fearing that officials had rashly accused Eric in the same way they had wrongly apprehended Richard Jewell after the bombing of Centennial Park in Atlanta, the Rudolphs allowed the lawyer to set up a press conference. But when the time for the conference came, none of the family showed up. A few weeks later, Eric Rudolph's older brother, Daniel, addressed a videotaped message to the journalists whom he had shunned.

According to those who viewed it, the videotape shows Daniel Rudolph in his garage, removing his suit coat, placing a tourniquet around his left forearm, turning on a circular saw, taking a minute or less to contemplate his action, then completely sawing off his left hand at the wrist.[62] He then wrapped his bloody stump in a towel or some other white fabric and left. Reportedly, he drove to a hospital, from which crews were dispatched to retrieve his hand, which was reattached surgically. Everyone was astonished at this radical, sensational display. Journalists scrambled to make meaning of Daniel's only words of explanation spoken on the tape: "This is for the FBI and the media."

Most journalists assumed Daniel's videotape included a religious reference, attributing his action to the Bible verse "if your right hand causes you to sin, cut it off [because] it is better for you to lose one part of your body than for your whole body to go to hell."[63] A few recognized that the disdain expressed for the media and the federal government was common among locals and family friends of the Rudolphs. One revealed that Tom Branham, a close family friend who had helped raise the Rudolph children but who had since had a falling out with Eric, refused to talk with reporters after an initial encounter.[64] Apparently perturbed, he requested that neighbors who resided in Rudolph's former home distribute a "photocopy of a statement that has circulated among white supremacists for a number of years." The statement reads, in part, "the business of the journalist is to destroy truth; to lie outright; to pervert; to vilify; to fawn at the feet of mammon and to sell his country and his race for his daily bread." This report speculated further on racist beliefs shared by the Rudolphs. Some journalists quoted experts on hate groups and extremism; one said, "The way it looks to me, he was rather vigorously protesting what [Daniel] Rudolph imagined to be the persecution of his brother and his family. It's difficult to read it any other way."[65] By all accounts, the Rudolphs felt wrongly targeted and harassed by the FBI and newspeople. No report related the gory incident to the fact that Eric Rudolph was alleged to have blown up an abortion clinic—or to the gory images of mutilation that characterize pro-life protests and testimony.

The actual mutilation Daniel Rudolph inflicted on himself resonates profoundly with the fantastic mutilation to which the previously quoted clinic bomber had subjected himself. In preparation for making the political statement of blowing up an abortion clinic, the bomber had forced himself to imagine the brutal severing of his own arm. Likewise, as a political statement, Daniel Rudolph brutally severs his hand. His anxiety over political persecution (actual or perceived) is projected as abject dismemberment. The videotape shows the process of the mutilation, forcing the viewer to experience the act in real time, projecting the image of a man willing to sacrifice his own hand for the sake of making a statement. Perhaps Daniel Rudolph wanted the video to be played on national television as an example of what the FBI, in pursuing his brother, had brought him to do.

Daniel and Eric Rudolph's actions so engaged one militia member that he commented on them at length via the Internet, in the process making clearer how abortion—and racism—figure into the cultural logic of some factions of the paramilitary right. Most of the following commentary has bases in fact. Eric Rudolph considered himself a mountaineering survivalist and for a time was an enlistee in the U.S. Army.[66] He had no connection to any financial institution, paying rent and making purchases only with cash. As a youth he had submitted a paper to a high school English teacher in which he argued that the Nazi Holocaust and persecution of the Jews had never occurred.[67] Thus, the commentator suggests, he is part of a particular brand of paramilitary culture.

> Fact is, Rudolph is one of us. He is a soldier and an outdoorsman, an agrarian Christian and an Israelite. He has no bank account, no credit line, no social security #, no phone. He learned about avoiding a paper trail when he was 13. He disputed the holahoax [the Holocaust] in a well written term paper in high school when he was 14. He registered his now infamous pick-up truck at a residence in Ashville, NC where he never lived, but where an abortionist resides. (heh-heh) Do not underestimate the lack of fear in the heart of a true Israelite. God's word is written on his heart. The spirit of fear is gone. Eric's brother, Daniel, cut off his hand to give the jewsmedia and the feds their 'pound of flesh.' Now leave his mother alone! (That is one video the jewsmedia and the FBI do not have the stomach or the spine to share with the rest of us.)[68]

The "us" that Rudolph belongs to, according to this writing and many other articles, is a group that subscribes to a white supremacist theology known as Christian Identity. Christian Identity "teaches that whites are the true descendants of the lost tribes of Israel and that Jews, blacks, and other minorities have sprung from Satan and are subhuman."[69]

As a boy, Rudolph had lived in areas in which Christian Identity, or other racist religions, predominated. Rudolph's hometown had a strong Christian Identity presence. The "late [Christian] Identity leader Nord Davis, who founded the Northpoint Tactical Teams, built a compound there that includes a farmhouse, numerous outbuildings, an underground bunker and fortifications made of granite, placed there as a shield against invading government agents."[70] A spokesperson for the group denied having any knowledge of Rudolph prior to the bombings. But Tom Branham, the previously mentioned close family friend who had helped raise the Rudolph boys, was associated with Nord Davis, according to a civil case in federal court from the mid-1980s.[71]

As a teenager, Rudolph had spent as much as six months in Schell City, Missouri, with his mother in a community devoted to the Church of Israel. Its pastor "is adamantly opposed to abortion, homosexuality, miscegenation, and rock music." The pastor has written that Jews "have good mental ability" but are "guided by their father, the Devil." Although he rejects the Christian Identity label that experts have given his 150-member congregation, the pastor says, "we do teach that the Anglo-Saxon people of the earth are the genetic descendants of the Biblical Israel of the lost ten tribes."[72] This teaching is congruent with the racist theology of Aryan Nations, a white supremacist umbrella group founded by a Christian Identity leader. Like the Church of Israel, Aryan Nations teaches that the Aryan race (composed of many "tribes of Israel which are now scattered throughout the world and are now known as the Anglo-Saxon, Celtic, Scandinavian, and Teutonic people of the earth") is the "true Israel of the Bible." This belief goes hand in hand with the idea that "the Jew is the adversary of our race and God."[73] Regardless of what we call it, Eric and Daniel Rudolph were regularly exposed to white separatist and anti-Semitic religiosity from an early age.

The militia member writing in cyberspace thus claims Eric Rudolph as one of his own because Rudolph's profile is in keeping with Christian Identity. In the same vein, Daniel Rudolph is embraced for offering a "pound of flesh" to the "jewsmedia." This anti-Semitic slur refers to a well-worn conspiracist belief that Jews control and manipulate all media as well as the federal government, which is therefore known as the Zionist Occupied Government. Rudolph apparently shared such conspiracist ideas, which explains why he avoids governmental bureaucracy; he "does not have a Social Security number because he believes it is part of a government plot to monitor the actions of U.S. citizens."[74] A farmer and seller of marijuana, Rudolph reported no income, considered television "the electric Jew," and told his sister-in-law that abortion is a means of rendering the white race a minority.[75]

For those ensconced in paramilitary culture, such as Bo Gritz and the North Carolina Militia Corps, Rudolph is a warrior worthy of support and respect because he is, like Rambo, a target of corrupt law enforcement. To those familiar with the racist side of the militia movement (including professionals, whose expertise on white supremacy was solicited, as well as self-identified militia members, whose electronic commentary was offered freely during the manhunt), Rudolph is an exemplary race warrior. As a fugitive, Rudolph has engaged the paramilitary right, if not emerged from its principles. His case exemplifies how New War culture connects opposition to abortion (such as blowing up a clinic) with militia practices (such as avoiding bank accounts and Social Security numbers) and racist or anti-Semitic beliefs (such as denouncing the Holocaust as a hoax).

Paramilitary culture does not presume racism, however. The contemporary militia movement and the Christian Identity movement are hardly synonymous. Approximately one-fourth of the "estimated 225 far Right paramilitary formations in the United States had explicit ties to white hate groups" in 1997. It is therefore a "distortion to characterize the militias in toto as consciously racialist or anti-Semitic."[76] A look at blatantly white supremacist arguments against abortion as distinct from the militia movement demonstrates the tensions and the compatibility between the new abortion warrior and the new race warrior.

New Race War

As the case of Eric Rudolph suggests, the resurgence in organized white supremacy in America after the Vietnam era coincided with the emergence of paramilitary culture. If 1979, the year that ushered in anti-abortion apocalypticism and ushered out right-to-life rhetoric, was a turning point in pro-life politics, it was also a turning point in white supremacist organizing. In 1979, a Christian Identity leader named Richard Butler convened the first annual Aryan Nations World Congress, which brought together white supremacists of various sorts, including Ku Klux Klan members and neo-Nazis.[77] As the paramilitary manifestation of Christian Identity, the Aryan Nations became a strategic hub for all kinds of white race–based groups motivated by the notion that whites, God's chosen people, are engaged in a racial holy war against nonwhites and Jews.

Another momentous event of 1979 was the Greensboro massacre, which occurred in Rudolph's home state of North Carolina. Members of a local

Ku Klux Klan outfit ambushed participants from an anti-racist, civil rights demonstration, at whom they opened fire without warning or mercy, and killed five people.[78] One of the Klansmen, Glenn Miller, later changed the name of his group from the North Carolina Knights of the Ku Klux Klan to the White Patriot Party. Like many leaders in what has been called the "fifth era" of the KKK, Miller fused Southern populism with paramilitary New War culture.[79] The Klan also began to make alliances with neo-Nazis as never before, fashioning what one author has called the "nazification of the Klan."[80] Instead of robes and hoods, members began wearing camouflage fatigues. Eventually, Miller's group espoused "vintage Christian Identity" views, linking, for example, the "farm depression in North Carolina to international Jewish bankers."[81] The new race warrior now thrives in paramilitary garb and takes the "international Jew," even more than African Americans or immigrants, as his primary enemy.[82]

The Klan did not meld completely with the militia movement or Aryan Nations. Especially in opposing abortion, Klansmen adopted some slogans and practices of neo-Nazis and militia groups, repackaging some old white supremacist ideas in pro-life language. When fifteen Ku Klux Klansmen joined about ten neo-Nazi skinheads in a protest at a Florida abortion clinic, the public witnessed a rare demonstration of different generations and different types of American white supremacists coming together to fight abortion.[83] Klan members in ceremonial hoods and robes with purple and gold accents, which date back to the nineteenth century, carried signs warning of "Big Sister Federal Tyranny" (see fig. 1). The Klansmen seemed influenced by and accommodating of the contemporary conspiracist language of New World Order tyranny. In addition, they were uniting with a newer brand of race warrior, the skinheads, a type of neo-Nazi to emerge since the 1970s.[84]

One of the Klansmen who helped organize the protest at the clinic, J. D. Alder, felt the need to distinguish the KKK's involvement in pro-life efforts. Alder therefore recorded a message for a KKK telephone hotline in which he commends Paul Hill, the killer of Dr. John Bayard Britton and clinic escort James Barrett at a Pensacola clinic in 1994, and others who take aim at "baby killers." Alder's message is representative of an older type of white supremacism endemic to the Klan. He attributes abortion to white people's propensity for "racial suicide," a fear dating back to the late nineteenth and early twentieth centuries.

Abortion is mostly a white thing. Abortion is racial suicide for the white race. As white people kill their babies, the jigaboos and other

Fig. 1. *"Abortion is racial suicide for the white race." The Klan pickets outside a clinic in Florida. Reprinted by permission of* Body Politic *and Patricia Baird-Windle.*

mud races are hatching little nigglets as fast as roaches. So-called doctors who commit murder on unborn white babies deserve our undying hatred. It's a miracle that more of them haven't been terminated. Men such as Paul Hill are heroes for eliminating baby killers and saving the lives of unborn beautiful white babies. We of the Klan would be willing to pay higher taxes to pay for tar baby abortions if it meant a whiter and brighter future for our people. There is such a thing as Justifiable Homicide. Baby killers need to know that the Klan is not asleep.

And now for the Tip of the Week. We find the best prices for guns are at Anchor Guns at Port St. Lucie and the Arms Depot in Stewart. We found Mom and Pop's gun store in Fort Pierce to have prices that are just a little too Jewish for us, but I guess the lame brains in some local kook outfit calling themselves The Militia, prefer to pay higher prices for their fire arms. As long as the

[Ku] Klux Klan is in town, we don't need toy soldiers or boy scouts with guns. Tough times call for real men and women—not weekend warriors. So for all you weekend warriors, stay in your fantasy land and drink your cheap beer and clear the battlefield for the real patriots.[85]

Whereas other race-based white groups that have emerged in the latter of half of the twentieth century have rejected charges of being hate mongers, Alder is unabashed in pledging "undying hatred." He sees this virulent racism as distinguishing the Klan from other far-right factions.

In his statement, Alder differentiates the Klansmen from the local militia group, which he sees as engaged in a paramilitary "fantasy land." His characterization of a local "kook outfit" that drinks "cheap beer" is derogatory and based on socioeconomic class stereotypes. Alder's offer to "pay higher taxes" to provide abortions for people of color indicates perhaps that Alder is comfortably middle class, and certainly it presumes a congenial relationship with the government. Historically, the Klan has enjoyed good relations with local and federal officials, some of whom were suspected Klan members themselves.[86] Alder insists that Klansmen are not merely "weekend warriors" but more established, less flighty "patriots" whose history—and presumably significance—extends beyond the weekend.

The basic premise of Alder's commentary—that the white race is not reproducing fast enough—is nearly as old as the Klan itself. At the beginning of the twentieth century, many people—not just Klansmen—feared that the declining birth rate of whites would result in race suicide. The decline was attributed to middle-class white women who were avoiding motherhood and to a new enterprise called birth control—the use of contraception with the intention of "spacing" pregnancies over time to reduce infant and maternal mortality.[87] Alder's message retains and reproduces a white supremacist fear that dates back to the Klan's inception.

Just as old ideas and fears have recirculated among white supremacists who oppose abortion, old Klan tactics have crossed over and become pro-life tactics.[88] These include distributing "wanted" flyers that designate specific individuals as targets of vigilante lynch law. Similarly, as espoused in *Closed: 99 Ways to Stop Abortion*, effigies can be used to further the pro-life cause.[89] A method of political dissent employed worldwide, the effigy focuses on an individual whose corruption or cruelty warrants death. In the pro-life context, effigies signal death to those who provide or obtain abortions. Other symbolic death threats used by pro-lifers include nooses and metal plates riddled with bullets placed on the gates of abortion clinics.

The displaying or posting of crosses in yards—another pro-life tactic—also has roots with the Klan. This tactic has a history with anti-war activists as well, who occasionally constructed fake graveyards to memorialize the numbers killed in Vietnam. But the crosses of pro-life protest call to mind their more sinister use, as the "aunt of a Black clinic employee" once attested. She "said her lawn was planted with small white crosses by 'rescue missionaries'" and "told clinic defenders that such activities reminded her of harassment tactics employed by the Ku Klux Klan in the South."[90]

Another terror tactic of the post-Emancipation Klan, lynching, was often concluded with participants removing body parts from the hanged (or burned or otherwise murdered) body as souvenirs and trophies. People collected teeth, toes, ears, fingers. According to Klan culture, these pieces served as evidence that a wrong had been righted, that further injustice had been deterred, and that lynch law had prevailed. The lynching of black men accused of having raped white women, for example, sometimes included castrating them and dividing pieces of the penis among triumphant members of the lynch mob.[91] Similarly, the *Army of God* manual suggests a method of driving "the abortion industry underground with or without the sanction of the government": by "disarming the persons perpetuating the crimes by removing their hands, or at least their thumbs below the second digit." It continues, the "removal of abortionists' thumbs [is] an act of mercy toward all concerned."[92]

Here again we encounter the politics of abject dismemberment, which need to be put into historical perspective, in addition to the previously discussed context of psychological and semiotic analyses. Like "removed" thumbs and souvenir genitals, the displayed flesh of stillborns or fetuses calls forth such psychoanalytic terms as projection, fetishism, or the uncanny.[93] But seen in the context of crosses, nooses, effigies, and "wanted" posters, the display of actual fetuses as practiced by the pro-life movement may be a cultural relic that has migrated into the movement from the Ku Klux Klan and retains a historical residue of lynching.

Not only cultural practices but members themselves have migrated from the Klan to the pro-life cause. Florida-based John Burt, for example, once was a Klansman and now is an influential pro-life leader who has been photographed repeatedly with a stillborn in his hand.[94] During a trial of clinic bombers in Pensacola, Burt "picketed the courthouse throughout the trial, parading while carrying a jar containing a dead fetus that he nicknamed 'Baby Charlie,' provoking disgust, outrage—and attention—throughout the city."[95] Not satisfied with a picture or a poster, Burt used actual fetal flesh to signal moral depravity, sexual deviance, and religious blasphemy.

Just as Alder's opposition to abortion was derived from an older premise of race suicide, Burt's practice of carrying fetal parts may derive from Klan heritage, specifically from its anti-Catholic campaigns. Although Burt has adamantly and earnestly denounced his membership in the Klan, he seems to memorialize the Old South. According to one reporter who visited his home, "there was a Stars and Bars battle flag of the Confederate forces, and there were huge prints of 'Johnny Reb' soldiers, including one with a gray-uniformed young man whose head was bowed as he stood somberly above the slogan, 'The South will rise again.' "[96] In addition, Burt has kept anti-Catholic literature in his home, according to one pro-life visitor who took offense to it.[97] Burt's penchant for displaying fetal flesh bears a historical resemblance to similar displays used in early-twentieth-century anti-Catholic tours sponsored by the Klan.

In the 1910s and 1920s, when race suicide was a common fear among the white middle class and the Klan was a very popular middle-class member organization, the Klan circulated salacious stories of sex, sadism, infanticide, and abortion to promote anti-Catholic sentiment nationwide. Not unlike pro-life presentations that feature female speakers who used to work in abortion clinics, Klan events billed Helen Jackson as an "escaped nun" whose effectiveness was ensured by props: "Jackson traveled across the country, regaling her sex-segregated audiences with tales of sexual horrors behind convent walls. She claimed to have firsthand knowledge of infanticides and abortions forced on nuns by the priests who fathered their babies. Displaying little leather bags, Jackson told her riveted audience that these were used to dispose of the convents' murdered newborns and aborted fetuses."[98] Jackson's memoirs were published as *Convent Cruelties* and distributed widely by the Klan with other anti-Catholic books and pamphlets.[99] Some of the printed material purported a Catholic Knights of Columbus pledge against Protestants and other "heretics" that supposedly instructed Catholic initiates to "rip open the stomachs and wombs of [non-Catholic] women and crash their infants' head against the walls in order to annihilate their execrable race."[100]

It seems to be part of Klan heritage to accuse enemies, in the most sensational manner possible, of sexual debauchery, infanticide, abortion, and the desire to annihilate the white race. However, the Klan has changed its opinion of who their enemies are and of who really wants to annihilate the white race. Now that abortion is tantamount to race suicide, as Alder makes clear, naming Catholics—whose opposition to abortion has been so keen—as enemies would be counterproductive. There is another group to blame for the supposed decline of the white population through abortion. According to the new race warrior: "More than ten million white babies have been murdered through Jewish-engineered legalized abortion since 1973 here in America and more than a million per year are being slaughtered this way. The Klan understands this is just one of many tools used to destroy the white race and we know who it is."[101] Instead of blaming Catholics, Klansmen now blame the Jews.

New Genocide, New Holocaust

As adopted by the United Nations in 1948, *genocide* is a legal term that describes the mass killing of a national, racial, or religious group. It was coined after Nazi Germany exterminated millions of Jews as part of Hitler's plan to secure the future for a master race. To accuse a person or a group of genocide is to assert their criminality and request their punishment. Thus when the Ku Klux Klan asserts that "Jewish-engineered abortion" is committing genocide against the white race, the Ku Klux Klan is not only locating a source of the supposed decline of the white population but also is suggesting its arrest and some sort of punishment. This notion is clearly stated by the White Aryan Resistance leader who said, "Jews must be punished for this holocaust and murder of white children."[102] When they focus on Jews as those responsible for abortion in the United States today, white supremacists displace the victims of the Nazi Holocaust and replace them with a fantastic white unborn population that is subject to genocide and holocaust.

To achieve this displacement, American white supremacists have revised the history of fighting the Nazis in World War II. Richard Butler, who first convened the Aryan Nations in 1979 and served in the U.S. military during World War II, later claimed, "I fought on the wrong side of the war because I fought against my own race."[103] This sentiment is expanded in an Aryan Nations newsletter article titled "The Tragedy of the White Race," in which a U.S. World War II veteran reflects on his part in military history, calling the defeat of Hitler "the last flicker of white life" and otherwise using the word *life* as shorthand for white life.[104] The "tragedy of the white race," he claims, is brought about by a "hatred for life itself." American white supremacists often employ the language of "life itself" to express their fears of genocide and extinction, and in effect to pose white survival as a pro-life issue. Their anti-Semitism and racism lie not so much in portraying unborn white generations as victims of genocide as in the corollary to this move: demonizing those who are not white and Christian.

This demonization is clearly pronounced in the cover illustration for a book titled *The Real Holocaust: The Attack on Unborn Children and Life Itself*.[105] The image is one of a man standing outside a clinic and throwing small coffins into a mass grave, while in the background three men are riding camels under a star that resembles an old German cross. The caption reads: "Fewer and fewer will escape if we can keep Christians from listening to the Wise Men!" The man is identified as an abortionist and anti-Christian by a sign on a fence that reads "Dr. Herod's Abortion Clinic." On the night Christ was born (referenced here by the wise men following the star of Bethlehem), Herod the Great supposedly committed a "slaughter of the holy innocents," a bloodbath of the children of Bethlehem, in his attempt to find and kill the child Jesus. When pro-life proponents refer to abortion as another indiscriminate "slaughter of the innocents," they are recalling the story of Herod and reinscribing abortion as a conflict not between fetal rights and women's rights but between Christian life and anti-

Christian forces. Should we sense only indirect, implicit anti-Semitism in the notion of presenting modern-day abortion as a slaughter of innocents, *The Real Holocaust* defines anti-Christian as Jewish, making its cover blatant and explicit. It is a Jewish man who is throwing small coffins into the mass grave. Thus the reversal is complete: Jews are responsible for a holocaust of the unborn white population and are sabotaging Christian "life itself."

This reversal works in tandem with a campaign to convince people that the midcentury Holocaust of six million Jews never occurred, that the mass graves in Nazi Germany were never filled. This campaign began in the 1980s, about the same time that pro-lifers escalated their arson attacks against abortion clinics.[106] The kind of blatant racism and anti-Semitism endemic of Holocaust deniers or of texts such as *The Real Holocaust* is rare in pro-life writing. Nevertheless, racism and anti-Semitism are accommodated and sometimes are latent in pro-life campaigns that argue that abortion is as reprehensible as genocide, or that it actually is genocide.

Black Americans have long considered the public health policies of coerced abortion and sterilization to be part of a genocidal politics aimed against them. This charge of attempted genocide through reproductive control of people of color has some merit, as scholars have shown. Native Americans, African Americans, and Latinas historically have been the targets of U.S. reproductive regulation and sterilization abuse, which many have argued comprise genocidal tactics.[107] Yet it is predominantly white pro-life groups that use the genocide argument unabashedly. In claiming that abortion is a holocaust of the unborn, or a new genocide, pro-life politics thus seem to some extent to be linked to anti-racist and anti-fascist campaigns.

But this link is weak and twisted. It presents the unborn not as a subset of religious or racial groups, like Jews and blacks, but as a group whose experience parallels that of Jews and blacks. An awareness of abortion as genocide requires an acknowledgment of the unborn as a group persecuted, like blacks or Jews, as a racial or religious minority. A pro-life campaign called the Genocide Awareness Project (GAP), which has toured more than twenty-five colleges and universities in the United States since 1997, exemplifies this move.[108]

Tactics of GAP include using large, professionally produced banners whose panels display different scenes of supposedly genocidal destruction (see fig. 2). The size of the banners, six feet by thirteen feet, allows images of fetal parts to appear as large as bodies of fully grown men. The old pro-life trick of magnifying fetal images is used to suggest that the aborting of a pregnancy is as serious an offense as the mass murder of generations of

Fig. 2. *Images from the Genocide Awareness Project help expand definitions of genocide to include abortion, breast cancer, and the Oklahoma City bombing. Photograph by Luis Sanchez Saturno.*

people. A banner featured as an exemplary product in Paul de Parrie's *Life Advocate* magazine sports three panels depicting a grisly mass of Jewish victims of the Holocaust, a lynched man hanging from a tree, and an equally grisly fetal skull, supposedly representing the victims of abortion.[109] Each image has a caption: "Ungentile," "Unwhite," and "Unborn," respectively. The implication is that each group is persecuted by genocide on the basis of its racial or religious difference.

A cynical reading of these captions reveals that they operate as a rhetorical trope. The "un" in each functions in a way similar to the "un" in "uncola." Also known as 7-Up, a product of the Coca-Cola company, uncola was a marketing ploy that played on the countercultural trend to buck established norms but that nevertheless bolstered the sales of an established cola company. Likewise, the "un" in these captions appeals to liberals and leftists while promoting the conservative, right-wing message that abortion should be outlawed. In the context of white supremacist thought, it is easy to read the "Ungentile, Unwhite, Unborn" banner as an indictment of—not solidarity with—the abject of society (massacred Jews, lynched blacks, and expelled fetuses). According to this thinking, liberal, leftist accounts of the Holocaust, lynching, and abortion have in fact tried to "undo" gentile, white, born men.

The designers of GAP pledged to "refine the messages" for fullest im-

pact. And so, as GAP has g[...]
costing a thousand dollars.[...] [...] twenty banners now exist that
compare the unborn with whales, laboratory animals, breast cancer survivors, Cambodian and Rwandan children, and infant victims of the Oklahoma City bombing.[111] Although GAP draws comparisons with children of
other countries, it defines the victims of abortion as specifically American.
This definition is made clear on the website of the organization that created GAP, where the director (a decorated Vietnam veteran) explains that
there are "several dictionary definitions of 'genocide.' One is the extermi-
nation of a national group. The national group is unborn American children."[112] Elsewhere, the GAP director suggests that a dictionary's "reference to the murder of 'whole' groups and nations" in its definition of
genocide "was already obsolete." Furthermore, "dictionary definitions of
genocide have little to do with total numbers of victims," according to
GAP officials, and thus GAP has refined and redefined the original intent
of the word.[113]

The slippery way in which GAP defines genocide is exactly what allows
racists to argue that abortion is genocide of white people. Not content
with a mere dictionary definition, one white supremacist contends that
"the people of European descent of this world are the targets of a constant,
consistent, systematic, sustained campaign of genocide, with the intention
of humiliating, subjugating, and eventually eliminating our people." After
examining the United Nations' definition of genocide, he neatly lists all
the things that supposedly comprise a genocidal campaign against white
people:

> Is multi-racialism genocide? Yes it is. Is multi-culturalism genocide?
> Yes it is. Is teaching minorities self-esteem while teaching Whites
> "sensitivity" genocide? Yes it is. Is diversity indoctrination geno-
> cide? Yes it is. Is toleration of illegal immigration genocide? Yes it
> is. Is any non-White immigration, except perhaps for diplomatic
> and consular representatives, genocide? Yes it is. Do anti-discrimi-
> nation laws constitute genocide? Yes they do. Do "hate crime" laws
> constitute genocide? Yes they do. Does support of convenience
> abortion constitute genocide? Yes it does. Does promotion of ho-
> mosexuality constitute genocide? Yes it does. Is suppression of in-
> formation on racial difference genocide? Yes it is. Is "affirmative ac-
> tion" genocide? Yes it is. Is the subliminal or overt promotion of
> interracial sex on TV genocide? Yes it is. Does failure to provide
> equal media time to Whites to further their cause, constitute geno-

cide? Yes it does. Does the undermining of loyalty of Whi... cans to their own people constitute genocide? Yes it does. Does undermining the sovereignty of our nation and the promotion of world government constitute genocide? Yes it does. It is not necessary to use gas chambers to commit genocide.[114]

Although GAP does not purport the conspiracist notions exhibited here, it certainly accommodates them when it argues that abortion is "systematic killing."[115] The similarity of GAP's definition to this explicitly white supremacist argument about genocide invigorates the question about which racial or religious differences the unborn are meant to represent.

This question is complicated further by the fact that GAP was originally designed to appeal to members of the Promise Keepers men's movement, which convened for a huge revival in Washington, D.C., in November 1997.[116] The convention was called "Stand in the Gap," in reference to a biblical verse, and the acronym GAP was intended to resemble this slogan of the Promise Keepers. A Christian evangelical group known for gathering its large congregations in sports arenas (the natural habitat of ex–football coach and Promise Keepers' founder Bill McCartney), the Promise Keepers aim to live their personal lives for Christ, to structure their family lives according to patriarchal order, and to "take back the country" for Jesus. As a predominantly white phenomenon, the Promise Keepers movement has had to defend itself from accusations of being exclusively white or of incorporating demands for racial purity with its quest for spiritual purity. Promise Keepers president Randy Phillips told one newspaper that "the goal is not [racial] integration . . . the goal is reconciling through relationships."[117] Thus, Promise Keepers is seen as promoting "essentially regressive racial politics."[118] By 1997, the Promise Keepers had formulated seven promises for the new Christian soldier to keep, one of which is to promote racial "reconciliation" rather than racial equality or integration.

The GAP sought to add an eighth promise, a promise to oppose abortion.[119] One of the banners the group displayed in Washington depicted a first trimester abortion and read, "Promise #8 I am committed to not killing my children." Suggesting that the in utero "children" of these white men are targets of genocide racializes the unborn as white. Thus when Promise Keeper founder McCartney "addressed a rally of Operation Rescue, which was trying to close a local women's clinic, [he was able to declare] that abortion had become 'a second Civil War.' "[120] Other war cries are inevitable at Promise Keeper meetings, which are overtly apocalyptic:

"One PK director says it is a fulfillment of the Bible's prophecy of a great force that will destroy sinners in the period preceding Armageddon."[121]

As a post-Vietnam Christian men's movement, the Promise Keepers illustrates how the revitalization of America masculinity has become more blatantly religious. Other illustrations of this trend are handbooks targeted to born-again American men, such as *Tender Warrior*.[122] The paramilitary machismo implied in being a warrior for Jesus is tempered with a call to be tender and loving toward those the Christian warrior is ordained to subdue. Men are meant to be submissive to God and to demand submission from women, especially wives. In defining tenderness as a manly attribute to be distinguished from weakness or effeminacy, *Tender Warrior* encourages domination by a kinder, gentler, more Christ-centered male.

Although the relationship between American masculinity and godliness has a history too long to engage here, we can see the premise of *Tender Warrior* and the Promise Keepers as a variation on the theme of "self-imposed restraint," which thwarts godly, American manhood.[123] Just as the U.S. government is to blame for restraining U.S. soldiers in Vietnam so they were unable to win the war, American culture (supposedly secularized and feminized during the Vietnam era) is to blame for restraining American husbands and fathers from taking their rightful place as leaders of the family. Thus Michael Bray, who defends killing for life in *A Time to Kill*, complains of a "testosterone deficiency" that has resulted in "an emasculated church."[124] GAP's outreach to the Promise Keepers sought to guarantee that the thwarting of women's self-determination and reproductive freedom is part of this tender Christian agenda to remasculinize America. By arguing that abortion is a new genocide, GAP does not assert but certainly resembles and accommodates some of the most virulently racist and anti-Semitic attitudes that have repackaged white supremacy as pro-life patriotism. In this post-Vietnam cultural context, the new abortion warrior has emerged essentially as a religious figure who may believe (as did Goldwater) that we are all equal in the eyes of God, but not in any other respect.

The fall of Saigon ended the Vietnam War in 1975. That year also saw the first issue of *Soldier of Fortune* magazine and new handbooks with instructions for forming militia "bands of patriots" to challenge a new federalism and restore states' rights.[125] David Duke, undeterred by the lowest national membership in Klan history, initiated the Knights of the Ku Klux Klan in Louisiana, transforming "rednecks in sheets to good ol' boys in wing-tip shoes."[126] The National Right to Life Committee was the largest secular anti-abortion organization, and the first volume of *Human Life Review* rolled off the presses, in hopes of expanding the right-to-life argument. In 1975, the soldier of fortune, the patriot, and the Klansman had not yet met the right-to-lifer.

By 1979, however, the same year that gave us the nazification of the Klan and the founding of Aryan Nations, rights rhetoric was being replaced by more warlike, apocalyptic pro-life language, distributed through organizations such as the Moral Majority and American Life League. And so the abortion warrior emerged from the baby-killing imperialism of America in Vietnam to fight the baby killing on the home front. As a revitalization of Christian masculinity, the guerrilla politics of pro-life America stealthily moved ahead.

2

From Protest to Retribution

The Guerrilla Politics of Pro-Life Violence

Finding an accurate vocabulary with which to discuss pro-life violence is not easy, given that in the 1990s, "life" became in some anti-abortion circles a justification for killing rather than an argument against it. Michael Bray, author of *A Time to Kill* and Paul de Parrie, editor of *Life Advocate* magazine, are two pro-life leaders who publicly defend killing for life on biblical principles.[1] After the first assassination of an abortion provider, Dr. David Gunn, by Michael Griffin in 1993, Bray helped Paul Hill write a statement that claimed murdering abortionists is "justifiable homicide."[2] This "Defensive Action" statement was signed by thirty pro-life leaders and circulated to the media a year before Hill himself fatally shot two men outside a Pensacola clinic. Since the shooting, Bray and other pro-life organizers have hosted an annual White Rose Banquet, at which letters by Hill and other incarcerated pro-life activists are read; their cars parked outside the banquet hall sport such bumperstickers as "Execute Murderers/Abortionists."[3] For these pro-life leaders, it is not a contradiction to kill for life.

Pro-life organizations, however, denounce all violence, and many pro-lifers I have personally spoken with have told me that those who commit anti-abortion violence are not "real" pro-lifers. Many insist that they deplore violence, which they say is antithetical to the principles of the pro-life movement. They speak with a conviction that I respect—a conviction that seems to be one heartfelt aspect of witnessing their faith. But witnessing is only one form of pro-life discussion. It is an oral, performative discourse designed to spur religious conversion, to proselytize. I have witnessed a lot of witnessing, and I am grateful for those pro-lifers who have shared with me their life stories and their views. My analysis, however, is based more on primary pro-life texts written by and for the pro-life community. These texts, unfettered by the compulsion to proselytize, supply accurate vocabulary with which to discuss pro-life violence and insights with which to analyze it.

Pro-life texts in the 1990s articulate an acceptance of violence that is not generally acknowledged beyond militants such as Bray and Hill. In this chapter I focus not on the calls for violence they wrote but on a text that describes a strategy for working within the system, a strategy for restoring "respect for life" through legislation and litigation. The text, an underground manual circulated in 1992 by Mark Crutcher, is titled *Firestorm: A Guerrilla Strategy for a Pro-Life America.*[4] Many confidential pro-life strategies have preceded *Firestorm*, including campaigns delineated in the *Abortion Buster's Manual, Closed: 99 Ways to Stop Abortion,* the *Army of God* manual, and "No Place to Hide." All of these, like *Firestorm*, seek not to outlaw abortion but to stigmatize and demoralize by subjecting those who provide and seek abortions to exposure, sabotage, and harassment. Unlike the strategies set forth in these earlier publications, however, those outlined in *Firestorm* hope to carry out this harassment through "guerrilla legislation."

Like the term *pro-life murder*, the expression *guerrilla legislation* seems to be an oxymoron. Legislation is the result of a formalized and painstakingly slow legal process, or the collection of state-sanctioned laws procured by such a process. Guerrilla action is radical, random, and often violent and illegal. But *Firestorm*, in coining the phrase *guerrilla legislation*, calls into question these general assumptions and hints at a relationship between pro-life violence and pro-life legal strategy.

In *Firestorm*, guerrilla legislation refers both to a collectivity of pro-life laws and to the litigious and legislative processes by which pro-lifers can propose, pass, and enforce those laws. For example, Crutcher suggests promoting malpractice litigation by passing more than twenty new regulatory and punitive laws; he then provides a partial description of the organizational infrastructure needed to make such laws and litigation work together in a cumulative way. The term *guerrilla legislation* is a self-conscious choice of words that draws from and perpetuates the paramilitarization of pro-life thought and strategy. Indeed, Crutcher gives a standard dictionary definition for *guerrilla*: "one who engages in irregular warfare especially as a member of an independent unit carrying out harassment and sabotage" (36). The intent of *Firestorm* is "guerrilla" in that it relies on independent operators and independent cases of litigation and legislation to sabotage and harass, on an irregular and arbitrary basis, those seeking or providing abortions.

Crutcher, sometimes known as "the most dangerous anti-abortionist in America," is president of two nonprofit corporations in Denton, Texas— Life Dynamics Incorporated (LDI) and National Lifesource. According to investigative reporter Donna Fielder, these two corporations' 1997 IRS 990 forms (on which tax-exempt organizations report their finances) show that during 1997, at least, a lot of money was moved back and forth between them.[5] National Lifesource, whose headquarters are the Crutcher residence, received $2,258,662 in gifts or grants and itself donated $480,214 to LDI. LDI turned around and donated $600,000 in cash and $63,774 in office equipment to National Lifesource, ending 1997 with net assets of $509,090. Each 990 form records "none" in the space that asks for "donee's relationship." In 1997, Crutcher's salary was $72,929. The two cars he and his family appear to drive are listed in the county tax office as property of National Lifesource. In addition to these two cars, National Lifesource lists six other automotive vehicles as property on its 990 forms, including a Chevy suburban, a Cadillac, a GMC Yukon, a pickup truck, a van, and a BMW. Perhaps this oddity is related to the fact that before becoming a pro-life crusader, Crutcher sold cars.[6] Crutcher may indeed be dangerous, or he may be merely opportunistic. He has repackaged existing pro-life strategies as new and innovative and is now professionalizing the paramilitary mentality of the new abortion warrior; in the process he is making a good living.

Regardless of whether or to what degree *Firestorm* or Mark Crutcher is dangerous, the very idea of guerrilla legislation indicates an ideological relationship between pro-life violence and pro-life litigation and legislation. Instead of viewing pro-life violence as either lunatic fringe behavior or reasonable force necessitated by a repressive state that prohibits peaceful protest, we can situate pro-life trends toward the use of violent tactics in the context of pro-life trends in legal strategy. Such contextualization demonstrates how pro-life violence and pro-life litigation or legislation function together politically, even if they are not orchestrated. Pro-life litigation and legislation capitalize on pro-life violence, and as primary pro-life texts reveal, pro-life ideology accommodates violence not only implicitly and in practice, but also explicitly and in principle.

Trends in Illegal, Violent Tactics

Journalists and scholars have detailed how pro-lifers came to use violent means to protest abortion.[7] Few, however, have considered the historical trends within that violence, which since the first killing of an abortion provider by Michael Griffin, has become more and more like guerrilla warfare. Three trends in particular suggest a definite shift from protest to guerrilla warfare.

First, pro-life assassins no longer fit the description of religious martyrs, protesters, or proselytizers. Assassins no longer confront abortion providers face to face, as Michael Griffin approached David Gunn a few days before the murder.[8] Neither do they hope to serve as martyrs, as Paul Hill had intended, sacrificing his freedom (and possibly his life) to challenge pro-choice laws (specifically the 1994 Freedom to Access Clinic Entrances Act) and save babies. The trend has become one of anonymous snipers shooting at abortion providers from undisclosed locations. Gunmen and bombers alike flee the scene after attacking instead of standing their ground as either political protesters or religious exemplars. The trend is toward becoming a fugitive guerrilla rather than a martyr, as in the case of the alleged assassin James Kopp, who is suspected of shooting various doctors in their homes in upstate New York and Canada. Specifically, Kopp is accused of killing Dr. Barnett Slepian; he disappeared eleven days later, just before a warrant was issued because authorities wanted to question him. Kopp had the resources and connections that allowed him to flee ultimately to France, which had abolished capital punishment in 1981. French authorities recommended extradition on the condition that "the death penalty will not be requested, pronounced or applied."[9] Kopp denies all of the charges. However, if he is not responsible for Slepian's death and the other sniper fire, one or more gunmen who have been taking aim at abortion providers remain at large, fugitives rather than martyrs.

Second, most recent bombs, unlike those detonated in Pensacola in 1984, are made not only to destroy buildings that house clinics but to kill and maim people.[10] For example, later bombs (such as those detonated in Atlanta and Alabama) were designed to ignite while people were in the clinic. It has become more usual for multiple bombs to be planted, so that one explodes or is detected first, and then the other detonates after police or paramedics have arrived on the scene to investigate the first.[11] The objective to not only sabotage facilities but to maim or kill personnel is especially evident when bombs contain nails or shrapnel; when detonated, such bombs propel these small metal shards or spikes through the skin of anyone in proximity.

Third, civil disobedience in the form of direct action has given way to domestic terrorism. Direct action tactics such as clinic blockades have been replaced by more underground activities such as butyric acid attacks and anthrax scares, in addition to the bombings and shootings. Pro-lifers explain that a repressive, unfair government has prevented them from protesting peacefully by enacting laws such as the Freedom to Access Clinic Entrances (FACE), and thus they have been forced to take illegal, violent action. But the FACE law went into effect in 1994, after David Gunn was murdered and after George Tiller, an abortion provider in Kansas, had been shot. To argue that lethal force was made necessary by the FACE laws ignores basic chronology and cannot account for the desire to cause bodily harm, which is evident in the shootings, anti-personnel bombings, and butyric acid attacks.

By making this shift toward terrorism and guerrilla warfare, pro-lifers are able to translate the element of surprise into a sustained psychological fear derived from the arbitrary and irregular nature of the attacks. In 1998, butyric acid attacks were launched on a wide scale. From May 18 through 23, the highly toxic chemical that can cause severe nausea and irritation of eye, throat, nose, and skin was spilled or squirted into ten clinics in Florida. From July 6 through 8, eight more clinics were hit with the acid in New Orleans and the Houston area.[12] These concentrated attacks aim to deter clinic employees from working and to force clinic owners to spend a lot of money removing the toxic residue from both personnel and clinic walls and floors. Although eruptions of butyric acid attacks have seemed to occur simultaneously, not all clinics are targeted each time, and it is impossible to predict which clinics will be doused in the future. Before 1998, according to the National Abortion Federation, seventy-nine incidents of butyric acid vandalism had caused damage totaling $863,050.

Anthrax scares are also deployed arbitrarily and irregularly. Anthrax, classified as a biological weapon, is a deadly bacterium that can be sealed in an envelope or left on any surface. In October 1998, seven clinics in Indiana, Kentucky, and Tennessee received letters that claimed, "You have just been exposed to anthrax." As a result of coming into contact with such letters, employees and patients of a clinic in Indianapolis, as well as two police officers and a postal worker, were scrubbed down by special hazardous chemical emergency crews.[13] In February 1999, another rash of anthrax scares occurred, this time at clinics in Missouri, Washington, and West Virginia. Approximately thirty fire fighters and employees "were quarantined and washed down with bleach" in one location; in another, the building was evacuated.[14] All of these incidents were hoaxes; the bacterium had not been used. Nevertheless, even Attorney General John Ashcroft, a devoutly pro-life evangelical, had to admit finally that anthrax scares aimed at abortion clinic personnel constitute domestic terrorism. This admission came only after anthrax scares made national news in the aftermath of the terrorist attacks of September 11, 2001. Traces of anthrax were found in congressional and media offices, where some employees were treated with antibiotics. Then, hundreds of reproductive health care clinics across the country received letters that "contained a white powder and a note that read: 'You have been exposed to anthrax. We are going to kill all of you. Army of God, Virginia Dare Chapter.' "[15] Ashcroft at first refused to meet with "alarmed abortion providers, preferring to delegate such matters to subordinates."[16] But when Clayton Waagner, a prison escapee who called himself an anti-abortion terrorist, claimed responsibility for the mass mailing of fake anthrax letters and vowed via the Internet to kill forty-two abortion providers unless they quit their jobs, it was impossible for Ashcroft to deny that the threats fell under the category of domestic terrorism. He put Waagner on the FBI's Ten Most Wanted list, along with Osama bin Laden.

Waagner's highly public campaign to terrorize abortion providers into resigning their jobs confirms the trend away from mere protest and challenges the notion of the lone, psychotic, extremist martyr. The mailings for which Waagner took responsibility were a sophisticated campaign featuring return addresses ostensibly from the U.S. Secret Service and the U.S. Marshall Service; correct spellings of names and addresses; and authentic Federal Express packaging and account numbers, access to which indicates a keen understanding of clinic security. "This is not a crazed, ragged, fiery-eyed bunch," said one sociologist who had examined some of the letters.[17] Nor is it probably the work of one man alone.

It is difficult to understand how Waagner, as a hunted fugitive, could have gathered the materials for the anthrax letters, prepared them, and then mailed them all by himself, as he claims. After the mailings, he enlisted the help of Neal Horsley and his notorious website, the Nuremberg Files, to advertise how abortion providers could register their job resignations and thereby avoid death. According to Horsley, Waagner threatened him with a gun and tied him up, but some officials suspect collusion rather than a hostage situation.[18] Regardless, Waagner's meeting with Horsley was not irrational and psychotic but shrewd and strategic.

Some pro-life leaders publicly admired the effects of Waagner's strategy, applauding the possibility of terrorizing people into leaving their employment. Michael Bray wrote on the Internet,

> The use of anthrax or the threat of the same is not popular, especially
> in the wake of 911. But it was certainly effectual. Abortuaries were
> closed all around the county. Babies were, by all facts of statistics,
> saved from death. Waagner disrupted abortuary operations through-
> out the country with the very fact of his being on the lam following
> his simple statement to the agents. He added to the fears of abortuary
> personnel by re-issuing direct threats when he held Neal Horsley at
> gun point while informing him that he would proceed to kill 42 spe-
> cific [clinic workers] on whom he had already gathered data. The
> chosen could be seen on Horsley's web site as having ceased to prac-
> tice abortion and relieved. Several abortionists did contact Horsley
> and notified him of their decision to abandon baby killing.[19]

Although no pro-choice organizations or individuals confirmed Bray's claim, the general attrition of abortion providers nationwide since the 1980s is undeniable.[20] Anthrax scares and direct threats such as Waagner's are only the latest methods in decades of increasingly clandestine and sophisticated efforts to terrorize citizens devoted to reproductive freedom and health care services for women.

Not knowing when an anthrax scare, butyric acid attack, sniper attack, or bombing will hit is, to say the least, unnerving. Since 1990, 150 incidents of arson, 39 clinic bombings, and more than 100 cases of assault and battery have gone on record. Since 1993, 7 people have been murdered, and 15 murders have been attempted.[21] The psychological terror these efforts have induced is accompanied by the financial sabotage they procure. The costs of rebuilding facilities, cleaning hazardous chemical spills, replacing staff, paying hiked insurance rates, and increasing security are extraordinary.

Such trends in illegal, violent tactics are not elements of protest. They are more accurately described as sabotage waged by guerrillas. But our earlier definition of a guerrilla as one who engages in "irregular warfare especially as a member of an independent unit carrying out harassment and sabotage" can also accurately describe one who engages in both lawful and legal pro-life strategies.

Trends in Legal Strategies

Despite its military-apocalyptic title, *Firestorm: A Guerrilla Strategy for a Pro-Life America* is an eighty-six-page manual that delineates the rationale for and components of a legal and nonviolent strategy. It is not a well-known text because, like most underground manuals, its effectiveness depends on its obscurity. Written and circulated by Mark Crutcher in 1992, *Firestorm* is emphatically "CONFIDENTIAL and is intended to be used only by those people to whom it was directly sent" (87).

Those who want "to win" the "battle" for "an America which protects its unborn" (1) are the intended audience for *Firestorm*. In the volume, Crutcher relinquishes the goal of reversing *Roe v. Wade* and outlawing abortion; instead, much like the authors of the *Army of God* manual, he seeks to increase the financial and psychological costs of providing or obtaining abortions until the procedure is no longer feasible.[22] Unlike the overt promotion of violence in *Army of God*, however, *Firestorm* seeks to increase those costs by using only lawful and legal means—that is, by breaking no laws and by promoting pro-life legislation and litigation. Proposing a "steady stream of regulatory legislation that's specifically designed to run [doctors] out of business," *Firestorm* emphasizes "a requirement that all abortions have to be done by licensed physicians" who carry "mandatory malpractice insurance, or proof of financial responsibility" (50).

Unlike Crutcher's publicly distributed writings, this underground manual predicted much of the legal maneuvering and illegal terrorism that has characterized pro-life politics in the 1990s.[23] For example, *Firestorm* predicted that pro-life assassinations would occur; a year later, Dr. David Gunn was killed. It also predicted that "abortions done late in pregnancy" would be prohibited—a prediction made three years before the ban on late-term or so-called partial birth abortions were introduced in Congress. Although *Firestorm* is not an exact blueprint for pro-life legislation, much less a discussion of the relation between pro-life laws and anti-abortion violence, the legal strategies it describes resemble guerrilla warfare in design and effect.

Like trends in illegal pro-life violence, plans for legal guerrilla campaigns reject the idea that "it's OK to martyr yourself for the unborn"; instead, tactics are designed so that they not appear to be part of an orchestrated strategy (1). Both guerrilla warfare and what *Firestorm* refers to as guerrilla legislation are executed as isolated incidents. To this end, Crutcher created Life Dynamics Incorporated (or LDI) as a front organization for the monitoring of separate "guerrilla campaigns." Rather than creating "another national organization with its own state affiliates," Crutcher emphasizes that LDI should legally operate as and be seen as "a 'company' that provides education and support materials to existing state groups who want to make a commitment to this guerrilla campaign" (83). This facade masks the organization's roles in orchestrating the guerrilla campaigns, labeled G-1 to G-5 ("G" for guerrilla), and detailed in *Firestorm*. Other duties of LDI, as conceived in 1992, are as follows:

(b) develop and produce the "hard products" necessary to carry-out those activities (ad slicks; post-cards; operating manuals; training materials; videos; etc.);

(c) develop sales and marketing strategies for each of the G-3 regulatory legislation proposals, and educate state leaders in those strategies. LDI will also provide the educational tools needed to teach the "business approach" needed for some of the G-2, G-4, and G-5 activities;

(d) become a central clearing house to constantly monitor the guerrilla campaign in every state. LDI will identify what works and what doesn't, and track the abortion industry's defense tactics;

(e) see that [G-1 through G-5] is carried-out as evenly as possible from state to state. (82–83)

The individual guerrilla programs are specifically designed to appear to be working as independent campaigns. But the ulterior motive is to achieve an optimal, culminating impact: "We don't want one state's guerrilla program getting too far ahead of the others. That would simply become a warning to the abortion industry in other states of exactly what our future intentions are for them" (83).

As a front organization, LDI is designed to use other pro-life organizations under the guise of serving them. LDI is publicized as a clearinghouse of educational materials, but *Firestorm* reveals that the real agenda is to be a "clearing house to constantly monitor the guerrilla campaign." Reports of LDI's activities have sounded the alarm that a new pro-life strategy is afoot, and that it has a propensity for sneakiness. For example, one journalist emphasizes the shady dealings in his reportage:

> In March 1993, Life Dynamics, under the guise of an abortion rights advocacy group called 'Project Choice,' took a survey of physicians who provided abortions about their personal fears and misgivings about the procedure, then released the findings to the media. In April 1993, the group published a book of crude jokes and cartoons about abortion providers. It then mailed copies to half of the medical students in America. But Life Dynamics' latest project, pushing malpractice suits, may prove the most controversial.[24]

In general, reports of LDI do not portray the organization in a favorable light; it is often described as controversial and dangerous. But neither do reports indict LDI as the front organization for a larger guerrilla strategy called Firestorm.

Although the media have reported that LDI is a "self-proclaimed center of a guerrilla movement," they seem to have accepted that this idea is only a military metaphor.[25] *Firestorm*'s description of LDI as the cover for a decentralized and clandestine guerrilla strategy is not a rhetorical trick. It indicates, rather, a desire to make pro-life action as decentralized and leaderless as possible. *Firestorm*'s description of guerrilla operatives or agents reveals an intention to rely on a loosely knit coalition of individuals, not a massive, unified movement compelled by majority consensus.

> Of course, in some states the agent might be an independent pro-life organization that's not affiliated with any particular national organization. In fact, an agent could probably even be just an individual who wants to make the guerrilla campaign a reality in his or her area. The responsibilities of Firestorm agents would be to assemble a team of pro-life organizations (referred to as operatives) within their state who agree to assume responsibility for *one specific part* of the guerrilla campaign (G-1 through G-5). What we want is a coalition of specialists who focus their efforts in one area. Once this team of operatives is created, the agents would then be responsible for coordinating and monitoring their activities. (84)

In claiming that the "agents would then be responsible" for executing certain plans, *Firestorm* also implies that culpability for these actions rests entirely with those individual agents. The activities cannot be traced back to LDI, Crutcher, or any donors or employees.

In this way, Firestorm deploys a guerrilla strategy comparable to leaderless resistance, which was popularized in the 1990s within the militia movement.[26] The advantages of leaderless resistance, which consists of a cell-based structure of organizing, not a central leadership or hierarchy, are that it thwarts suspicions of conspiracy and makes acts of terrorism appear as isolated incidents. According to one man who spent time in the pro-life underground, Paul Hill articulated precisely how leaderless resistance would work for the anti-abortion cause. During the trial of Michael Griffin, just months before Paul Hill himself would kill two at an abortion clinic, Hill revealed the plan for an "IRA-type reign of terror." He explained: "There's too much pressure on all of us, too many people watching us to do anything major under direct orders from the national level, so what you're gonna see is individuals or small groups of people takin' action in their own hands to do what the leaders want to see done, but since there won't be any direct orders given, no one can prove conspiracy."[27] Both guerrilla warfare and guerrilla legislation reduce the likelihood that leaders or strategists can be held accountable for the consequences of pro-life action, and they give pro-life actions the appearance of being the work of individuals or small groups motivated only by their own conscience. Just as Paul Hill's "reign of terror" is designed so that "no one can prove conspiracy," Firestorm is a strategy designed so that participants can disavow culpability.

Such disavowal is evident in Crutcher's discussion of the reduced number of doctors willing to perform abortions. He writes as if, as a "twenty-year veteran of the pro-life movement," he and that movement are not progenitors of—or even related to—clinic blockades, bombings, arson, picketings, and death threats. Despite accounts such as Joseph Scheidler's *Closed: 99 Ways to Stop Abortion*, Crutcher suggests that forcing doctors and clinic workers out of business has been unintended.

> Until now, this situation [of "running out of people who are willing to do abortions"] has been mostly created by the law of unintended consequences. The competition between us trying to stop abortion, and the other side trying to stop us, has been so ugly that it has made a lot of people decide that they don't want to have anything to do with abortion one way or the other. And this is especially true for the very image driven medical community.
>
> So while we never had this as stated goal, we have in practice dis-

couraged from doing abortions a lot of people who might otherwise have been willing to do them. We are winning a battle we didn't even know we were fighting! I might insert here that this situation has been immeasurably helped through activities like those of Operation Rescue, although they never intended or predicted this consequence either. (38)

Saying that Operation Rescue and other pro-life militants "never intended or predicted" that their protests would have the effect of reducing the number of doctors willing to perform abortions denies the pro-life leaders' stated rationales for harassing doctors and women. It contradicts, for example, Scheidler's discussion of picketing, which is clearly acknowledged as a means of driving doctors out of business:

We go to the homes of abortionists and to places they work other than the clinics precisely because they don't like it. They usually are not proud of being abortionists, and often they even guard the fact that they are involved in abortion from their community.

If it were widely known that they are abortionists, they might be very uncomfortable in their communities, and the communities might be uncomfortable with them. There is even the possibility that they may be forced to stop doing abortions. In some smaller communities, this has happened.[28]

If doctors are beleaguered by noisy, menacing, picketing crowds, so are their communities. Pro-life harassment produces discomfort with having an abortion provider in town. Scheidler understands that doctors can "be forced to stop doing abortions" as a result of the pro-life picketers' disruptions of the community. This consequence is intended. Patricia Baird-Windle and Eleanor J. Bader, in *Targets of Hatred: Anti-Abortion Terrorism*, detail the harassment of reproductive health care providers, including doctors, nurses, administrative staff, and their families, over decades. By daring to document what some pro-choice groups often will not, Baird-Windle and Bader have resisted the unfortunate trend in both academic and journalistic accounts of pro-life violence to not publicize the day-to-day effects of anti-abortion harassment and violence for fear of giving their opponents satisfaction, encouragement, and media attention.[29] This unofficial policy of silence sometimes keeps employees blissfully ignorant (and may put them in danger) if the management of a large, corporate clinic denies to its own employees the number and the kind of threats that the clinic and its personnel receive. Baird-Windle and Bader break that silence and allow the long-muffled voices of workers in small, independently owned, woman-oriented clinics to be heard. *Targets of Hatred* also explores the plight of those reproductive health care workers who live in rural areas and are not connected to financial resources that corporate urban clinics enjoy. Their voices are important for countering a myth that Crutcher popularizes in LDI's joke books and other materials—that abortion providers are rich, cowardly, and uncaring parasites feeding off of women's vulnerabilities. *Targets of Hatred* documents the lasting effects of such stereotypes and of the daily harassment tactics that Scheidler perfected.

Crutcher's aim to drive abortion providers out of business merely augments Scheidler's strategy, adding to it a more forceful commitment to capitalize on trends and consequences of militant activity. "In a nutshell, the mission of the G-1 program will be to take this situation [of doctors refusing to do abortions] out of the realm of unintended consequences, and place it squarely in the realm of calculated results" (38). For example, Crutcher advocates "coordinat[ing] our efforts [with those] of other organizations (like Operation Rescue)" for maximum, calculated effect (40).

Whether the strategy of Firestorm has been put into effect in the ways and to the extent that Crutcher describes is difficult to determine because by design it is an operation that is not easy to detect. Perhaps Crutcher has been successful and an orchestrated but decentralized network of guerrilla agents is in place and has been operating since 1992. No one can be held accountable for cumulative results of individual cases of litigation or regulatory legislation sponsored by lawyers and politicians unaffiliated with LDI. *Firestorm*, therefore, remains valuable not as proof of conspiracy but as an articulation of the dynamic among pro-life legislation, litigation, and violence.

Pro-Life Litigation, Legislation, and Violence Working Together

Firestorm provides a good vocabulary with which to describe the ulterior consequences, if not the ulterior motives, procured by pro-life litigation and legislation. It allows us to see how neatly the illegal and legal strategies line up in the social control of abortion providers, girls, and women. The following examples of malpractice lawsuits and regulatory laws demonstrate how pro-life litigation, legislation, and violence function together for devastating political impact.

One of LDI's main efforts is called ABMAL, short for abortion malpractice. In 1993, Crutcher mailed a seventy-two-page guide on how to litigate abortion malpractice suits to 4,000 lawyers.[30] He claims to have recruited 600 lawyers and 500 expert witnesses willing to litigate and testify, respectively, using his guidelines, but because Crutcher has always insisted on and operated under the guise of secrecy, there is no telling who the recruited may be and whether his claims are true. At one point, according to a legal reporter, three lawyers completely denied having attended an LDI seminar on how to profit from abortion malpractice litigation, even though attendance records proved otherwise.[31] It is also impossible to say which lawsuits may be the direct results of Firestorm strategy and LDI, the front organization. It is not, however, difficult to determine the political impact and consequences of such suits.

Like pro-life assassinations of doctors, pro-life malpractice suits do not seek to eliminate all abortion providers. Rather, the political objective is to sabotage the medical practices of doctors at random. Just as doctors are arbitrarily targeted by pro-life snipers and assassins, doctors are randomly taken to court. Not knowing when a lawsuit will hit may have a psychological effect similar to that of not knowing when a bullet will hit.

Psychology aside, the tactic of litigating abortion malpractice can wear down doctors financially. Even if Firestorm fails to achieve its goal of discouraging insurance companies from "writing abortion malpractice coverage at any price," a significant hike in insurance rates or the cost of a legal defense can run doctors out of business. Consider the case of Dr. Bruce Steir, who was forced to relinquish his medical license when he was faced with "three legal battles at once: the battle to retain his license, the battle to prove he was not negligent, and the battle to stay out of jail."[32] Because he was not able financially to fight all three battles, he reluctantly surrendered his license. Even so, Dr. Steir had to come up with $250,000 in bail to stay out of jail because the charges he faced included that of murder.

Unlike abortion malpractice litigation that seeks compensation for emotional damage—suits that are largely seen by legal experts as frivolous[33]—the case against Dr. Steir involved the death of a woman whose uterus was perforated during a second-trimester abortion. Significantly, the death was initially reported as an accident by the county chief medical examiner. Controversy ensued when the examiner changed the cause of death and Dr. Steir subsequently was arrested for second-degree murder. It was later determined that the examiner had changed the cause of death from "accident" to "murder" as the result of a report filled with inaccurate testimony and hearsay; he testified that had he not been given the misinformation, he would not have changed the cause of death to murder. The report that contained the false and inflammatory statements had been produced by the Medical Board of California, an agency charged with investigating patient complaints and ensuring medical quality, in conjunction with a pro-life activist who had connected the patient's survivors with a pro-life attorney.

To avoid conviction on charges of second-degree murder, which carried a mandatory prison term of fifteen years, Steir accepted a plea bargain and agreed to plead guilty to involuntary manslaughter. In spring 2000 he was sentenced to six months in jail; later he was released two months early for good behavior. In the end, Steir was financially and emotionally devastated by this incident, which he described as "the only death of a patient of mine throughout the 40 years of my career as a doctor."[34]

In comparison to the treatment meted out to other physicians brought before the Medical Board in a case involving a patient's death, Bruce Steir was subject to unusual tactics and standards. The ACLU of northern California compared his case with other disciplinary cases involving California doctors since 1993 and concluded that although, because of the circumstances of his patient's death, Steir "deserved to lose his license, . . . he did not deserve to be singled out for criminal prosecution." The report condemns the charge of murder and details the influence of Jeannette Dreisbach, the pro-life activist who had approached the patient's family and offered to introduce them to a pro-life lawyer. The ACLU suggests that Dreisbach's involvement with the Medical Board indicates its political collusion with pro-life forces to drive abortion providers out of business. Dreisbach was permitted to circumvent regular policy in obtaining names of doctors with pending accusations; her relationship with the board was described as "a very close liaison." She was the person who apparently gave the coroner the initial report that was later dismissed but which nevertheless compelled the coroner to change his original opinion of the cause of death from accident to homicide. Although the Medical Board has not always granted Dreisbach's requests, the ACLU claims that her involvement suggests that "Ms. Dreisbach's pressure caused disproportionate attention to be focused on abortion providers by the Medical Board, but also that the Medical Board welcomed this arrangement and provided fuel to an effort that was clearly politically motivated." Ultimately, the ACLU report calls for "openness by the Medical Board as to its policies and procedures; fairness and consistency by the Medical Board in pursuing complaints against doctors; and reform of Medical Board's practices or policies that allow bias to influence the agency's actions."[35]

According to the ACLU, Dr. Steir's case is a "hallmark of the effort to use regulatory agencies as a weapon against abortion providers." Targeted Restrictions on Abortion Providers (TRAP) laws have been enacted in thirteen states, and pro-life publications have used Steir's case to argue for their implementation, claiming that there is no such thing as a "safe abortion."[36] By regularly anticipating and tracking abortion complications and then connecting complainants with pro-life lawyers, Dreisbach and the Medical Board of California may be able to increase the numbers of pro-life malpractice suits—even murder charges—which may increase insurance rates for physicians who provide abortions. And such a strategy certainly increases the stigmatization of doctors, which is one of Firestorm's stated goals.

Crutcher's LDI produces and distributes various publications intended to dehumanize doctors who provide abortions. For example, they distribute several graphic books of crude jokes and cartoons, one of which is titled *Quack the Ripper*. In the monthly, hour-long, LDI-produced video magazine titled *LifeTalk*, doctors are routinely portrayed as incompetent but rich. In the first edition of *LifeTalk*, Crutcher lists seven examples of penalized and incarcerated abortion providers. The reasons for their legal entanglements range from tax evasion to manslaughter, but the cases are interpreted in sweeping terms by Crutcher as evidence of abortion providers' basic incompetence and "stupid life habits." By presenting doctors' legal troubles as news items, Crutcher thus implies that the strategy of litigating abortion malpractice is working.

As part of the litigation strategy, LDI provides an array of services for lawyers, including client referral networks, legal education materials, depositions and interrogatories, client training, case management, a co-counsel network, expert witnesses and consultants, research collected by "spies," information on abortion providers and clinic workers, and "abortion animation"—a video created for courtroom demonstrations. These services are detailed on LDI's website, which does not state Crutcher's calculated intent as clearly as *Firestorm* does: to get "these 'chain-store' law firms to start looking upon abortion malpractice as a lucrative field" (64).

One political effect of promoting abortion malpractice suits is to create a moral outrage that distorts the reality of abortion in America. Abortion is among the safest and most frequently performed surgeries in the United States. An estimated 43 percent of all American women will have an abortion by the time they turn forty-five years old, and approximately 1.5 million American women obtain abortions each year. According to the Alan Guttmacher Institute, "The risk of abortion complications is minimal; less than 1% of all abortion patients experience a major complication, such as serious pelvic infection, hemorrhage requiring a blood transfusion or major surgery." "The risk of death associated with childbirth is about 10 times as high as that associated with abortion."[37] Psychologically, too, abortion is shown to cause few adverse reactions (as mentioned in chap. 1). Thus hundreds of thousands of women terminate pregnancies safely and sanely every year, but this reality is shrouded by the pro-life movement's promotion of malpractice suits.

Another political effect of promoting abortion malpractice litigation is to make the defense of the right to an abortion synonymous with the defense of the medical profession. From a historical standpoint, this equation makes for some strange bedfellows, given that progressive women and the medical profession have often been at odds. In fact, the drive to outlaw abortion throughout the United States, especially up to and during the 1860s, was in large part the result of the professionalization of medicine by male physicians, many of whom hoped to de-legitimize those women who until then had provided abortions as well as midwifery services.[38] A century later, in the 1960s, the medical profession was still seen by progressive women as an enemy because hospitals and doctors did not fight for repeal of abortion laws but only for their reform. It was feminists and other progressive women who sought to undo the mystification of their own bodies that the medical profession had institutionalized. By "demystifying" the female body and the simple procedure of abortion, ordinary women launched a self-help movement that defied both the law and the medical establishment. For example, in the Chicago area, an underground women's collective known as Jane operated from 1969 to 1973, providing 11,000 safe, affordable, and successful abortions.[39] Pro-life malpractice suits play on this history of women's struggle to break free from the male-oriented and male-dominated medical profession in that they attempt to channel the distrust and anger derived from any actual medical mistreatment of women into pro-life causes.

But if *Firestorm* is to be taken as an indication of the objectives of pro-life legislation and litigation in general, one goal is not to stop the medical mistreatment of women. Oddly enough, according to Crutcher (34), outlawing abortion is also not a goal. Instead, it is to create a matrix of individual pieces of regulatory and punitive legislation that work in concert to prevent (sometimes forcibly) women from obtaining or doctors from providing abortions. Some legislation proposed by *Firestorm* has been put into effect since 1992. For example, *Firestorm*'s proposal that "a requirement that women obtaining an abortion must be a resident of the state" prefigures the 1998 Child Custody Protection Act, which prohibits minors seeking abortions from crossing state lines.[40] *Firestorm* also proposed prohibitions on "abortions done late in pregnancy"—a full three years before the term *partial birth abortion* was created by pro-life strategists and then introduced into a bill in the U.S. Congress.[41]

These two pieces of pro-life legislation combined (as guerrilla strategies are apt to do) to profoundly affect the case of a pregnant twelve-year-old girl who had been raped by her seventeen-year-old brother. The girl and her family, recent immigrants to Michigan from India, remained anonymous throughout the various court proceedings required to obtain an abortion for the girl. Her pregnancy had gone undetected for reasons that are not described fully in any media account but which certainly may have included the taboo of incest, cultural differences, and communication problems. A doctor apparently did not find the girl's physical complaints credible; consequently he misdiagnosed her symptoms until she had been pregnant for twenty-eight weeks. Because Michigan law prohibits abortions after the twenty-fourth week, the family had to appeal for permission for the abortion. (Meanwhile, pro-life organizers, apparently unaffected by the girl's age or the incest, offered to pay the family if the girl remained pregnant.[42] American Life League featured the story in a fund-raising letter, calling it a "sordid parable of abortion's impact on our society.")[43] The judge not only denied the request and "made the girl a ward of the court until a psychiatric examination was performed," but "prohibited the girl from leaving the state, blocking her parents' efforts to take her to Kansas for a late-term abortion." Thus two pro-life guerrilla strategies—a ban on late-term abortions and a ban on allowing pregnant minors to cross state lines for an abortion—teamed up to delay the abortion for two additional weeks. Once the travel ban was lifted and the girl was returned to her parents' custody, they drove to Kansas to terminate her pregnancy.[44]

In the case of this anonymous twelve-year-old, the culminating effects of guerrilla pro-life legislation amounted to more than just being denied an abortion. It also denied her recourse from rape. Bans on late-term procedures in particular affect young women and girls, who may not realize they are pregnant until the second or last trimester. Or they may deny it themselves and hide it from others. Incest and rape too are particularly pernicious for girls because they are too young to recognize or understand manipulation and coercion when it is part of their daily family or community life. Even in cases that do not involve rape, however, it is clear that compulsory pregnancy—enforcing the condition of pregnancy against the will of a woman—is the order of the day for some communities that use this legislation as justification for vigilante action.

Another example is the situation of a fifteen-year-old girl in Blair, Nebraska, who in 1995 was prevented from having an abortion, despite having the full support of her parents. In this case, her boyfriend's family orchestrated a pro-life intervention by enlisting the aid of a pro-life deputy sheriff, a pro-life doctor, and a pro-life county prosecutor. According to the *New York Times*, the house of the girl's parents "was violently invaded by the boyfriend, his parents and friends; their daughter was taken from them in the middle of the night by law-enforcement officers determined to stop her from having an abortion; she was put into foster care, and, finally, she was ordered by a judge not to abort the pregnancy."[45] The girl's family filed a suit after leaving their hometown of Blair, detailing in the complaint the invasion, kidnapping, and harassment. Remarkably, there was no denial of the actions. No one, according to the *Times*, "appeared to dispute the facts of the case. Rather the issue here appeared to center on whether the actions taken by a community strongly opposed to abortion were an acceptable use of the legal system or an example of anti-abortion extremism."[46] More precisely, this is an example of pro-life guerrilla strategy, of combining illegal forced entry and sanctioned law enforcement (court orders) to impose compulsory pregnancy.[47]

As these two cases attest, the distinction between legal versus illegal pro-life activity becomes ambiguous when guerrilla mentalities and strategies are focused on girls. The line separating protection from coercion, loving support from manipulation, and pro-life proselytizers from pro-life predators becomes very thin. This thin line is blurred by Terra Vierkant in a 1996 pamphlet, whose front page reads: "Twelve and Pregnant . . . What Choices Does She Have? Too Young to Bear?"[48] The pamphlet describes how Vierkant compelled a pregnant girl to reject abortion as an option. The job entailed describing the "side effects" of abortion and enlisting other pro-lifers to show family members the medically inaccurate pro-life movie *The Silent Scream*.[49] The movie convinced the girl's father not to drive her to the clinic. Then, Vierkant kept "in close contact with" the girl day after day until she reversed her original decision to have an abortion and committed to going through with the pregnancy. For months, Vierkant continued the relationship until the girl, at thirteen years old, delivered a baby.

What gives Vierkant permission to play such an active role was reportedly a call from the girl's mother, who knew of her child's pregnancy only because of the pro-life parental notification laws in effect in 1985. Again, we see pro-life legislation permitting activity that extends beyond the traditional means of proselytizing or witnessing one's religious convictions.

Such legislation gives license to pro-lifers who are increasingly warlike in their attitudes and calculating in their strategy. Part of this calculation includes circulating misinformation about so-called side effects of abortion. Another part of this calculation involves the missing information about the girl and her circumstances. Just as there is no discussion in the pro-life pamphlet of the psychological toll that pregnancy and childbirth take on a twelve-year-old, there is no discussion of how she got pregnant in the first place. Thus the pamphlet follows a general trend in abortion politics to eschew discussion of the only briefly mentioned "cases of rape and incest" and to ignore the relationship between abortion and rape or incest.

What some females are taught as raped girls is reinscribed in the midst of pro-life assassinations and bombs: some women deserve the random acts of terror that are forced on them. A sophisticated understanding of how blaming the victim works seems to have been eradicated in the so-called post-feminist 1980s and 1990s; no women want to present themselves as victims. But that twelve-year-old in Michigan is a victim not only of an incestuous family but of a pernicious legal system that, armed with guerrilla pro-life legislation, would deny her an abortion as a recourse from rape, impose compulsory pregnancy, and enforce mandatory motherhood.

The rape of teens, incestuous or not, provides another opportunity for pro-lifers to place unintended consequences "squarely in the realm of calculated results." The two cases of the twelve-year-old in Michigan and the twelve-year-old featured in the pro-life pamphlet illustrate this. Although it may be no one's intention that these girls get pregnant, their experience serves as an opportunity to draw from and reinforce the pro-life guerrilla legislation that regulates abortion, such as parental notification laws, interstate travel bans, and late abortion bans. Firestorm makes no apologies about using the misfortunes of girls and women as opportunities to further pro-life guerrilla strategy. Ironically, to exploit these opportunities and, by extension, the girls and women themselves, *Firestorm* suggests employing strategies that ostensibly are designed to fight for women's rights.

According to Crutcher's own words, *Firestorm*'s focus on women's rights is not genuine but a ploy to hide the real agenda and confuse opponents: "They are evidently so accustomed to our arguments being focused only on the unborn baby, for us to voluntarily talk about the woman catches them totally off-guard" (75). But ideally it is not pro-lifers who should be proposing regulatory guerrilla legislation. Instead, Crutcher prescribes that "pro-life organizations should not allow themselves to be publicly identified with this, or any other guerrilla type legislation" (59). All guerrilla "legislation should be sold as 'pro-women' and/or 'consumer protection' legislation" (57). For example, in proposing a "requirement that all abortion related counseling be done by people not employed by people in the abortion industry," Crutcher readily admits that

> We simply sell it as consumer protection that would prohibit any medical-related counseling from being done by people who might financially profit from the decision being discussed. Our goal would be to sneak this legislation through and once it's passed do whatever is necessary (lawsuits?) to see it applied to abortion counseling. (51)

Here the link between punitive lawsuits and pre-emptive, regulatory legislation proposed as consumer protection for women is made clear. Like the abortion malpractice cases and other pro-life litigation, regulatory laws appear to be made to benefit women as reproductive health care consumers. *Firestorm*'s disregard for women is never very disguised, however, as is evident in Crutcher's explanation for this strategic switch away from fetal protection to women's protection: "When it comes to regulatory legislation, always keep in mind that, generally speaking, it is not necessarily designed to directly protect the baby, but the mother. . . . While it may sound crude, the reality is that an abortionist has to go through the mother to get to the baby. And like it or not . . . her case is easier to make in the legislature" (62). It is even easier when women, not men, are spokespersons for the pro-life cause. *Firestorm* insists that "in all cases make sure the person delivering the message is female" (70). In *Firestorm*, if not in pro-life politics generally, protecting women is undeniably a ruse.

Unfortunately, it is a ruse that may prove effective. Take, for example, the case of Deborah Gaines, who sued the Brookline, Massachusetts, clinic where pro-life assassin John Salvi III killed two clinic workers and injured six others in 1994. Gaines's case reflects the pro-life guerrilla tactics described in *Firestorm* and illustrates how pro-life violence and punitive legislation against abortion clinics function together.

According to legal statements, Deborah Gaines was scheduled to have an abortion at PreTerm on December 30, 1994, the day John Salvi attacked the clinic. After firing inside the building, Salvi chased Gaines outside, which terrorized her to the point that later she was unable to terminate her pregnancy.[50] Suffering from post-traumatic stress, Gaines decided to avoid abortion clinics, hence abortion, and consequently delivered a baby girl many months later. She then sued the clinic because it had not provided her, as a patient, with enough security from the likes of Salvi. Gaines demanded financial compensation for mental anguish and the "wrongful birth" of her daughter, which had interrupted Gaines's plans to finish her GED and become independent from the welfare program.[51] Eventually the Brookline clinic owners settled out of court.

To stunning effect, this case reflects the strategy outlined in *Firestorm*. It positions the woman as a reproductive health care consumer whose protection and rights are the ostensible foci of the lawsuit. It aims punitive and regulatory legislation at the clinic owners and clinic personnel—not at abortion itself. Couching the case in terms of "wrongful birth," the prosecutors appear to have a callous view of the baby and seem to be privileging the mother. This too is a reflection of *Firestorm*'s aim to catch abortion rights advocates off guard by focusing on the woman's side of the mother/fetus dyad that has characterized the abortion debate.

Crutcher may not have been behind the Gaines case, but LDI certainly is responsible for having contacted employees of the Brookline clinic three years after Salvi's attack, urging them to "turn in their employer for tax and safety violations." In 1997, LDI sent letters to employees at their home addresses, warning them of the "potential illnesses" they could contract "by working at an unsafe abortion clinic."[52] The letters were sent in envelopes designed to look like official Federal Express or priority mail packages (a strategy that would be repeated in the mass mailings of fake anthrax letters to clinics after the September 11, 2001, attacks). As in Gaines's case, the letters appeal to a desire for security and protection by those working in or benefiting from abortion clinics.

Crutcher later launched a much larger campaign appealing to employees of reproductive health care facilities. Using the website Clinic-Worker.com, LDI advertises materials that aim to "reduce the number of physicians willing to perform abortions" by "educating" physicians and clinic employees about the legal and medical violations they may be held accountable for and about the "financial rewards" they could obtain by reporting what could be construed as incidents of income tax evasion, medical fraud, insurance fraud, money laundering, sexual harassment, sexual assault, physical assault, statutory rape, health/safety risks, and consumer fraud. Most vividly, ClinicWorker.com couches this appeal in terms of self-protection for workers. A yellow poster announces the imperative: "Employees Protect Yourself."[53] LDI's emphasis on this protection is a variation on Firestorm's intention to pose lawsuits and regulations in terms of women's protection.

Firestorm's emphasis on women's "protection" is revealing in another way in that it foreshadows the demand for governmental protection that women in the 1990s were forced to make in the wake of lethal pro-life violence. As Deborah Gaines's case shows, protection for women may be couched in the legal terminology of consumer rights, but the protection Gaines really needed was from a man with a gun, a guerrilla for life, a new abortion warrior. The emphasis on "women's protection" that pro-life legislation touts has gained more applicability as the years have passed. As pro-life violence has become guerrilla warfare, those who provide or seek abortions have apparently had no recourse other than asking the government to protect them from bombs, assassins, anthrax, and acid.

The Logic of Killing for Life

As pro-life violence became guerrilla warfare in the 1990s, pro-lifers conducted their own ruminations about how law, justice, and violence relate. Foremost among these prolific philosophers is law professor Charles Rice, author of "Can the Killing of Abortionists Be Justified?"; member of the Society for a Christian Commonwealth (featured in chap. 5), which founded the early pro-life group Americans United for Life; and one-time adviser to Human Life International.[54] In keeping with a vibrant tradition of pro-life scholarship geared toward resisting changes in social and sexual mores during the 1960s,[55] Rice uses sophisticated, natural law arguments to conclude that "The use of violence in the pro-life cause must be utterly rejected."[56] This emphatic rejection, however, is tempered within the general discussion. Rice argues that the use of violence should be rejected because it is (or at least it was in 1994) politically and strategically disadvantageous, and morally unjustifiable because pro-lifers have not yet reached the point of no other recourse. Rice's rejection of the use of violence, however, does not preclude the acceptance of violence at a later time or in different circumstances. In this article, as in others, pro-life violence is not rejected in principle.

Five months before "Can the Killing of Abortionists Be Justified?" appeared, another of Rice's pro-life discussions of lethal violence was published, "The Death Penalty Dilemma."[57] In this article, Rice bases his discussion of capital punishment on natural law, which is the cornerstone of Catholic Thomist thought. Saint Thomas Aquinas believed that "divine law, revealed through grace, perfects, but does not overturn, the human law that is based on natural reason."[58] Moreover, for those who subscribe to natural law, "recourse to violence poses no problems, since natural ends"—derived by natural reason perfected through the revelation of divine law—"are just." Natural law normalizes violence in the sense that "recourse to violent means is as justified, as normal as a man's 'right' to move his body to reach a given goal."[59] Drawing from natural law, Rice delineates several justifications for capital punishment, claiming that it is not "unjust to execute a murderer" because it may deter other murders from occurring, and because "retribution," though not vengeance, is a "sound principle of natural law and common sense."[60] Punitive violence is commonsensical to Rice when murder is the offense.

Rice's critique continues: "murder should be stigmatized as the crime of crimes" because it devalues life, which is defined as the dominion of God. Only God can give life, and only God can take life away. It is therefore not a contradiction for the government, on behalf of God, to execute a murderer: "the state derives its authority from God who is the Lord of life." The death penalty, says Rice, "promotes respect for innocent life." On these grounds, Rice makes punitive violence seem not only natural and commonsensical but also an obvious complement to anti-abortion politics: "Capital punishment is obviously a 'right to life' issue," he says. Like the banning of abortion, "the imposition of capital punishment can be seen as a means to restore respect for innocent life."[61] Rice advocates state-sanctioned killing for life because he sees it as ultimately sanctioned by God.

Rice takes for granted that his readers believe both that abortion is murder and that abortion providers are murderers. With these unexamined assumptions intact, the article approves punitive violence such as capital punishment not only as retribution but as a commonsensical, obvious, and natural way to deal with "abortionists or more conventional killers."[62] Killing for life is hardly a contradiction, according to Rice's logic; it is tantamount to restoring respect for God as Lord.

Rice's article makes explicit what is implicit in other pro-life discussions based on natural law: it naturalizes and normalizes violence as retribution for challenging God's dominion over life. Natural law was the basis of many early pro-life arguments, some of which were written by Rice and others by John Noonan, who edited the *Natural Law Forum*, published from 1956 to 1968 by Notre Dame Law School, where Rice is a professor.[63]

Rice's pro-life writing is important because of whom it has influenced, and where it has appeared, not because it represents particularly original thinking or is in any radical way a departure from erudite pro-life arguments. His writing has been a cornerstone for defenders of pro-life violence, including convicted clinic bomber Michael Bray, who quotes Rice liberally in his 1994 book *A Time to Kill*. Rice's arguments have been part of the legal defense of Curt Beseda, who was sentenced to twenty years for arson in the burning of four clinics in Washington state, and of Matthew Goldsby and James Simmons, the men who bombed the Pensacola clinic on Christmas day in 1984.[64] Rice's article "The Death Penalty Dilemma," published in April 1994 in the *New American*, a John Birch Society magazine, appeared around the same time that other publications were examining the legal issues of killing for life. *Life Advocate*, for instance, reported on the April 1994 trial of Rachelle "Shelley" Shannon, who had shot and wounded Dr. George Tiller a year earlier, and it published experts from Paul Hill's "defensive action statement," which had been inspired by Michael Griffin's murder of Dr. David Gunn. More discussion ensued that summer after Hill killed two at a Pensacola clinic. Later, in December 1994, John Salvi slaughtered people in a Brookline, Massachusetts, clinic. Evidently, Salvi was tuned in to these discussions about killing for life; in his apartment was found a copy of Rice's article from the *New American*.[65]

The fact that Salvi had Rice's article in his apartment does not suggest that Rice intended to promote violence, nor that the article incited Salvi to kill. Salvi, who ultimately committed suicide in jail, is considered by some to have had a "fevered mind" gripped by "the admonition that abortion requires a vigilante response," which Rice's work helped to justify.[66] Others attribute Salvi's murderous attack to his membership in an apocalyptic subculture, as demonstrated by Salvi's oral and written comments about fearing conspiracies against Catholics and wanting to join a militia.[67]

In the context of Rice's logic of natural law, Salvi's—and others'—attacks may be understood to function not as a protest of the "violence" of abortion but as retribution for the violation implicit in that so-called violence. Guerrilla warfare and guerrilla legislation aimed at those seeking or providing abortions constitute retribution for challenging God's dominion over life. In this way, pro-life retribution through guerrilla strategies is not as much a punishment for an individual's infringement on God's law as it is a way to restore the order of God.[68] In this light, the act of killing for life—like the strange notion of guerrilla legislation—is revealed not as an oxymoron but as an act with logical consistency and a political manifestation of religious retribution.

What does this turn from protest to retribution mean for the future of pro-life politics? According to Jerry Reiter, whose story as pro-life activist is recounted in *Live from the Gates of Hell: An Insider's Look at the Antiabortion Underground*, there will be more killing for life because "the mainstream anti-abortion movement has shrunk dramatically and now you just see more hard-core people." Specifically, Reiter reports a plan of "unprecedented violence" scheduled in response to the execution of Paul Hill.[69]

In stark contrast, historian David Garrow cautions not to exaggerate the "size of the terrorist [pro-life] underground or the long-term danger that its members pose."[70] Judging from attendance at the annual White Rose Banquet, Garrow suggests that the network of pro-lifers who believe in killing abortion providers is "composed of only about seventy-five people."[71] From a historical perspective, the incidents of pro-life arson and sniper attacks indicate that opposition to abortion is dying down, not escalating, says Garrow. He compares the pro-life violence of the 1980s and 1990s with the church bombings and death threats by Klansmen to civil rights workers of the 1950s and 1960s, arguing that such groups "may very well never evaporate completely, but history shows that across time they *are* indeed quite controllable by means of aggressive and thorough criminal investigation and prosecution."[72] (Implicit in this argument is the notion that racial terrorism is now more contained than it was in the Deep South of the 1950s.) Garrow concludes: "If and when we can get to the point of having doctor after doctor after doctor stand up and say, 'I provide abortion services,' that is when the terrorists will be fully and finally defeated."[73] Emphasizing the doctor as the hero whose words can dissolve terrorists does not seem to take into account the amount of guerrilla legislation and harassment that has been aimed at those doctors. Moreover, it ignores the history of progressive women, who know that the American medical profession does not always act in their best interests. Nevertheless, Garrow offers compelling points that temper Reiter's warnings of impending pro-life onslaught.

With a book on the market and a made-for-television movie in the works, Reiter may be cashing in on the cloak-and-dagger appeal of his story. On the other hand, Garrow's history of abortion-related conflict is bereft of the paramilitary and apocalyptic aspects of pro-life ideology, and he seems to ignore the experience of those clinic workers who must daily withstand death threats or harassment.

Will the logic of killing for life persist? Will more pro-life gunmen murder? Are the numerous anthrax scares following September 11, 2001, a prelude to actual chemical warfare launched by pro-lifers? Will the fugitive abortion warriors who have gotten away with bombing clinics and sniping at doctors resurface to commit more murder? Predicting the future is fruitless. It is better both to curb hysteria about pro-life violence—and thereby resist enhancing the right wing's construction of apocalyptic expectation—and to examine further how guerrilla legislation currently precludes social justice for women and the doctors who serve them.

3

Protection from and for the Fetal Citizen

The Crack Baby and the Partially Born as a
Millennial Pair

If we are to take Charles Rice seriously, retribution rather than
vengeance is part of the philosophical fabric of pro-life politics. Vengeance
is akin to revenge and counterattack. Retribution, in contrast, seeks to restore social order based on particular principles. Although this distinction
is no apology for the violent acts committed to "save babies," once we acknowledge that principled retribution rather than zealous, reactionary
vengeance is operating, we can better identify which particular principles
are at work. Accounts by scholars and investigative reporters reveal that
the principle behind killing for life is not the sanctity of life but the apocalyptic prophecy of millennialism. This chapter reviews accounts of guerrilla tactics that illuminate how millennialism is central to killing for life; it
then asks whether millennialism is not also the principle behind pro-life

guerrilla legislation. In particular, do fetal protection cases involving "partial birth" procedures or "crack babies" reflect an undercurrent of millennialism in which Christian purity is apocalyptically opposed to anti-Christian impurity?

I believe they do. When I compared these two types of fetal protection cases, I realized a curious inconsistency about how fetuses are represented in court. Proponents of banning so-called partial birth abortions routinely portray fetuses as innocent, whole, and intact babies worthy of the privileges of citizenship that will save them from death. But crack babies, who are explicitly presumed to be African American, are routinely portrayed as impure, tainted, and polluted babies who are a liability to society and from whom the tax-paying citizenry should be saved. Thus the fetus of partial birth legislation symbolizes moral purity, whereas the crack baby denotes genetic impurity. The cases designed to protect partially born fetuses and crack fetuses reflect the dichotomized millennial worldview of pure and impure domains. Illegal tactics and legal campaigns meant to enforce fetal protection reflect a millennialist viewpoint. But is it accurate to say that federal and state court cases are therefore reinscribing the racist tenets of those right-wing groups that consider abortion to be an indicator of the apocalyptic end times of white America?

Abortion as the End Times

To understand how people see abortion in apocalyptic terms requires some knowledge of millennialism. Millennialism is a theological interpretation of the biblical discussions of the end times of the mortal world and the Second Coming of Jesus Christ, who is prophesied to return and reign on earth for a thousand years, a millennium—hence the term *millennialism*. Over the last few decades, according to Michael Barkun, scholarship on millennialism has become less and less peripheral as Protestant fundamentalism, new religious movements, and secular apocalyptic visions of society became central to many political landscapes. Public awareness of millennialist movements has been fostered by "dramatic and highly publicized cases" such as the Peoples' Temple in Guyana in 1978, the Branch Davidians outside Waco in 1993, and the nerve gas attack on the Tokyo subway in March 1994, which "within a few days was unofficially attributed to [an] apocalyptic sect."[1]

Membership in apocalyptic cults is not required to participate in apocalyptic culture and prophecy belief. Frequently quoted statistics reveal just how prevalent millennialist beliefs are in contemporary America. In 1989 a Gallup poll registered that more than 60 percent of Americans have "no doubt that Christ will return."[2] Millions of Americans consciously embrace millennialist views.[3] Millions more engage in apocalyptic culture, unaware of the biblical derivation of images, metaphors, and narratives that shape daily news stories, television shows, and political rhetoric.

> It is vital to understand just how much the metaphors of Biblical Apocalypse guide perceptions of everyday events for most people in the United States, despite the fact that relatively few actually read the Bible. Two Gallup polls from the fall of 1991 indicate how widespread certain apocalyptic notions are. An October poll indicated that 52 percent of the "typical" adults polled said they believed in the devil. A November poll reported that 47 percent of the respondents agreed that "God created man pretty much in his present form at one time within the last 10,000 years" while 40 percent agreed that "man has developed over millions of years from less advanced forms of life, but God guided this process, including man's creation." These responses show that, even when people are not declared fundamentalists, they often hold to notions of divine origin and metaphysical evil. Even the overtly secular-minded speak of a nuclear blow-up, AIDS, rises in crime, and the greenhouse effect in apocalyptic terms.[4]

Whether we are consciously searching for signs of the end times or not, we are surrounded by the language of apocalypse and millennialist expectation.

As the world anticipated the coming of the year 2000, America capitalized on millennialist views and doomsday fantasy. Toward the end of the 1990s, the notion of apocalypse became commonplace because the "elastic" appeal of the term allows for a "convergence of religious and secular attitudes and practices."[5] Apocalypse was explicitly detailed in films such as *Deep Impact*, *Armageddon*, *Terminator 2: Judgment Day*, and *Prophecy*. Television programs such as *Millennium* and *The X-Files* were enormously popular and garnered top dollar from advertisers. The Y2K problem, which threatened chaos if computers were not deemed "compliant," required special servicing for millions of business and personal computers.

The American commodification of millennialist doom was never so succinctly pronounced as in a television commercial for the retail chain named Target. In the commercial we see the store's logo, the bright red bull's eye of a target, on fashionable clothes and in the shape of domestic items, such as a round kitchen table, a ring of red Jell-O, and the marking around a pet dog's eye. A jaunty jingle announces that "it's the sign of the times." The message of the commercial is that it is fun to own, watch, buy, wear, and eat the signs of the times. Thus the consumable "targets" of apocalypse are portrayed comically, in the cheery red of domestic fashion, which is counterpoint to the tragic rendering of apocalyptic doom achieved in the menacing, macho gore of so many action flicks.[6] Whether in its tragic or comic mode, apocalypse is not just imminent. It is entertainment. Americans are consumers of popular apocalyptic culture.

Consumers of religious or secular apocalypse can become producers of the apocalyptic worldview. As scholars, movements, and movies of American apocalypse reveal, millennialism promotes a dichotomized view of the world in which "we" represent the pure and the light and "they" represent the impure and darkness.[7] Conflict is considered inevitable and ultimate, lending itself to a self-perpetuating validation. The more opposition to their views, values, or actions millennialists experience or perceive, the more solidified their apocalyptic expectation becomes. If a situation elicits activist, legal, or military intervention, this intrusion only validates the prophecy that Armageddon is upon them—they are under siege by the forces of darkness. Such was the case in Waco, Texas, when David Koresh was unable to convey to the FBI how his mission was based on millennialist principles. The FBI heard only "bible babble" and proceeded to bombard the Branch Davidian compound with sights and sounds that strengthened Koresh's perception of being under attack by anti-Christian forces.[8]

The same dynamic occurs during clashes between pro-life and pro-choice activists. Pro-choice protests meant to discourage people from blockading clinics or preaching sexism and homophobia in the name of God often strengthen the perception—and resolve—of Christians who believe the world is divided between Christian and anti-Christian forces. Pro-life leaders take advantage of their congregation's ability not only to accept apocalyptic thought but also to reproduce it according to current events.

Jerry Reiter, for example, tells how Operation Rescue leader Randall Terry roused an assembly of pro-life activists when the opposition attempted to demonstrate a strong pro-choice presence, an intolerance for any disruption of area clinics, and a promise to match the outrageous harassment for which Operation Rescue had become famous. Reiter sat among the pro-life congregation and witnessed the pro-choice group disrupting the meeting.

Terry began his message by reading the gospel account of Jesus being tried in front of Pontius Pilate as the bloodthirsty mob shouted, 'crucify him, crucify him!' Almost on cue, the protesters who had been moved to the street rushed the church all at once like an angry herd of wild animals. They banged on the clear glass windows of the sanctuary running from floor to ceiling at the back of the church, and we turned around to see their hate-filled faces hissing and spitting and screaming in rage.

A chill ran down my spine at the sight. It was overwhelming, it was as though we were witnessing a mob guided by the very same spirit that two thousand years ago had driven another such mob to call for the blood of an innocent one. And it couldn't have worked out better for Randall Terry's message.[9]

Terry proceeded to "work the scene into his sermon," portraying the liberal church as a Judas that ignores the fact of abortion and replacing the blood of Jesus with the blood of the fetus. The pro-choice mob served as evidence of an ancient anti-Christian "spirit" that was again on the rise, signaling a spiritual war and, implicitly, the end times—a belief to which Terry is devoted. Terry's writings, specifically *Accessory to Murder*, reflect what fellow pro-life leaders have said is his adoption of a postmillennialist eschatology.[10]

Other pro-life leaders are explicit about their millennialist motivations, according to Reiter's reports. As an undercover agent for the FBI, Reiter learned how pervasive apocalyptic thought is among the pro-life activists who defend those who kill for life. He paints the "radicals" as a millennialist cabal, led indirectly by older public figures such as Don Treshman, Joseph Scheidler, and John Burt, who manipulate younger, unknown, impressionable men such as Michael Griffin and John Salvi—convicted assassins of abortion doctors. Reiter suggests that the enterprise of killing for life works less like a conspiracy of equal partners consenting to a single secret plan to kill abortion providers and more like a psychological dynamic between an older, more established "bully" and a less experienced, easily impassioned "doofus used as a pawn."[11] But the principle behind the psychological dynamic is indeed millennialism, a belief in the end times.

Reiter shows millennialism as a common denominator among pro-lifers both notorious and unknown. Pat Buchanan made his millennialism famously clear in his 1992 speech at the Republican National Convention in Houston, in which he detailed the apocalyptic culture wars upon us. What Buchanan, Randall Terry, Paul de Parrie, Michael Bray, and Pat Robertson write and speak about in their books and speeches is reflected in the testimony of a young pregnant woman living in John Burt's home for "unwed mothers." "The end times are upon us," Reiter quotes her as saying, "and we have to be ready to put on the whole armor of God, to be ready to do battle with the powers and principalities of darkness. The devil and all his demons will not prevail against us, though, we already know we have the victory in Jesus, amen."[12] With the self-deprecating qualifier that "we're just a bunch of women," she tells Reiter that she and pregnant friends living under Burt's roof are learning to shoot semiautomatic rifles. From the presidential candidacy of Pat Buchanan to the euphoric testimony of an unknown born-again mother, apocalyptic millennialism infuses pro-life views. Reiter's conversations with Paul Hill help provide a theological depth to pro-life millennialism.

Hill introduces Reiter to Reconstructionism in particular. When asked how he accounts for the New Testament's ethos of nonviolence, Hill "scrunched up his face with a sneer, saying in the kind of condescending manner that some adults use with a not-too-bright child, 'Don't you read any good theology? Haven't you ever read R. J. Rushdoony or Gary North or any of the Reconstructionists?' "[13] Reiter thus positions Hill as a follower of a theology that seeks to justify a complete fusion of church and state. Both Rushdoony and North seek to "reconstruct" the church as prevailing authority over any civil government. Hill's part in this, apparently, is to serve as the person who will inspire the insurgency against the government and its inevitable apocalyptic overthrow. "I am going to be the one who causes the abolition of abortion in America. It is my call. I am called to be a martyr. My death will cause the righteous to rise up and take to the streets and say 'no more' to the baby killing, 'no more' to the sin. When I am executed unjustly, you will see an uprising that will shock the nation."[14] At least this is what he tells Reiter after he has killed Dr. John Bayard Britton and his escort, Jim Barrett, in 1994. Before becoming a murderer himself, when he was only writing and speaking in defense of killing for life, Hill had predicted that his actions, not his execution, would procure that apocalyptic battle. "As we put our convictions into concrete actions, millions who are indifferent to abortion or accepting it as expedient will be forced to reconsider. . . . When this occurs, the time will have arrived for the lower civil magistrate and those in positions of power to call the multitudes to unified action."[15] This prediction, which did not pan out, not only demonstrates Hill's devotion to Reconstructionism but also reveals a relationship between Reconstructionism and other varieties of right-wing millennialism.

Hill's reference to the "lower civil magistrate" is "strongly reminiscent of the Posse Comitatus theory of the radical right wing," according to historian Jeffrey Kaplan, whose ethnographic interviews with incarcerated pro-life activists support Reiter's reportage on Hill and others.[16] Kaplan traces the millennialist themes in Paul Hill's "Defensive Action" document and in writings of the Posse Comitatus, charters for which were first issued in the late 1960s by a former member of the Silver Shirts, a domestic pro-Hitler trooper force.[17] According to Berlet and Lyons, "Like the Posse Comitatus and some other neonazi groups, Reconstructionists advocate a form of social totalitarianism, administered mainly through local governments and private institutions such as the church and the family, rather than the classical fascist goal of a highly centralized nation-state."[18] Kaplan suggests that Hill and the Posse Comitatus believe they will succeed because of "divine intervention on the side of the faithful."[19] In addition to Paul Hill and Randall Terry, the three leaders of a group called Missionaries to the Preborn (Matthew Trewhella, Joseph Foreman, and Gary McCullough) all are Reconstructionists.[20] They embrace the idea of divine intervention as part of their millennialist belief in a holy war, the coming apocalypse of Armageddon.

The apocalyptic plot thickens, moreover, when we take into account that the Posse's millennialism is manifested as envisioning a holy war not to save babies but to save the white race. Posse rhetoric and leadership are influenced heavily by Christian Identity theology, the same racist religion that is associated with Eric Rudolph.[21] It "teaches that whites are the true descendants of the lost tribes of Israel and that Jews, blacks, and other minorities have sprung from Satan and are subhuman."[22] Although not a proponent of Christian Identity himself, Hill has been praised "in the pages of Identity publications, including *The Jubilee*," where he was called a Phineas Priest.[23]

The Phineas Priesthood is a biblically inspired ideology or mission. To be a Phineas Priest requires taking vigilante action. The priesthood is not a member organization or militia, but its popularity among militias and white supremacist organizations is notable and "can be witnessed at the Aryan Nations World Congress and Identity gatherings. On these occasions, men have been seen wearing belt buckles fashioned with the Phineas Priesthood symbol or with '#25:6,' indicating the chapter and verse from the Bible that related Phineas's killing of the Israelite and his Midianite wife." In the book of Numbers in the Old Testament, Phineas, a male Israelite, "enters into an unlawful union with a woman from another tribe and brings down the wrath of Yahweh on the Israelites."[24] Thus the story may appeal to white supremacists because they oppose interracial unions, which they deem unlawful, according to their brand of racist religion. They believe that the appropriate response is to kill those guilty of miscegenation or those who have formed other "unlawful unions" such as gay relationships. "Phineas slays the couple and appeases Yahweh—hence the story's appeal to extremists who view the killing as biblical justification for homicides designed to restore 'God's law.' "[25] In the same vein of restoration and retribution, Paul Hill wrote about "the need for 'Phineas actions' a year before" he killed John Britton and James Barrett.[26]

Hill's reference to Phineas does not prove his membership or alliance with white supremacist organizations, but it is certain proof of his millennialism. According to Kaplan, "Hill's ethical basis for Defensive Action is strongly millenarian. Citing the example of Phineas, he asserts that the individual has an over-riding ethical responsibility to do all in his power to turn God's just wrath from the American people: 'Though sin has fanned God's righteous anger to a searing blaze, the shedding of guilty blood has cooled the flame and saved the people from destruction.' "[27] Hill sees killing abortion doctors as synonymous with the shedding of guilty blood. In acting out his millennialist belief by murdering Britton and Barrett, he earned the title of Phineas Priest.

Although Hill has denied the racist elements of the Phineas Priesthood, he put his pro-life action in racial terms by yelling to the camera that filmed his arrest to "fight this as you would fight slavery."[28] This statement fits his logic as told to Reiter; Hill has predicted an insurgency that would lead to the "abolition" of abortion. But does Hill's use of antislavery rhetoric preclude his free association with white supremacists? Another camera earlier caught Hill talking peaceably with a pro-life protester dressed in full Nazi uniform outside the Florida clinic at which Hill would kill for life.[29] Like the Genocide Awareness Project discussed in chapter 1, Hill's racialized statements may not stem from intentional racism, but they coexist with and can accommodate or spur on white supremacist arguments against abortion and fears of diminishing white dominance.

White supremacists explicitly equate the unborn with white culture, as previously discussed. Life becomes shorthand for white life. When white supremacism and millennialism converge, as they tend to do in Posse Comitatus and Reconstructionist writings, abortion is seen not only as the termination of one pregnancy (or, in pro-life parlance, the murder of a single baby); it is seen as the end times for the white race. Hill's prediction of an insurgency that will shock the nation is a manifestation of his millennialist belief that he is destined to play a part in biblical prophecy, to bring about the apocalyptic war that will usher in a new theocratic paradise.[30] Hill is willing to be a martyr because he sees himself and his Christian culture—not only fetuses—as abortion's victims. Similarly, white supremacists who argue that abortion is genocide see white culture as society's abject. This synecdochic equation of the collective unborn generations with white and/or Christian culture is a projection on a scale grander than that of the clinic bomber who imagined his own limb-by-limb dismemberment. Echoing the language of bombers he interviewed, Kaplan calls this projection a "total identification with the baby."[31]

Is this identification with the fetus replicated in the less militant, legal discussions of fetal protection? And if it is, are the accompanying white supremacist and millennialist implications also replicated? These questions require an investigation of rhetorical and legal strategy in fetal protection cases, beginning with the high-profile disputes over late-term or partial birth abortions.

Protection for the Fetal Citizen

What Kaplan refers to as "total identification with the baby" or fetus has been an effective tactic for those working toward a proposed ban on late-term abortions. As part of their 1995 campaign, pro-life strategists created the term *partial birth abortion* to attempt to foster this identification. The term is not used by the medical profession, however; nor has it ever appeared on a patient's chart or in a medical journal.[32] By coining this phrase, pro-life strategists created a purely political, neological category of late-term abortion.

Identification with the fetus has also been effective in promoting the total obfuscation of the woman obtaining the abortion. Rarely, for example, do proponents of this ban discuss the dilation part of the procedures, as in dilation and extraction (D & X) or dilation and evacuation (D & E). To do so would entail discussing the numbing by anesthesia and the physical plugging of the cervix so it becomes sufficiently dilated before the surgery. Such a discussion might make women more queasy than men and thereby underscore the gender differences among proponents of the ban; it would also undercut the notion that women terminate pregnancies for frivolous reasons that are validated because abortions are simple, easy, and too readily accessible. Besides, discussing dilation would require a focus on female anatomy. Therefore, throughout discussions of partial birth abortions, female anatomy is always talked about in relation to the position of the fetus.[33] In some depictions, female anatomy is merely the ground on which the battle for fetal citizenship is fought.

The report of the Judiciary Committee of the U.S. House of Representatives, which accompanied the proposed Partial-Birth Abortion Ban Act of 1995 out of committee, attempted to add a neological term and new category of citizen to U.S. law.[34] The Judiciary Committee, in an attempt to get around the U.S. Supreme Court's clear statement in *Roe v. Wade* that a fetus is not a person, began its 1995 report with the declaration that the "Court has never decided that human beings in the process of being born are not 'persons.' "[35] Thus, the report implies, "the baby involved is not unborn" and therefore is a person. The main goal of the Partial-Birth Act of 1995 had been to find a way to bypass *Roe v. Wade* and grant the privileges of citizenship to the "not unborn" "person"; the preferred method was one that would not require the Court to recant *Roe* and would not entail proving that the fetus is, constitutionally, a person.

Thus the Judiciary Committee, in its report, distinguished the "not unborn" from "the unborn" by use of space, not time—that is, it did not consider the lateness of the pregnancy. The report avoids directing discussion back to the stages of pregnancy, of fetal development, of viability—all of which were more or less settled (to the dissatisfaction of pro-lifers) by *Roe v. Wade*. Instead, the report states, "the only distinguishing characteristic is locale." "Clearly," the text reads, "the only difference between the partial-birth procedure and homicide is a mere three inches."[36]

In 1995 those "three inches" apparently referred to the birth canal, otherwise known as the vagina—the passageway from the uterus, also called the womb. According to the committee report, if any part of the "not unborn" "person" entered the vagina, this occurrence was to be considered a "partial birth." A definition is provided: "As used in this section, the term 'partial-birth abortion' means an abortion in which the person performing the abortion partially vaginally delivers a living fetus before killing the fetus and completing the delivery."[37] By this definition, if anything entered the vagina from the uterus, it would be illegal to follow through with the abortion in progress, despite the doctor's and the woman's expectation of terminating the pregnancy. Dissenters to the report described why the provided definition was practically limitless:

At one truncated hearing on this legislation before Subcommittee markup, Dr. Courtland Robinson, Associate Professor in the Department of Gynecology and Obstetrics at Johns Hopkins University School of Medicine, testified that " 'partially vaginally delivers' is vague, not medically oriented, just not correct. In any normal 2nd trimester abortion procedure by any method, you may have a point at which a part, a one-inch piece of cord for example, of the fetus passes out of the cervical os before fetal demise has occurred. This doesn't mean you're performing a 'partial birth.' "[38]

The press and pro-choice advocates immediately zeroed in on the overly vague language of the proposed ban. What their general criticism neglected, however, was the way in which a new term—a "not unborn" (and yet not fully born) "person"—had been introduced. Fetal personhood had certainly been proposed before, but this likely was the first time that the vagina, those three inches, had been claimed as public space, government territory. But the powers of vague language did not stop there.

By 1997, the concern was no longer that the "not unborn" person would be "partially delivered" into the vagina from the uterus but entirely delivered *through* the birth canal. The legislative report that accompanied H.R. 1122, the Partial-Birth Abortion Ban Act of 1997, uses a nonmedical description from the *Los Angeles Times* (a publication not known as an authority on gynecology or obstetrics) as its premise: "The procedure requires a physician to extract a fetus, feet first, from the womb and through the birth canal until all but its head is exposed." The report then builds on this idea: "it is essential that the procedure be completed *before* the fetus' head leaves the birth canal; once the fetus were completely clear of the mother's body, a live delivery would have occurred and the child would be protected by existing criminal statutes."[39] This discussion further obfuscates the reality of female anatomy and the late-term procedures. It misrepresents the dilation-and-extraction or dilation-and-evacuation procedure as taking place outside the woman's body—not just outside the uterus and in the vagina.

In 2000 the U.S. Supreme Court ruled by five to four, in *Stenberg v. Carhart*, that Nebraska's ban on late-term abortions was unconstitutional. In its arguments before the Court, pro-life proponents had avoided distinguishing the vagina from the uterus and thereby sustained the misrepresentation that late-term abortions occur outside the womb, and hence outside the woman. The American Medical Association, as amicus curiae, had supplied a "fact sheet" that lent professional credence to the implication that, for the purposes of the Supreme Court, women's reproductive anatomy consists only of the uterus. Should fetal parts fall or be pulled into the vagina during a dilation-and-extraction procedure, the Court should view it as a fetus being "killed *outside* the womb," where the fetus "has an autonomy which separates it from the right of the woman to choose treatments for her own body."[40] This wording implies that what lies "outside the womb"—the vagina—is not significant to the Court. The AMA successfully erased the vagina from the Court's consideration and claimed it as a space in which the fetus has autonomy, which the federal government has an obligation to protect. No longer is the vagina, as space that exists "outside the womb," a private space; indeed it is no longer a part of a woman's "own body." By this logic, if the fetus is not in the womb, it is not in (or of) the woman.

Justice Anthony Kennedy's dissenting opinion illustrates how the vaginal area "outside the womb" is easily mistaken for the far more expansive area outside the woman. In his opinion, Kennedy cites eyewitnesses who had testified that "when the scissors are inserted in the back of the head"—a procedure they cannot see, since it is by their own account inside the womb—"the fetus' body, wholly outside the woman's body and alive, reacts as though startled and goes limp." Clearly appalled by the horrific nature of testimony for the anti-abortion prosecution, Kennedy quotes the AMA brief without making a distinction between the vaginal space "outside the womb" and the expansive space "wholly outside the woman's body." As one of the pro-choice lawyers understands this opinion, Kennedy "is saying that once the fetus is in the vagina, women lose constitutional protection."[41] This point was especially grievous to reproductive rights advocates because Kennedy had coauthored the 1992 majority opinion in *Planned Parenthood of Southeastern Pennsylvania v. Casey*, the decision that was once regarded as resolving "the basic constitutional question of abortion *for all time*" in favor of women.[42] In this about-face from 1992, Kennedy "is narrowing the definition of what abortion is."[43]

In 2000, the pro-life arguments in *Stenberg v. Carhart* also attempted, as had previous partial birth cases, to redefine the fetus. In the legislative campaign for the Partial-Birth Act of 1995, pro-life lawmakers had tried to grant privileges of citizenship to the "not unborn" "person" and had purported that late-term abortion "partially vaginally delivers a living fetus." In 2000, the Supreme Court engaged the language of the Nebraska statute, which claimed that the "abortion partially delivers vaginally a living unborn child." Although Justice Kennedy struggled with the semantics of whether a dilation-and-extraction procedure constitutes a "delivery," he never questioned the slippage from "living fetus" to "living unborn child." Even if he had accepted these terms only for the sake of argument, he admitted them into the legal record, which is no insignificant event.

Legislators may accept terms such as *living unborn child* or *partial birth* for the sake of argument one year, only to find in another year that they have been taken for granted and adopted in the Court's opinion. Phrases may be assumed to be legally adopted terms simply because they are found in the Congressional Record. Justice Kennedy relies on this assumption when he argues that the term *partial birth abortion* is not vague language at all; he says it denotes precisely the dilation-and-extraction procedure. When he notes how "partial birth" has been used in the legislatures, Kennedy is either ignorant or dismissive of the fact that pro-life strategists created the term as a political ploy. The term, he writes, "has been used in state legislation on 28 occasions and by Congress twice. The term 'partial birth abortion' was adopted by Congress in both 1995 and 1997 in two separate pieces of legislation prohibiting the procedure."[44] Therefore, according to Kennedy, it is a legitimate term that denotes a particular medical procedure, dilation and extraction. Never mind that those 1995 and 1997 discussions rejected the term as inadequately representing actual late-term procedures. The phrase is on the books. Without a doubt, the series of "partial birth" Supreme Court cases has succeeded in entering into the legal lexicon phrases that can now be used as arguing points in future hearings and court cases. Moreover, the pro-life lawyers in *Stenberg v. Carhart* were successful in painting a word picture of a whole baby dangling outside a woman's body, when in fact late-term abortions occur in the womb and sometimes in the vagina.

This image of a baby dangling from a torso is one that can be found in pro-life drawings. For example, an anti-abortion advertisement for "a Doctor's Illustrated Guide to Partial-Birth Abortion" shows a fully formed child, except for its head, hanging outside an abdominal cavity (see fig. 3).[45] A child, not a fetus, is illustrated, and its proportions are grossly exaggerated. Visually the illustration is illogical, because the child shown looks as though it would not fit into the body cavity that is drawn. That space is ambiguous too. It is a single cavity, presumably the uterus, the womb. At second glance, one might guess that the vagina, represented by two long loops on either side of the cavity, has collapsed the way a vagina does after the uterus has contracted in full labor during actual birth. But the first glance presents the woman as just a gaping hole out of which a doctor is extracting a baby. Because the uterus does not contract during late-term abortion but only during labor, this illustration is inaccurate. Also inaccurate, and even medically counterintuitive, is the position of the doctor's fingers and the child's shoulders. If the cervix were dilated enough to allow

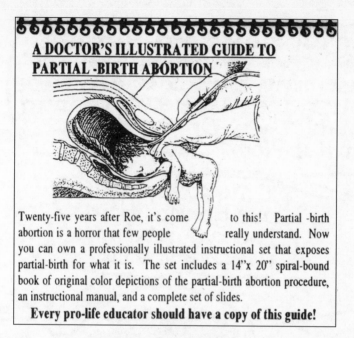

Fig. 3. *Where is the vagina? This unsolicited "medical" diagram was sent to a Planned Parenthood office.*

fingers, a scalpel, and the shoulders of a fully grown child within its circumference, there would be no need to collapse the skull, as is done in a dilation-and-extraction procedure. The goal of an image such as this is not to promote medical understanding but to promote identification with the fetus and to reduce women to the ground over which the abortion war is fought.

An extreme version of this idea is found in a cartoon first published in the *Life Advocate* and reproduced on the website of Life Enterprises Unlimited (see fig. 4). Barbara Kruger's statement that "your body is a battleground" has never been more apt in describing the abortion conflict, especially as depicted in this cartoon. The fully formed child stands in utero holding a smoking gun. It is an absurd image that is not intended to be realistic (even the most bombastic pro-lifer would not actually claim that a fetus can stand erect, aim, pull a trigger) or plausible (how did it get the gun in there?). The woman is presented as not only a vessel for the fetus but as the ground on which the fetus takes his position of self-defense. Aside from making the liberal feminist observation that the woman—at least all her internal organs—is erased, this cartoon reveals other things as well.[46]

Fig. 4. *The pistol-packing fetus waits for no rescue. Found posted on a telephone pole in Minneapolis, Minnesota, 1995.*

This depiction of the fetus marks not so much a change in fetal imagery as a shift away from defending fetuses in terms of civil rights or human rights (as discussed in chap. 1). As Karen Newman has demonstrated with a history of fetal images, the idea of the autonomous fetus is not new, and the rhetoric surrounding both fetal rights and women's rights is part of Enlightenment ideals of possessive individualism and humanism. For example, according to Newman, the language of warfare—killing, murder, weapons, strategies, tactics, Operation Rescue—and, recently, the escalation from language to physical violence against both property and persons serve to domesticate war by producing it safely within the boundaries of the nation-state. . . . Abortion, opponents claim, is war "on our unborn children. The veterans died to protect freedom everywhere, yet for the unborn there are no rights." . . . Such nationalist rhetoric might seem to evoke the social and a concern for the larger community, in contrast to individualism; it should not be forgotten, however, that the concept of nation is historically linked to the privileging of the individual.[47]

Newman makes an important observation when she notes that society and the individual are indivisible according to Enlightenment thought, which remains the dominant Western ideology. It is also important to recognize, however, that the new abortion warrior departs from right-to-life rhetoric that is philosophically based in individualism, humanism, and rights discourse. The profound influence of millennialism on abortion warriors such as Hill must be taken into account to recognize how far afield pro-life violence is from civil rights rhetoric or a human rights rationale. Abortion warriors who believe they are engaged in a holy war that transcends man's law, who believe that the end of history is imminent, eschew a rights discourse because they believe it is not God's law. The pistol-packing fetus is not seeking rights but retribution through self-defense.

This cartoon departs from the idea that pro-lifers should defend the unborn as innocent, vulnerable, and voiceless children. The position it serves does not appropriate civil rights arguments to claim that the fetus is enslaved, persecuted, and slaughtered and that therefore pro-lifers must free, save, or rescue them. Instead, the pistol-packing fetus fits more the besieged mentality and rhetoric of millennialism. The abortion warrior's "total identification" with the fetus results in action taken not on behalf of fetuses. Rather it is action played out on one more battlefield in the apocalyptic war against the federal government, which is under satanic/Jewish/nonwhite rule. Just like the Weavers at Ruby Ridge, the Branch Davidians at Waco, and Eric Rudolph in the woods of North Carolina, so is the fetus in the womb. The abortion warrior is not so much acting on behalf of the unborn as he is saying, "I am the unborn."

The abortion warrior's total identification with the fetus thus evolves to the point that the warrior comes to equate himself with the unborn, who then is viewed not as defenseless but as self-defensive. The unborn stands erect, extends his phallic gun, and shoots the doctor. In the case of the particular cartoon reproduced here, which was posted on a telephone pole on a Minneapolis street some months after John Salvi's attacks at clinics near Boston, the dialogue suggests there is nothing irrational or psychotic about killing abortion providers, which countered the prevailing media accounts of Salvi as a mentally disturbed loner unconnected to the pro-life movement and its principles. Whoever posted the cartoon was indicating that Salvi was not crazy or alone in his rationale for killing clinic staff. According to the cartoon, there is little difference between the fetus that would pull a trigger in self-defense and the pro-life assassin who has pulled a trigger. Like the new abortion warrior outside the womb, this unborn is besieged but able-bodied, with the faculties of awareness, language, and reason. This unborn waits for no rescue.

In fact, the cartoon turns the rhetorical tables by suggesting that abortion providers are the ones who need protection—protection from the self-defending unborn. In this way, we glimpse an alternate reading of the notion of fetal protection. To investigate how some laws infer that the term *fetal protection* means protecting society from an undesirable unborn, it is necessary to consider the keen discrepancy among the descriptions of fetuses subject to late-term abortion, on the one hand, and those subject to crack cocaine on the other.

Protection from the Fetal Citizen

The cartoon version of the unborn as a pistol-packing fetus is anomalous, especially among other "partial birth" images of fetuses as vulnerable and defenseless—except in one way. Like all the other fetuses described in terms of late-term abortion, the pistol-packing fetus is presented initially and notably as intact, whole, and unmarred. This condition reflects a dispute over the developmental status of fetuses that is part of late-term abortion discussions.

Pro-choice advocates have tried to focus debates about partial birth abortion on the fact that late-term abortions are performed on women whose pregnancies are considered catastrophic, that is, pregnancies in which the fetus is grossly deformed to the point of being unable to function and survive should it be born.[48] For example, when Dr. George Tiller testified against a proposed ban on late-term abortions in Kansas, he was "armed with statistics and photos of catastrophic pregnancies he aborted."

He brought pictures of fetuses with significant abnormalities such as partially missing skulls and spinal cords, and one photo showed what appeared to be a single fetus but was really "twins fused in a single body." Only 3 to 5 percent of pregnancies beyond twenty weeks involve these kinds of severe distortions, Tiller said, and of these cases of abnormalities, a full third "escape detection until after the 24th week."[49] Tiller argued that therefore late-term abortions are necessary to terminate pregnancies that would result in dead or severely deformed babies, whose birth often would put the woman's health at risk.

To underscore Tiller's logic, the *Wichita Eagle* featured the personal stories of five Kansas families. Each story focused on an abnormality, such as hydrocephalus or spina bifida, and the daily existence of mature people living with such abnormalities, highlighting their inability to feed or dress themselves, bathe, walk, or talk using an adult vocabulary.[50]

On the East Coast too, during debates on banning late-term abortion, pro-choice advocates emphasized fetal abnormalities. They challenged proponents of the ban to provide a better option than late-term procedures:

> What safe alternatives would they offer a woman who wants to
> abort a nonviable fetus with anencephaly (lack of brain) or one of
> 400 other types of catastrophic anomalies that cannot be detected
> until after 20 weeks of pregnancy? Would they recommend she be
> forced into labor, have a Caesarean section or other invasive proce-
> dure to expel a dead or deteriorating fetus that has no possibility of
> independent life?[51]

As in Kansas, the debate became a showdown of horrific images of bodily deformation. "Medically inaccurate drawings of the intact D & E procedure have upset many people. But most Americans would be more horrified to look at photographs of a fetus with anencephaly (lack of brain) or one of 400 other fetal abnormalities for which women seek late-term abortions."[52] To win the debates over late-term abortions, pro-choice advocates repeated information on bodily disfigurement and catastrophic pregnancies.

Pro-life forces countered that these catastrophes occur in a very small number of cases. To offset the discussions of gross deformity and severe abnormality, proponents of a ban on partial birth abortion repeatedly portray the fetus as a whole baby. To this end, they employ language that emphasizes normality, health, and wholeness. In the legislation of several states, Louisiana and Michigan among them, the terms *infant* and *fetus* are defined as "interchangeable" to denote a fully formed and cognitively developed child. The Utah legislation repetitively describes the fetus as "intact."[53] The legislative notice discussing the 1997 federal Partial-Birth Abortion Ban Act insists that late-term abortions terminate pregnancies even when the fetuses are "normal" and "healthy."[54]

More specifically, these abortions are said to be performed not on women but on "normal fetuses." Moreover, these abortions are emphatically said to be performed "not on fetuses suffering genetic or other developmental abnormalities."[55] In other words, the fetuses discussed in these bans are whole, "intact," "normal," "healthy," and free from "genetic or developmental abnormalities." These are the kind of fetuses that legislators want to protect, the kind they want to count as persons and as citizens, unborn or in the process of being born.

In contrast, fetal protection of another sort focuses on fetuses that are perceived to be not healthy, normal, intact, whole, or "free from genetic of developmental abnormalities." This kind of fetal protection is epitomized by the case of *Whitner v. South Carolina* (1992), in which the South Carolina Supreme Court reinterpreted its criminal child endangerment statute to include protection of a viable fetus.[56] A summary of the case as written by Whitner's legal team follows:

> In 1989, two South Carolina solicitors began applying the state's child endangerment law . . . to pregnant women whose conduct was presumed to pose a risk to fetal health. Since that time, the overwhelming majority of women arrested pursuant to this new interpretation, including petitioners Cornelia Whitner and Mallisa Crawley, have been low-income, African-American women who sought health care, and who, instead of being offered treatment for their substance dependency during pregnancy, were arrested after the hospital reported their condition to the local police department.[57]

In fact, the hospital in which Whitner and Crawley were seeking maternity care had "cut a deal with the police that virtually deputized doctors and nurses."[58] These medical professionals tested urine samples without patients' consent and sent the results to police, who initially had provided the hospital with a profile of whom to test. With one exception, all those tested were African American and poor. The rationale for such profiling was to "defend" those unborn exposed to crack cocaine. Thus the context of *Whitner v. South Carolina* was a phenomenon called the crack baby syndrome, which presented fetuses and newborns as hopelessly debilitated by drugs used by pregnant women.

In stark contrast to those fetuses considered to be "intact" by pro-life advocates hoping to pass legislation detailing partial birth abortion restrictions, fetuses gestating in women who use cocaine were and are widely portrayed as "undergrown, brain damaged and congenitally stigmatized, who as children would be unlovable, unadoptable, and unteachable. They were the 'innocent victims' of selfish and uncaring women who had lost their maternal instincts under the influence of drugs. Other news stories branded babies exposed to 'crack' as 'genetically inferior,' 'troubled,' 'tormented,' and unable to cope with kindergarten."[59] These fetuses are the exact opposite of those discussed in the context of late-term abortion restrictions. It is as if the fetuses that might be aborted inhabit the pure domain of millennial thought, whereas the fetuses labeled as crack babies dwell in the impure domain. This millennialist pairing of two pieces of pro-life legislation manages to exalt the unborn as innocent victims of abortion, while suggesting that some "unborn babies" are dangerous even in their innocence.

Although they may be innocent, crack babies are seen as perpetuating the impurities from which they come, burdening society with a "permanent subhuman biologic underclass" that could not know God.[60] According to one account, "their IQs would range in the low fifties. They would barely be able to dress themselves, dependent on the taxpayers for life—'a life of certain suffering, of probable deviance, of permanent inferiority.' Informed that the bill for a single child might run to a quarter of a million dollars, the president of Boston University questioned spending this kind of money on 'crack babies who won't ever achieve the intellectual development to have consciousness of God.' "[61] Like a photographic negative, the so-called crack baby is the biologically and morally darker, a reversed image of those fetuses referenced in partial birth legislation—those "normal," "healthy," "intact" fetuses who do not suffer "genetic or other developmental abnormalities." The crack baby is also literally the darker image of the partial birth baby: crack babies are explicitly presumed to be black.

These discrepant images of fetuses illustrate Dorothy Roberts's understanding that "the powerful Western image of childhood innocence does not seem to benefit Black children. Black children are born guilty. The new bio-underclass constitutes nothing but a menace to society—criminals, crackheads, and welfare cheats waiting to happen."[62] If *Whitner v. South Carolina* is a case about fetal protection, it appears to be as much about protecting society from "degenerate" black fetuses who presumably will become burdensome black babies as it is about protecting fetuses from their presumably degenerate black mothers. As one news headline put it, events that led to *Whitner v. South Carolina* were part of a "crack-baby prevention program," one designed, as some believe, to prevent the kind of children who are perceived to be crack babies, those who are born from crack users, who notoriously are presumed to be black. Crack is "the drug of choice for blacks," South Carolina Attorney General Charles Condon—the leading proponent of prosecuting pregnant women who use crack—has been quoted as saying.[63]

The discursive discrepancy of portraying fetuses as innocent, whole, and genetically normal for the sake of restricting late-term abortions but as innocent, infirm, and biologically inferior for the sake of prosecuting drug-using women would be logical if crack babies were a proven phenomenon. But they are not. In fact, much has been written about the crack baby myth. Mike Gray discusses the focus on crack babies in historical terms:

> when the expected tidal wave of brain-damaged, unteachable monsters failed to materialize, a handful of thoughtful people started looking into some of the original assumptions. They discovered that the crack-baby epidemic, like the Nixon heroin scare, was a total fabrication—a blend of distorted data and sloppy journalism. The tiny infants trembling in their incubators were real enough—no question about that—but they were usually the victims of an older, more established ailment. What the cameras were capturing were the well-documented effects of malnutrition and poverty.[64]

Gray goes on to detail how previous cocaine studies were reviewed by doctors and researchers, who "found no link between cocaine use and the so-called crack baby syndrome." Dr. Ira Chasnoff, whose 1985 *New England Journal of Medicine* article launched the " 'crack baby' story in the mainstream press," reconsidered his preliminary research, conducted a new study, and recanted the original findings. "It is wrong," Dr. Chasnoff emphasized, "to paint a stereotypical picture of the so-called 'crack babies' as a lost generation."[65]

The media, whose "pack journalism," according to Gray, created the stereotype that Chasnoff and other health professionals later debunked, made recuperative if not penitent moves similar to Chasnoff's. They began retracting the image of what *Rolling Stone* called the "subhuman biologic underclass" that purportedly was produced by black cocaine users. For example, Jim Stossel narrated an ABC network program devoted to explaining why the crack baby syndrome constitutes "junk science." The television news magazine *60 Minutes*, however, refused to recant its piece titled "Cracking Down," which was first run in 1994 and then rebroadcast in 1998, at a time when lawyers for *Whitner* were petitioning for certiorari, asking the U.S. Supreme Court to review the decision, a request that was denied.[66]

In "Cracking Down," all the trappings of the crack baby stereotype are in place, and *60 Minutes* drew from anti-abortion rhetoric both visually and verbally. Shots of premature, raw-looking, excessively small infants cowering in the bright lights of the camera crew recall the anti-abortion images and discussions of helpless victims presented by pro-lifers. The name "crack baby" itself resonates with an American Portraits video titled "Who Broke the Baby?" which is based on a child's remark after seeing a picture of fetal parts that were sifted from the more gelatinous products of abortion and assembled to resemble a dismembered body. In this context, the word *crack* serves as a signifier of both cocaine and brokenness. The *60 Minutes* piece describes crack babies in the same manner that pro-lifers describe the dismembered, broken, cracked baby of abortion: they are "innocent children hurt severely." With this sort of rhetoric, "Cracking Down" sustains the premise of the inescapable, long-standing, deleterious effects of prenatal use of cocaine—a premise that by now has become questionable, if not entirely proven false.[67] "As I study more and more," Dr. Chasnoff said, "I think the placenta does a better job of protecting the child than we do as a society."[68]

In the midst of these refutations of the crack baby myth, what lends credence to the *60 Minutes* piece and the prosecutions in South Carolina? Generally, the answer is that they arouse an established anti-abortion sentiment. More particularly, it is the pro-life practice of total identification with the fetus that makes imprisoning pregnant women seem like a palpable and good idea. But identification does not necessarily occur on an individual level. Proponents of crack baby/fetal protection legislation do not identify fetuses with themselves, on a corporeal level, as did the clinic bomber who imagined his own abortion. Instead, they identify fetuses as members of their own community. To defy any accusation of racism in the *Whitner* case, for instance, South Carolina officials quoted "black

Charleston Police Chief Reuben Greenberg, who said he 'was glad that somebody was finally doing something to help kids in the black community.' "[69]

Attorney General Condon counts fetuses among his community, too. In fact, he routinely calls fetuses "citizens of South Carolina" and dubiously describes *Whitner* as a "ruling that a viable fetus is a fellow South Carolinian and therefore entitled to protection under the law."[70] Condon thus promotes a social and political identification with the fetus to secure an absolutist approach to prosecuting pregnant crack addicts.

Prosecuting pregnant crack users, who are explicitly presumed to be black, is Condon's priority as a "Defender of God, South, and Unborn."[71] It is important to keep in mind the ways in which God, the South, and the unborn are related. Among abortion warriors influenced by racist Christian Identity tenets, they are related in so far as abortion is the end times of the white race. Although Condon and his coterie deny that such an idea is their motivation, their views are in others ways complementary to traditional Southern views that hark back to the days of the Confederacy and its defense of a race-based slave economy. As such a defender, Condon "pushed to preserve the State Capitol's Confederate flag—a symbol that even the conservative Senator Strom Thurmond, Republican of South Carolina, reluctantly said was too contentious."[72] More to the point, Condon's push to criminalize pregnant black women is not incongruent with Southern history, in which defenders of the Confederacy enslaved black women. Condon's defense of "God, South, and Unborn" seems to preclude a defense of black women's freedom, reproductive and otherwise.

Even Condon's defense of the black unborn is qualified. His promotion of prosecuting black women on behalf of their unborn children is not an opposition to abortion. In fact, the regulations Condon has promoted, notably those involved in the *Whitner* case, make abortion more attractive to a pregnant black woman who could be prosecuted for her addiction. If Condon were protecting the unborn, rather than protecting society from unborn black kids, why would he promote regulations that encourage women to have abortions as a way to prevent promised prosecution? Both pro-lifers and pro-choicers have commented on how this result seems to fly in the face of Condon's fetal protection stance. But Condon's efforts are not contrary to the idea of fetal protection if we acknowledge it as securing protection *from* fetuses rather than extending protection *to* fetuses. Condon's efforts appear to secure the protection of society from the expense and burden of genetically cracked fetuses, which supposedly will become degenerate black babies.

Condon's claim that the "fetus is a fellow South Carolinian" functions not only as an identification with the fetus; it also functions to identify the unborn as a citizenry whose value is based on biological wholeness and genetic integrity. This sentiment is completely compatible with, if not derived from, the white supremacist definition of racial purity as biological integrity. Regardless of the derivation of these ideas, the fact is that the moral outrage over crack babies—who are presumed to be genetically abnormal, morally bankrupt, and black—emerged in the midst of resurgent anxieties about the perceived demise of the Christian white race. These anxieties have been amplified by millennialist views of abortion as the end times of America. Efforts to dispel the world of cracked babies are not therefore explicitly racist, but they have implications that are built on and feed racist assumptions.

A controversial program that pays drug users to become infertile, named Children Requiring a Caring Kommunity or C.R.A.C.K., offers sterilization rather than criminalization as a way to protect society from undesired cracked babies. Predicated on and perpetuating the crack baby myth, C.R.A.C.K. offers individuals $200 as an incentive to undergo tubal ligation (which permanently prevents conception) or to use one of the most notoriously unsafe methods of birth control: Norplant, Depo-Provera, or an intrauterine device (otherwise known as an IUD).[73] C.R.A.C.K. does not offer money for using barrier methods of birth control, such as condoms, or for taking contraceptive pills, nor does it arrange for drug rehabilitation for the women. Women's rights groups have criticized C.R.A.C.K. for working under three erroneous assumptions: "(1) that women who are addicted to substances will be perpetually addicted; (2) that treatment options for women who are addicted are not worthy of being pursued; and (3) that drug addicted women are expendable."[74] This last assumption is essentially eugenic, derived from the idea that "undesirable" people should not be able to procreate, lest the human race degenerate.

C.R.A.C.K. is not a forced sterilization program, as were some American eugenic campaigns of the early twentieth century, some Nazi programs based on the U.S. eugenics movement in the 1930s, and some U.S. government–sponsored population control programs of 1970s.[75] But C.R.A.C.K. is coercive in the sense that it exploits the desperation of drug users. According to one analysis, C.R.A.C.K. takes advantage of the vulnerability of substance abusers by use of advertising slogans such as "Don't Let a Pregnancy Ruin Your Drug Habit" and "If You Use Drugs, Get Birth Control, Get $200 Cash." The founder of C.R.A.C.K. has compared drug users to animals: "We don't allow dogs to breed. We spay them. We neuter them. We try to keep them from having unwanted puppies, and yet these women are literally having litters of children."[76] With these attitudes and assumptions, "C.R.A.C.K. denies poor, marginalized women with substance abuse problems their procreative ability, and this is a human rights violation."[77] Moreover, this violation is a plan that has been tried before by undeniably racist politicians.

In 1991, three years before C.R.A.C.K. was founded, David Duke, a notorious racist who has been in and out of electoral politics, proposed a similar program that encouraged marginalized women to forfeit fertility for income. In the 1970s Duke had been explicit about his white supremacist beliefs, founding the Louisiana Knights of the Ku Klux Klan. In the 1980s Duke distanced himself from the Klan, founded the National Association for the Advancement of White People, and otherwise toned down his blatant KKK racism. In 1989 he was elected to the Louisiana House of Representatives, where he was chastised for selling neo-Nazi literature from his legislative office. He then began promoting cash incentives for sterilization of welfare recipients, and in April 1991 he introduced a bill into the legislature that would pay cash to welfare recipients who agreed to accept Norplant implants or an equivalent long-term contraceptive. The inherent racism of the program comes from the fact that most Louisiana welfare enrollees are African American: "Duke restricts the bill to Aid For Dependent Children (AFDC) recipients, 74% of whom are black, and offers a yearly cash grant incentive of $100 for as long as the participant retains the implants."[78]

In 1985, after he claimed to have renounced racism, Duke said he sought to purify the white race through genetic engineering and a sterilization program for welfare recipients. In proposing a voluntary program, "Duke patterned his genetic engineering plan after Nazi-sponsored voluntary eugenic programs that eventually decimated millions."[79] After failed gubernatorial and presidential campaigns, Duke eventually returned to overt, organized white supremacism as a radio talk show host and recruiter for a neo-Nazi group founded by *Turner Diaries* author William Pierce.

Duke's 1991 plan was a government-sponsored voluntary sterilization program; C.R.A.C.K. is a privately funded voluntary sterilization program. Both are derived from the eugenic idea that "undesirable" people should be prohibited from procreating.[80] Duke's undesirables are poor people dependent on welfare; implicitly they are African Americans. C.R.A.C.K.'s undesirables are women who use crack; presumably they are not only black but bestial in their sexual reproduction. Like animals they breed unwanted litters, according to C.R.A.C.K.'s founder. The very name of the program feeds off of and perpetuates the racial stereotypes of blacks as crack users and of crack babies as degenerate black children.

Certainly there is good reason for working to eliminate the damage that drug use can cause before birth.[81] But there is no good reason for perpetuating the ideas that women who use drugs are all uncaring addicts and that children of drug users cannot function normally or know God. A 1999 study found that a "decade ago, the cocaine-exposed child was stereotyped as being neurologically crippled—trembling in a corner and irreparably damaged. But this is unequivocally not the case. And furthermore, the inner-city child who has had no drug exposure at all is doing no better than the child labeled a 'crack baby.'"[82] Poverty, not intrauterine traces of cocaine, is more damaging to "a child's developing brain."[83]

By 2001, the U.S. Supreme Court's opinion about prosecuting pregnant women in so-called defense-of-crack-babies cases remained standing. Although the Court had not caught up with medical fact, it did reconsider the manner in which Cornelia Whitner had been tested and then prosecuted for cocaine use.[84] The Supreme Court found that the Charleston, South Carolina, hospital had erred in testing Whitner's urine without her consent. According to Ellen Goodman, the decision provided that "pregnant women are entitled to the same medical privacy as any other patient."[85] Although Ms. Whitner remains in prison, lawyers popped the champagne cork over the victory for women's rights.

A few months later, however, a jury in South Carolina convicted a twenty-four-year-old black woman of homicide when, after she tested positive for cocaine use, her pregnancy ended in stillbirth. One pathologist for the defense said it was unlikely that the cause of the stillbirth could be determined; two other medical specialists testified that cocaine was undoubtedly the cause of death. The woman, labeled "callous" by the prosecutor, had no previous criminal record, no experience with drug treatment programs, and no prenatal care until she was eight-and-a-half months pregnant. She was sentenced to twelve years in prison.[86]

The legislative tactic of fetal protection is not simply a matter of extending privileges of citizenship to fetuses while thwarting women's rights as citizens. Viewed comparatively, the banning of late-term abortion and the prosecuting of black women presumed to use crack betray the double meaning of fetal protection. On the one hand the state is protecting fetuses perceived to be biologically pure and normal; on the other hand the state is protecting itself from fetuses perceived to be morally abnormal and genetically impure. In the millennial pressure cooker of turn-of-the-twentieth-century America, this double meaning of fetal protection best serves those who see abortion as the end times of the white race.

For those who do not consciously see abortion in either apocalyptic or racialized terms, the fabrication of the concepts of crack baby and the partially born nevertheless remains a compelling testament to the millennialist flavor of the United States around the year 2000. These concepts embody the two genres of apocalyptic narratives, the tragic (doomed) and the comic (utopian). With its degenerative godlessness, the crack baby suffers the tragedy of a soulless life filled with angst, violence, and social catastrophe. The "living unborn" of partial birth abortion, on the other hand, embodies hope for the country; it is the progeny whose wholeness is sure and whose deliverance secures our national humanity.[87] Millennialism is an undercurrent to discussions of fetal protection as surely as it is central to the notion of killing for life.

The Gideon Story

Millennialist Conflict as Mainstream Pro-Life Narrative

The undercurrent of millennialism reflected in fetal protection laws flowed into the mainstream with the publication of *Gideon's Torch*, a novel coauthored by Ellen Vaughn, a *Christianity Today* writer, and Charles Colson of Watergate fame.

Colson was eventually convicted for his role in the 1974 Watergate scandal, an event that coincided with the end of the Vietnam War and obliterated what was left of many Americans' trust in the U.S. government. In the midst of the scandal, Colson became a born-again Christian—a change in spiritual orientation at which many scoffed. A political cartoon of the era depicts an astonished President Nixon recognizing Colson, who had been one of his most loyal advisers, now dressed as a monk and carrying a sign reading "Repent—the End is Near" (see fig. 5).[1] The

' COLSON ?!...'

Cartoon by MacNelly—*Richmond News Leader*, © 1974 by *Chicago Tribune*.

Fig. 5. Richard Nixon recognizes Charles Colson, who was born again in the 1970s, when millennialism became mainstream. © *Tribune Media Services, Inc. All rights reserved. Reprinted with permission.*

joke, of course, rests on the triple significance of "end." The cartoon emphasizes Colson's prominent rear end, suggesting that his new religious convictions prove him an ass. Moreover, Colson's newfound millennialism, which included believing in the eschatological end times, signals the political end of the Nixon administration.

According to Colson's account of his spiritual rebirth and political demise, as detailed in *Born Again*, the cartoon was prophetic. As a consequence of his new acceptance of millennialist religion, Colson pled guilty to devising a scheme that had resulted in the burglary and electronic bugging of Democratic headquarters in the Watergate complex. Colson's admission of guilt profoundly implicated Nixon, who resigned from the presidency months later.

Like Colson's autobiography, the story in *Gideon's Torch* involves the failure of a presidency and the moral collapse of America. The saving grace in each book is millennialist born-again conversion. In 1974 Colson's conversion had been ridiculed, but by 1976 *Time* magazine was heralding the country's bicentennial year as "the year of the evangelical" to raise awareness of the growing phenomenon and acceptance of born-againism. In fact, the new president of the United States, Jimmy Carter, made no secret that he was born again. In the midseventies, millennialism was becoming mainstream.

Gideon's Torch, published twenty years later in 1995, demonstrates how millennialism crosses over into mainstream culture from extreme or far-right pro-life politics. Those who produce and consume pro-life millennialism are not only the "lone wolf" snipers who gun down doctors, the clinic bombers who sabotage and run, or the "guerrilla" legislators who promote anti-abortion proposals under the guise of consumer protection for women or humanitarian aid for crack babies. Indeed, *Gideon's Torch* proves that pro-life millennialism is packaged and consumed by a much larger population.

The significance of packaging pro-life millennialism as narrative, which is what *Gideon's Torch* does, became more clear to me when I heard a national pro-life leader tell the biblical tale of Gideon during a protest in Buffalo, New York, in 1999. Operation Rescue National's leader, Philip (aka Flip) Benham, told the media this Old Testament story to portray pro-lifers as a minority in God's charge. I listened and recognized the story from Colson and Vaughn's novel. "That's the story of Gideon!" I said. Benham seemed pleasantly surprised that I knew it. In addition to sharing the Old Testament tale, Operation Rescue National and *Gideon's Torch* share a millennialist formulation of the pro-life struggle, a narrative of biblical proportions. In this chapter I examine the apocalypticism in Operation Rescue's 1999 visit to Buffalo as well as in *Gideon's Torch*, a novel that, like its author's conversion, demonstrates the mainstreaming of pro-life millennialism.

U.S. versus Them in Buffalo

Reporters circled the Rev. Philip Benham, director of Operation Rescue National, as he discussed how a small band of God's men defeated an army of pagans. Benham was telling the story of Gideon, who led a small number of besieged men to an implausible victory on Mount Gilead. He was telling the biblical story, perhaps, because pro-lifers were outnumbered that day, April 20, 1999, in Buffalo, New York. More than a hundred police stood in intimidating should-to-shoulder lines to separate the pro-lifers from those going into and out of a women's clinic. Veteran activists from pro-choice Refuse and Resist's Reproductive Freedom Task Force had flown to Buffalo and had followed Benham since his arrival, determined to be everywhere he and the media went. A large, vocal, and angry group of pro-choice youth and concerned citizens organized by Buffalo United for Choice outnumbered the pro-lifers, who were reading from Bibles, singing, and witnessing their faith to anyone who would listen.

Founded in 1987 by Randall Terry, Operation Rescue did not always aim to look this meek, prayerful, and lawful. In fact, the organization had become famous for mobilizing thousands of people to unlawfully blockade clinics. But through the years, as guerrilla violence has become more prevalent, Operation Rescue has not only complied with the laws protecting clinic access but has striven to bring a more prayerful, peaceful vigilance to pro-life action. During these years the leadership of Operation Rescue has changed hands twice, and by 1999 Flip Benham was in charge.[2] Under his direction, Operation Rescue is geared more toward symbolic action and media stunts than toward actual "rescue" of the unborn by blockading clinics and preventing women from keeping appointments.[3] Benham's 1996 swimming-pool baptism of the actual plaintiff in *Roe v. Wade*, Norma McCorvey, had grabbed some attention. But McCorvey's conversion to born-againism, as I discuss in chapter 6, was for her one of a long series of religious experiments, and her continuing commitment since the 1970s to a female partner tainted the conversion in most evangelical eyes. In 1998, Benham took Operation Rescue to Disney World to protest gay and lesbian visitors, but even with that colorful backdrop, the event was hardly noticed. So in Buffalo in 1999, here Benham was, quietly explaining the biblical story of Gideon to the relatively small turnout.

Operation Rescue's legacy as a law-breaking vigilante force was intact, however, despite the small turnout. The local evening news in Buffalo showed file tapes of the 1992 Spring of Life campaign, which had resulted in more than 600 arrests.[4] In comparison to the truly massive turnout of 25,000 pro-lifers in Wichita, Kansas, in 1991, the Buffalo action of 1992 had been a disappointment.[5] Nevertheless, thousands of pro-lifers had gathered there on April 19, 1992, and some had thwarted police efforts by dropping to their knees and crawling en masse between the legs of law enforcement. This image had not faded by 1999. In the days before Operation Rescue's arrival, a local judge had ordered that extra-large buffer zones be created around any clinics in the area. The enormous showing of local and state police—not to mention the officers from the ATF, FBI, and CIA rumored to be there—was also prompted by the fact that Operation Rescue had called for this April meeting soon after the murder of an obstetrician-gynecologist who also had performed abortions in Buffalo.

In October 1998, a sniper had shot Dr. Barnett Slepian in his kitchen, just after he had returned from synagogue. A picture of Slepian with the words "Jew" and "killer" scrawled across his face was found in the Buffalo police department.[6] Slepian was the fourth Jew out of five abortion providers who had been shot at by a sniper in upstate New York and the surrounding area since 1994.[7] In conjunction with this rash of sniping aimed at Jews, the Hamilton, Ontario, *Spectator* had received packages that contained picture puzzles intended for the police and the media.[8] The pictures were decidedly apocalyptic in nature, and they included reproductions of Dürer's *Four Horsemen of the Apocalypse*. Within days of Slepian's murder, Rev. Bob Behn, founder of Last Call Ministries, announced that "on April 19, 1999, there would be a Spring of Life reunion during a week-long Operation Save America action in Buffalo."[9] That Operation Rescue was convening in Buffalo during the week of April 18–25 was therefore seen not only as incendiary to those appalled by Slepian's murder but also as reflective of the millennialism connected with the other pro-life sniper attacks in the area.

Millennialism was evident in the scheduling of Operation Rescue's gathering and in its geographic location. The timing of the event coincided with the anniversaries of Waco, Ruby Ridge, and the Oklahoma City bombing (April 19), and with the birthday of Adolf Hitler (April 20). All of these anniversaries are ensconced in apocalyptic conspiracy theories and millennialist rhetoric. The timing of the event also coincided with a prophecy conference, sponsored by Midnight Call Ministries, which was meeting across the border in Niagara Falls, Canada. Attendance at the two-day conference was large enough to fill a ballroom and to patronize a huge book exhibit that featured apocalyptic literature and prophecy Bibles. The theme of the conference, Israel and the Church beyond 2000, highlighted the millennialists' concern with the Middle East and Jews. This concern had made headlines just a few weeks before, when the Rev. Jerry Falwell had stated publicly that he believed the Antichrist was alive. Moreover, Falwell said, the Antichrist, who according to millennialist prophecy is not the same as Satan but who will consolidate a one-world government on behalf of Satan during the Tribulation, is an adult Jewish male. Falwell apologized for what many considered to be an anti-Semitic statement, but he would not retract it.[10] In the context of so much apocalypticism, Operation Rescue met in Buffalo (see fig. 6).

This Spring of Life reunion, announced so soon after Slepian's murder and convened in this apocalyptic context, helps illuminate the nature of the relationship of millennialist prophecy, pro-life action, and anti-Semitism. Historically, millennialists have had a profoundly ambivalent view of the Jews, because "prophecy believers . . . simultaneously honor the Jews

Fig. 6. In Buffalo, 1999, a grim reaper explains to the author that abortion is a sign of the end times. Courtesy of Jacqueline Soohen and Big Noise Films.

as God's chosen people and fore[see] a terrible fate for them in the Tribulation."[11] This terrible fate is the result of the Jews' so-called rejection of Jesus, and modern-day defamation and persecution of Jews can be seen as consequential and preordained. Millennialist Christians may wince at the suffering of Jews and simultaneously embrace it as a sign of Christ's return and the ultimate redemption of all suffering.

This ambivalence has led scholars to question outright whether millennialist belief encourages anti-Semitism. Rather than suggesting that there is a fixed and causal relationship between millennialism and anti-Semitism, it may be more helpful to acknowledge the historical ambiguity between the two as it relates to pro-life politics. In recognizing that ambiguity, what Timothy Weber calls Christian millennialists' "ironic ambivalence" toward Jews, we see how easy it is for millennialists both to empathize with suffering Jews and to accept their persecution unquestioningly, perhaps even gratefully, because it validates the millennialists' understanding of biblical prophecy.[12] This dynamic of identifying with victims of persecution while permitting or even perpetuating the conditions that give rise to that persecution is an element of what Charles Strozier describes as the psychology of millennialism.[13]

In millennialism, there is a thin line between the tendency to empathize or identify with enslaved and persecuted people and the tendency to see oneself as enslaved or persecuted. This thin line is crossed in pro-life discourse that counts abortion as only one "attack on life." White supremacists who organize against abortion do so because they see themselves—as well as the unborn—as victims of abortion, a procedure designed to eliminate the white race or at least to dispossess whites of any cultural and political power in the United States. In this case, however, pro-lifers not only identify with the unborn as a persecuted group but they then identify themselves as a persecuted minority.

Pro-lifers who identify themselves as a persecuted minority—as those outnumbered few who are fully convinced of the evil of abortion and of these wealthy and powerful conspirators who promote it—often compare themselves with groups persecuted on racial and religious grounds. These comparisons, however, do not necessarily indicate an affinity with, or even tolerance of, those groups that historically have been persecuted because of their race, religion, sex, or sexuality. In fact, as Michael Barkun explains, millennial movements often appropriate the status of victimhood that their perceived adversaries claim.[14] Following this logic (as discussed in chap. 1), white supremacists argue that the "real holocaust" is the abortion of white unborn generations and simultaneously deny that six million Jews were exterminated in Hitler's camps. Similarly, men in the Promise Keepers movement argue that they are victimized by society's ideas of gender (specifically by society's—not God's—norms of masculinity) and simultaneously demand nonnegotiable gender codes for their own families.[15]

The tendency of pro-lifers to identify themselves as a persecuted minority is not restricted to the guerrilla extremists and white supremacists discussed in previous chapters. Some pro-lifers view themselves—not only the unborn—as the victims of abortion because abortion is part of Satan's war against Christ and Christians, which the Bible prophesies as occurring before Jesus returns to earth.

This millennialist formulation of abortion is evident in the promotional literature that Operation Rescue distributed in Buffalo, which portrays the group's weeklong activities as an apocalyptic, as well as an anti-abortion, campaign. Benham and his cohorts promoted it as a battle in the ongoing spiritual war between "pro-life Christians," to whom their literature was exclusively addressed, and the rest of the godless country. The program for the Solemn Assembly that inaugurated the Buffalo events itemized particular battles of that spiritual war, including abortion, murder, corruption, homosexuality, and radical feminism. These hindrances to a Christian society are explicitly disregarded as "problems" and embraced instead as "a sign and judgment from God." A biblical account of each item reinforces not only the idea that the Bible has timeless words that respond to such happenings and individuals but that the Bible prophetically announces them:

1. Bill Clinton is not our problem, he is a sign and judgment from God. "Therefore the Lord was angry with His people. . . . and their foes ruled over them." Ps 106:40–41.
2. Abortion is not our problem, it is a sign and judgment from God. ". . . But Ephraim will bring out their children to the slayer." Hos 9:13.
3. Losing our kids to drugs, gangs, and murder is not our problem, it is a sign and judgment from God. "Even if they rear children, I will bereave them of everyone. . . ." Hos 9:12.
4. Kids killing kids is not our problem, it is a sign and judgment from God. ". . . bloodshed follows bloodshed. Because of this the land mourns. . . ." Hos 4:2–3.
5. Homosexuality is not our problem, it is a sign and judgment from God. ". . . They exchanged truth of God for a lie. . . . Because of this, God gave them over to shameful lusts . . ." Rom 1:25–26.

A total of twenty-five "signs" are listed in the program for Operation Rescue's Solemn Assembly. The biblical quotations serve as evidence of God's judgment and of his plan. Because of the repeated assertion that each of these items is a sign, it is difficult to deny that Benham's congregation is watching for signs of the end times. Not only do abortion and other social issues call pro-lifers to assemble in Buffalo, but it is a "last call." The sense of urgency is clear in a news release from Operation Rescue, which says that we must repent of such wrongdoing. Implicitly, this repentance may ease the judgment of God, whose anger is reaching fever pitch, as is evident in all the increasing signs of the times.

Flyers announcing the events made the apocalyptic tone clear by listing all the forces at war against pro-life Christians:

ALL THE POWER AND WEALTH OF

THE TOWN OF WEST SENECA

ALL THE POWER AND WEALTH OF

THE CITY OF LOCKPORT
ALL THE POWER AND WEALTH OF
THE TOWN OF AMHERST
ALL THE POWER AND WEALTH OF
THE TOWN OF TONAWANDA
ALL THE POWER AND WEALTH OF
THE CITY OF ROCHESTER
ALL THE POWER AND WEALTH OF
THE CITY OF BUFFALO
ALL THE POWER AND WEALTH OF
ERIE COUNTY
ALL THE POWER AND WEALTH OF
MARILYN BUCKHAM
ALL THE POWER AND WEALTH OF
UNIVERSITY OF BUFFALO
ALL THE POWER AND WEALTH OF
PLANNED PARENTHOOD
ALL THE POWER AND WEALTH OF
THE U.S. DISTRICT COURT
ALL THE POWER AND WEALTH OF
THE STATE OF NEW YORK
(SPITZER, PATAKI, SILVER)
ALL THE POWER AND WEALTH OF
THE UNITED STATES OF AMERICA

VS

THE CHURCH OF
JESUS CHRIST

From the top to the bottom of the page, these words were printed in increasingly large font, so that "THE CHURCH OF JESUS CHRIST" were the biggest, most easily read words.

The repetition of "ALL THE POWER AND WEALTH" resonates with working-class critiques of government. But it does not rely on socioeconomic analysis or encourage organizing around labor issues or against capitalist exploitation. Operation Rescue has always insisted that pro-life action be Christ-centered. As Operation Rescue's founder, "Randall Terry was never about economics" but about "sacred history."[16] Operation Rescue has "sacred history"—not class critique—as its ideological foundation. This sacred history is as dichotomous as it is populist. It is a biblical struggle between the rich, powerful, and depraved and the poor, persecuted, and pure.

The flyer detailing "all the power and wealth" that oppose pro-lifers matches Flip Benham's rendition of Gideon. As Gideon's troops before them, Benham and his group are outnumbered, but not ultimately overpowered. The logic is clear: because God is on their side, pro-lifers will prevail, despite the apocalyptic odds against them. This is the basic message of the story of Gideon that Benham was telling the reporters. It is also the basic, millennialist message of the Gideon story as told by Charles Colson and Ellen Vaughn in *Gideon's Torch*.

Light versus Darkness as Millennialist Conflict

Gideon's Torch translates millennialist conflict into pro-life sentiment by using the theme of light versus darkness.[17] The battle between light and darkness becomes a millennialist conflict when it surpasses a generic sense of an ending in apocalyptic anticipation of the coming of Christ. An apocalyptic conflict involves two diametrically opposed sides whose battle over their differences will bring about worldwide destruction. Millennialist conflict involves an apocalyptic conflict—or a promise of it—that is precursor to a thousand-year, or millennial, reign on earth by Christians. According to biblical prophecy, apocalyptic conflict of necessity occurs before—and is a promise of—the thousand years of Christian peace and justice on earth.

There is substantial debate about when Christ himself will return in relation to this millennium, this prophesied thousand years of peace and justice. Some believe he will return to inaugurate the millennium; others say he will return once the contemporary Christian saints have reigned for a thousand years. This debate has influenced many pro-lifers, including the authors of *Gideon's Torch*.[18] Charles Colson, before publishing *Gideon's Torch*, had written about when Christ will return in ways that define Colson as premillennialist.

Like all premillennialists, Colson believes that no one but Jesus can "usher in the Kingdom of God on earth. Only Christ Himself would do that when He returns."[19] Jesus' Second Coming, in other words, will occur *before* the millennial reign of Christians on earth, hence the term *pre*millennialism. Postmillennialists, on the other hand, believe that Christian men have been given dominion over the earth to create and uphold a good and just society for a thousand years, after which Jesus will return, hence *post-*

millennialism. Colson disagrees with the latter view and chastises leaders of the New Right for subscribing to it through their strategies and actions.

New Right politicians and strategists, says Colson, are wrong in "attempting to take dominion over culture through legislation and court decisions."[20] Yet Colson acknowledges that those presumed postmillennialist New Righters have aided his pro-life work by getting thousands of previously complacent Christians to register to vote, lobby, call senators, donate money, and otherwise be active in the political process. According to Colson, "For years many Christian fundamentalists shunned the 'sinful' political process, even to the extent of not voting."[21] Or, as Flip Benham says, "We were so heavenly bound we were no earthly good."[22] Although Colson does not advocate taking dominion over the earth, he has promoted political activity for Christians not only by writing pro-life books such as *Gideon's Torch* but through a prison ministry and other media outlets, such as his "Breakpoint" radio show.

This politically active version of premillennialism is new. Colson is accurate when he credits the New Right with taking the lead in convincing premillennialists to break with tradition and become politically active. As discussed in chapter 1, New Right leaders mobilized these dormant voters and activists around the issue of abortion. In 1979, the New Right convinced Jerry Falwell to launch the Moral Majority and use abortion as a main issue, and it helped Paul and Judie Brown form the radically conservative American Life League. These organizations were two of the "electoral vehicles" built by the New Right outside the Republican Party after the early 1970s.[23] They promoted conservative values through extensive direct mail campaigns and Christian mass media, which resulted not only in a bevy of newly registered voters but in six million American evangelicals switching from the Democratic to the Republican Party for the November elections.[24] There was, in addition, another force in 1979 responsible for rousing Christians to action with millennialist verve. The evangelical team of Francis Schaeffer and C. Everett Koop toured the country that fall to inspire Christians to reject their traditional complacency and take an active stand against abortion. I address Koop and Schaeffer's work later in this chapter.

For now it is enough to say that regardless of whether they were pre- or postmillennialists, right-wing politicians and evangelicals used abortion as the issue around which to mobilize previously inactive premillennialists and other Christians in 1979. Also, regardless of their pre- or postmillennialist stance, these right-wing politicians and evangelicals cast abortion in absolute terms that reflected the millennialism of Falwell, Schaeffer, and, if we take Colson at his word, the architects of the New Right. Those absolute terms also can be seen in Colson's 1995 novel *Gideon's Torch*, the cover of which was designed to resemble a John Grisham or Tom Clancy bestseller, to package millennial conflict as another popular novel full of intrigue, suspense, and drama.

The novel begins with the murder of a female abortion provider in the Midwest and its impact on an incoming White House administration. Chief among the main characters in the White House is a Clintonesque, liberal Connecticut governor turned president, J. Whitney Griswold, who has a wife and daughter. Bernie O'Keefe, a Catholic trial lawyer from Boston, is counsel to and an old friend of the president. Paul Clarkson, a born-again pro-lifer, becomes associate attorney general as the result of horse-trading by a conservative, pro-life senator Byron Langer. By maneuvering Clarkson into the associate position, the senator manages to offset his own disappointment in the appointment of a too-liberal attorney general, a pro-choice Harvard law professor named Emily Gineen, a pivotal character in the novel.

In contrast, we are presented with a second set of characters—a group of small-town pro-lifers struggling to understand the best Christian way to protect the unborn. Daniel Seaton is a Virginia minister whose commitment to nonviolent leadership of a pro-life group does not save him from being convicted on conspiracy charges, incarcerated, and killed in jail. His more radical brother, Alex, is the one really responsible for bombing a clinic, and he too dies—this time in a shoot-out with federal officers. Also present in this face-off with the Feds (and reminiscent of the actual confrontations in Ruby Ridge, Montana, and Waco, Texas, which inspired the militia movement) is a minor character, a black Gulf War veteran, who eventually cracks under pressure and reveals their location. These men are intended to be seen as martyrs for the pro-life cause, which in this novel involves opposing not only abortions but specifically late-term abortions used to harvest fetal brains for AIDS research, a procedure to be conducted in government-funded clinics called regeneration centers, the first of which is built and nearly ready to open for business.

Much is implied in this fantastic premise of harvesting fetal brains for a cure for AIDS, the always fatal sexually transmitted disease. The novel's juxtaposition of AIDS with abortion is, writ small, an expression of the ultimate conflict between (satanic) depravity and (Christian) purity—or darkness and light—which structures millennialism. Generally in evangelical literature, people with AIDS are portrayed not as victims of an indiscriminate epidemic but as depraved people who have engaged in ungodly homosexual activity (or, to a much lesser degree, unchaste heterosexual activity or criminal drug use). With its concept of the regeneration centers—where, in pro-life parlance, doctors kill unborn babies in hopes that people with AIDS will not die—*Gideon's Torch* both reflects and reproduces the millennialist sense of conflict between representatives of depravity (people with AIDS and the government that supports them) and representatives of purity (the "innocent" unborn and the Christians who defend them). It is important to realize that the novel pointedly portrays the regeneration centers as funded by both the government and private citizens. The pro-life characters who find it abhorrent to spill the "innocent blood" of unborn "babies" in order to find a cure for those with the "contaminated blood" of AIDS are thus in conflict with private funders, the federal government, the medical establishment, and anyone duped into going down a deliberately deceptive "rosy path" by believing that the regeneration centers' search for a cure for AIDS is a humanitarian effort.[25]

This fictional conflict is not unlike the populist conflict that Flip Benham portrayed: "all the power and wealth of the United States of America versus the Church of Jesus Christ." The church, as represented by Rev. Daniel Seaton and his Christian cohorts, face military and legal challenges from the federal government. *Gideon's Torch* depicts a government and a citizenry in which godly people are in the minority, and in which there is a fight to the death between purity, truth, and light, on one hand, and depravity, darkness, and evil on the other.

As with Gideon's soldiers in the Bible, the characters of this novel rely on God's help to "expose the darkness," which is the explicit objective of the strategic plan called Gideon's Torch. When the FBI director gets wind of this plan, he assumes the torch in question refers to a bombing. Assistant Attorney General Paul Clarkson silently marvels at the director's biblical illiteracy and explains that the story of Gideon is from the book of Judges. In a battle between the Israelis and the Midianites, a leader named Gideon equipped his troops to fight with only "a ram's horn trumpet, a clay pitcher, and a torch" (178). More importantly, he kept cutting back the number of his troops, down to a mere three hundred men, to ensure that their victory would be attributed to God. After a story about an ominous dream had circulated among the pagan Midianites and made them skittish, Gideon instructed his reduced troops to break the clay pitchers that had been shielding the light of each man's torch and simultaneously to blow the rams' horns. The subsequent clash of sound and light sent the already spooked Midianites into a frenzy. "The abrupt convulsion of light and noise terrified the jittery sentries, who leaped to their feet, drew their swords, screamed, and slew one another in the chaos" (179). This tale of "psychological warfare" (177) draws "parallels between the ancient victory [of Gideon] and [pro-lifers'] modern mission—the victory of light over darkness, of truth over fear" (179).

Because of his knowledge of the Bible, Clarkson knows that the strategy of Gideon's Torch is not, as the FBI director suggests, to use "torches as weapons," but Clarkson has no actual foreknowledge of the pro-life plan. Gideon's Torch, as it turns out, involves hijacking the airwaves of a national television network to broadcast a training video prepared for the regeneration center. The video shows a doctor performing a late-term abortion and identifies the procedure as the technique needed for harvesting the fetal brains sought for AIDS research. Exposing the darkness is tantamount to exposing the "truth" about abortion through pirated television.

This plan is the second of three independently executed guerrilla actions in the novel. The first is the aforementioned murder of an abortion provider in the Midwest, and the third is Alex Seaton's bombing of the newly built regeneration center. After Alex's death, the pacifist Rev. Daniel Seaton is convicted for conspiracy because he cannot bring himself to lie in court about having told his brother and pals to "follow their conscience." But the novel implicitly and explicitly denies that these three guerrilla actions are the result of national "conspiracy" (273) or the work of "cultists" (413).

These actions, rather, are portrayed as examples of leaderless resistance against the war on the unborn, and it is work described as "absolutely providential" (198). In response to government opposition, the novel explains,

> new cells mutated from the pro-life movement. Some advocated violence. Some proposed blowing up empty clinics. Others simply stepped up their efforts in every creative though illegal way possible, short of violence.
>
> The decentralized nature of the pro-life movement made it impossible for authorities to control it. Just when the government thought it knew all of the threats and had everyone identified, new groups emerged. It was like the French Resistance in World War II: an underground, spidery web of activists spun through every level of society. (26)

This decentralized guerrilla activity is emphasized throughout the novel. Daniel Seaton is tried and wrongly convicted on conspiracy charges, even though conspiracy never took place, because the government does not understand the guerrilla nature of the pro-life movement.[26] There are no connections between those who killed the doctor, those who hijacked the airwaves, and those who bombed the regeneration center, but Seaton becomes the scapegoat for all three.

In the trial of the United States of America versus Daniel Seaton (453), the authors present arguments reminiscent of those made at the actual trial of the pro-lifers who bombed a women's clinic in Pensacola, Florida, on Christmas day, 1984. The Pensacola bombers were found guilty of planning and executing what they called the Gideon Project, and the case made by the defense was argued in the same way that Seaton's defense was argued in *Gideon's Torch*. "We are in spiritual warfare, a war between God and Satan," the defense attorney told the court in Pensacola. "If we are not careful, the forces of darkness will prevail. Our country is in trouble. Our people perish for a lack of knowledge."[27] When each of the three Pensacola defendants were found guilty, the judge sentenced them with the recommendation that they "be considered for release at the minimum of the guideline period or earlier." Reflecting on the relatively light sentence, one of the defendants commented, smiling, "It [the verdict] was God's doing. It proves He answers prayers."[28] Like *Gideon's Torch*, the Gideon Project succeeded in presenting a bombing as God's will, not as conspiracy. And as with the Gideon Project, the conflict that motivates the guerrilla act of Gideon's Torch (as well as the entire novel *Gideon's Torch*) is expressed as a battle between light and darkness, Christians and the government. Or, as Operation Rescue's 1999 literature puts it: all the power and wealth of the United States versus the Church of Jesus Christ.

The similarities between the actual Pensacola bombing called the Gideon Project and the fictionalized guerrilla actions of *Gideon's Torch* warrant an examination of the theme of exposing the darkness as it is used in nonfiction pro-life writings. In *Gideon's Torch*, exposing the darkness is synonymous with raising awareness of the unprecedented escalation of evil and, consequently, of God's growing anger, which will result in his wrath and Christ's return. In the novel, the major rhetorical vehicles for raising this awareness are the analogies of abortion as slavery and abortion as holocaust, two comparisons that can be found throughout pro-life discourse.

These two analogies—abortion-as-slavery and abortion-as-holocaust—are not necessarily best understood as calculated rhetoric. Connie Paige has argued that the emergence of the abortion-as-slavery analogy was a deliberate attempt to offset charges of racism leveled at pro-life groups.

These groups, comprised mostly of "white ethnic Catholics" who were "perceived, however incorrectly, to be racist themselves," had forged an "alliance with anti-busing forces" in the 1970s.[29] Paige could not be more explicit in her assumption that this was a conscious effort: "The right-to-lifers' desire to make their campaign against abortion appear less racist led them to compare the unborn fetus to the slave."[30] I am less concerned with what may have instigated the analogy of abortion-as-slavery than I am with how that analogy continues to function, especially in relation to the theme of exposing the darkness. The same is true for the abortion-as-holocaust analogy, which, before *Roe v. Wade*, was much more prevalent than that of abortion-as-slavery.[31] Both analogies have long outlasted other analogical rhetoric from the 1960s and 1970s, such as abortion as napalm, abortion as a search-and-destroy mission, or abortion as a Trojan horse. To examine how these two analogies fit into the millennialist conflict of light versus darkness in *Gideon's Torch*, we must understand how those analogies were purposefully packaged in ways that would promote Christians to take an activist, absolutist stance against abortion.

Translating Millennialist Conflict into Pro-Life Narrative

In the history of the pro-life movement, Francis Schaeffer is attributed with rousing evangelicals and fundamentalists from their political complacency to take up the cause of abortion. In fall 1979, Schaeffer and C. Everett Koop, who would later serve as surgeon general for the Reagan administration, set off on a lecture tour during which they promoted an aggressive, absolutist stance against abortion. The tour targeted those same fundamentalists and evangelicals who had been urged to register as voters by both the American Life League and the Moral Majority, founded earlier in 1979. For four months, Koop and Schaeffer presented their message "over three days in each city," where the events were "mobbed like rock concerts," convening sometimes as many as 2,500 to 3,000 people in urban centers.[32] Those who did not receive the message through this venue surely found it through one of Jerry Falwell's venues. It "was through Falwell and Moral Majority that Francis Schaeffer's call for Christian political action to stop abortion was popularized and disseminated to a mass audience, one far larger than Schaeffer could ever reach directly through his books or documentaries."[33]

More than "a call," however, what Schaeffer and Koop presented was an emotional appeal to stop abortion—an appeal structured in a way that resonated with an apocalyptic logic endemic to secular, popular culture as well as to evangelical prophecy.[34] Schaeffer and Koop's tour featured a lecture and a movie titled *Whatever Happened to the Human Race?* A companion volume by the same name was also available.[35] Schaeffer is acknowledged with providing the "theological cover" for mobilizing Christians, from Jerry Falwell to Operation Rescue,[36] but the shift in theological reasoning that Schaeffer argued could not have been nearly as powerful had it not been packaged in a readily consumable form. Schaeffer and Koop's *Whatever Happened to the Human Race?* not only disseminated the call to action but it popularized a millennialist narrative that moved pro-lifers to action. As both a published book and a movie that was circulated in twenty cities before the November 1979 election of Ronald Reagan, *Whatever Happened to the Human Race?* may be called the *Birth of a Nation* of pro-life politics, if not of the "Reagan revolution."

Whatever Happened to the Human Race? presents the abortion-as-slavery and abortion-as-holocaust analogies as related, as part of a historical sequence and millennialist drama. And it connects them with a sense of urgency, humanity, and conflict that literally moved people to tears. Such was the case with future founder of Operation Rescue, Randall Terry. In a class on apologetics at Elim Bible College, young Terry "wept openly during the film" and declared it had helped him decide that he "had to do something about" abortion.[37] The film is as important for its visual rendition of ideas as for its theological maneuvering. Even in the printed version of *Whatever Happened to the Human Race?* the analogies of abortion with slavery and holocaust are depicted visually, dramatized by a sequence of high-contrast, black and white photographic images that make good use of light and darkness.

The first image represents three forlorn black people, who are chained around the throat and standing in a crate made of wood and chain-link. Light coming from the left, outside of the cage, casts the right side of their faces in shadow. The woman is pregnant, and all three are barefoot. Their clothes are tattered. There is no sense of resistance or unity; each pair of eyes is glazed and looking in different directions. This is the pro-life representation of slavery: people entrapped and waiting for deliverance.

The second image shows a smaller wooden-frame crate with chain-link walls fencing in another trio of people, again two men and a woman. The right side of their faces and the lower part of their bodies are cast deeply in shadow. A Star of David is visible on the woman, who is kneeling, and on an older man, who is wearing a Hasidic-style beard and hat. The bearded man reaches out between the chain-link in a plaintive gesture. They are as unfocused as the first group of three.

The third image is a radical departure from the first two. It presents a small bin of a crate similarly constructed of chain-link and wood. Unlike the other crates, which look as if they are resting solidly on the ground, this one is suspended high in the darkness. There is a bright luminescence emanating from within the crate, within which an infant lies on his back. Naked and illuminated, this baby is isolated, helpless. The whiteness of his body emerges from—and is at some points merged with—the whiteness of the light. This whiteness of light, coupled with the elevation of the crate, draw from classic Western Christian iconography of the Christ child. The pathos and victimization of the two previous images are displaced by this elevated icon of the babe bathed in light. And this child, unlike the other victims, is crying out.

Two other images follow. A young white girl sitting in a wheelchair, against which a crutch rests, looks out from her crate to the light coming from the left. And finally, three old people sit in a crate—two women and one man, who are also white. They too look forlorn, bereft, and passive. The light is angled from the upper left to show high contrasts and definite lines.

Only the image of the child is underlit in a way that shows him as emerging from the light, and the whiteness of his skin is indistinguishable from the whiteness of the light. However, twice in *Whatever Happened to the Human Race?* Koop and Schaeffer insist that "all human life" includes babies of all colors and races.[38] This message is portrayed visually as well in that they depict masses of presumably aborted children, represented by baby dolls, some of which are Caucasian looking and some of which are obviously meant to look black. But in the sequencing of what pro-lifers consider to be the greatest atrocities of humankind, the white child alone is the victim of abortion. Especially given the child's luminosity, this image transcends mere symbolic status; it is an icon. Scholars who have discussed the importance of lighting in visual representations from painting to photography to television believe that for Westerners, light conveys not only a sense of spiritual purity but also a racialized sense of whiteness.[39] Thus, this pro-life iconography is undeniably and unmistakably white, Western, and Christian. This babe bathed in light is a white child, a Christ child.

All five images present human victims of inhuman and inhumane atrocities. As a group, the images depict the slippery slope argument that pro-lifers have used since the 1960s: legalized abortion will *lead* to indiscriminate killing because the "abortion mentality" has a propensity to devalue individual lives and life itself. But *Whatever Happened to the Human Race?* converted this intellectual argument into a human drama by using these racialized and religious images, and it placed the drama on a historical timeline: first the slaves, then the Holocaust, then abortion. If abortion is allowed, the sequence implies, what will follow will be indiscriminate killing of the unfit and the elderly—a practice of eugenics and euthanasia not unlike the horrors of the Holocaust, but to a greater and more insidious degree.

By providing this sequence of single images, *Whatever Happened to the Human Race?* succeeds in squelching comparative analyses that acknowledge how reproductive control was intrinsically part of the institution of slavery in the United States and German Nazism. It separates out the "issue" of slavery and the "horror" of the Holocaust from abortion. In doing so, *Whatever Happened to the Human Race?* ignores the possibility that enslaved women used abortion as a method to thwart the reproductive tyranny of rape by slavemasters, and it ignores that abortion was banned by Hitler for German Christians but enforced for Jews and other "undesirables" for the sake of breeding a master race. Moreover, the sequencing of slavery–Holocaust–abortion presents these phenomena as not just a series of human atrocities but as an increasingly atrocious series of historical events. Abortion thus becomes the culmination of these human atrocities, the ultimate evil that will certainly result in unprecedented destruction.

These images then produce not just a millennialist *conflict* but an apocalyptic, millennialist, pro-life *narrative* that succeeds in dramatizing abortion as an apocalyptic end of humanity, a narrative that demands *Whatever Happened to the Human Race?* The narrative also succeeds in displacing the horrors of slavery and the Holocaust with the "evil" of abortion.

This displacement can be seen in the statue Schaeffer built to commemorate the prophesied apocalyptic end times of humanity. Those end times are, according to Schaeffer, the last days of the twentieth century. The dedication to the book version of *Whatever Happened to the Human Race?* as well as the legend carved in a shrine to the victims of darkness, reads: "To those who were robbed of life, the unborn, the weak, the sick, the old / during the dark ages of madness, selfishness, lust and greed / for which the last decades of the twentieth century are remembered." This dedication leaves behind slavery and the Holocaust, which happened before "the last decades of the twentieth century" (and therefore are not considered part of the "dark ages"). The dedication thereby focuses only on abortion and the atrocities that presumably will follow abortion—killing of the disabled and the elderly, who in the earlier photographs appear white.

Thus the documented persecution of enslaved Africans in America and imprisoned Jews in Germany gives way to a futuristic persecution of "the unborn, the weak, the sick, the old." The perpetrators of this persecution are not racism, anti-Semitism, nationalism, or fascism but "madness, self-ishness, lust and greed," caused by turning away from God and embracing secular humanism. Schaeffer positions us in the future, as looking back on abortion in the twentieth century. In the process he displaces concern with slavery or the Holocaust; they were only precursors to the ultimate suffer-ing of "those who were robbed of life" in the "last decades of the twentieth century" (read: the last days of humanity). Like the silhouetted man who runs across the midsection of the statue, the human race appears to get lighter in color as it runs around the edge of the monument, beyond its dark stages, and, presumably, into the next millennium. At the apex of the monument is an adult male hoisting a baby, whose genitalia mark it as a male. Masculinity is at the apex of this monument. Here are, carved in stone (or something that looks like it), the ones to whom we should dedi-cate ourselves, the ones who most certainly will have suffered most, the icons of an apocalyptic era: a man and his progeny.

The pro-life narrative presented by *Whatever Happened to the Human Race?* displaces the persecution of blacks and Jews with the persecution of not only the unborn but also the pro-life men who support the unborn. Like the iconographic babe bathed in light who symbolizes the victim of abortion, pro-lifers are also portrayed, however implicitly or un-consciously, as Western, Christian, white, and male. In fact, *Gideon's Torch* presents a prose version of this tripartite pro-life narrative of slav-ery–Holocaust–abortion. In it, the evil of abortion displaces the horrors of slavery and the Holocaust, and the persecution of blacks and Jews is dis-placed by persecution of the white, Christian, pro-life man, who is himself persecuted on the basis of his race, religion, and sexuality.

Racial and Religious Implications in the Pro-Life Narrative

The idea of an apocalyptic persecution of the unborn and pro-lifers performed on the basis of race and religion is found throughout *Gideon's Torch*, as are references that compare slavery and Nazism with abortion. Because most of these allusions are made by token Jewish and black char-acters, *Gideon's Torch* seems to give the "black" or the "Jewish" perspective on abortion. However, these characters do not oppose abortion as a racist or anti-Semitic means of controlling the reproduction of blacks or Jews.

They do not see abortion as stemming from institutionalized or individual racism or anti-Semitism but from a general disregard for "equality."

For example, an African American character opposes abortion in a way that eschews analysis of racial injustice while accommodating classic conservative arguments about the divine nature of being created equal. Sophisticated arguments have been made by scholars and communities of color about coercive abortion as part of a history of reproductive control exerted by white-dominated bureaucracies and economies to hinder reproduction of their race.[40] But the African American character in *Gideon's Torch* does not draw from these. Instead, the reader is introduced to Lance Thompson, a Gulf War veteran, as a brooding man with a sign that reads "Abortion: the new black lynching." Thompson does not object to abortion qua lynching on the basis of intentional or institutional racism but on the basis of inequality. "To him the politics of abortion were simply the most recent threat to true equality for African Americans" (63). He recognizes that the "goals of the civil rights movement [are] still largely unrealized," and the fundamental goal of that movement is presented in terms of "true equality"—not in terms of an end to racism. The character of Lance Thompson represents a desire for equality within the existing social structure. However, as previously discussed, in the pro-life context, equality is often defined in terms of divine creation rather than democratic participation. The conservative insistence that all Americans are created equal is in direct opposition to the notion of an egalitarian society in which political and social power is equally accessible to all.

The dubious nature of Thompson's character undermines the lynching parallel and accommodates this conservative understanding that all men may be equal in the eyes of God but are not equal in any other respect. Despite a limited omniscient narration, Thompson is one character whose motivations are never provided as direct, internal thoughts, so readers never hear his point of view. Suspicions are raised when he decides to contact a fellow conspirator through the personal ads section of a newspaper: "If I need you, I'll put an ad in the personals section of the *Fairfax Journal*: 'Gay black man seeks same for discrete, explosive good times.' Check every day. If you see that ad, meet me here at noon" (170). Why he chooses to cast suspicion on his sexual orientation in this manner is questioned by a second character but never explained. The possibility that Thompson is a homosexual is presented as something suspicious, and this feeling is confirmed during his confrontation with the SWAT team sent to flush him and Alex Seaton out of hiding in the dense West Virginia hills.

There, Thompson has a flashback to the Gulf War, becomes delusional, cracks under pressure, and begins firing his weapon. As a result, he discloses their location and eliminates any possibility of peaceful surrender. He thereby causes his own death and that of Alex Seaton, who despite a head injury acts more rationally than does the spooked Thompson. In combat, and implicitly in other arenas, Thompson is not the equal of Alex Seaton.

But Thompson is not the novel's only source for the slavery-as-abortion comparison. That comparison is most extensively explicated by Emily Gineen, the president's choice for attorney general, who must address the moral and legal ramifications of the Dred Scott decision during her confirmation hearing. *Gideon's Torch* presents this hearing in a style generic to any television courtroom drama or congressional hearing. The pro-life Senator Byron Langer dramatically and stealthily leads Professor Gineen through a series of questions, which lead to "the one impossible dilemma": the ostensible moral contradiction of opposing slavery and defending abortion. Senator Langer says, "The majority in America once believed that slavery was in the best interest of the greatest number. The majority approved slavery when the Congress passed the Kansas Nebraska Act. And the Court in the Dred Scott decision then affirmed it on the grounds that the black slave was not a person under the Constitution" (74). Comparing the 1857 Dred Scott decision (*Dred Scott v. Sandford*) with *Roe v. Wade*, the 1973 Supreme Court decision that prohibited states from banning abortion, is a favorite among pro-lifers. Some as notable as Ronald Reagan have argued that it is *Roe v. Wade*'s fate to be wholly despised and discredited just as *Dred Scott v. Sandford* was in its time. Dred Scott, a slave who had lived freely in Wisconsin territory for years, was denied the status of freedman. When his case reached the Supreme Court, Scott's claim was denied, in the notorious words of Chief Justice Taney's majority opinion, because black people were "considered as a subordinate and inferior class of human beings" with no rights.[41] Widely regarded as an abominable ruling against "Negro citizenship" which has been "hooted down through the pages of history," *Scott v. Sandford* eventually was rendered moot with ratification of the Fourteenth Amendment in 1868, which Dred Scott himself did not live to see.[42]

In *Gideon's Torch*, the discussion of *Scott v. Sandford* sets up Gineen and Langer as characters with conflicting worldviews. Langer uses *Scott* to ask whether Gineen believes "there is a higher law beyond the law." This question, in turn, leads to his appraisal of the United States as a "government under God," a nation that is, he says, to quote Thomas Jefferson and invoke natural law, "governed by 'laws of nature and nature's God' " (75). Gineen eventually wins over the audience at her confirmation hearing with a relativistic notion of truth, which is reversed by the end of the novel as a result of her conversion to born-again Christianity, to which Langer has subscribed from the start. He tells her, "I believe Jesus when He says He is *the* truth," and that "if God is God, faith cannot be simply personal. . . . All law ultimately finds its roots in God's Word. All legitimate law, that is. That's where our natural law comes from." Reminiscent of Barry Goldwater, in *Conscience of a Conservative*, Byron Langer says, "one cannot be a conservative without believing in natural law" (81). Eventually Gineen changes her mind and her disdain for the idea of being "saved," and becomes born-again by believing in Christ as the source of the Truth, as her personal savior. But at the point in the novel at which *Dred Scott* is invoked, during Gineen's confirmation hearing, Langer and Gineen represent a dichotomy: "Two different cultures were facing each other across the witness table" (73).

This dichotomy—these two different cultures—is precisely what has given the *Scott/Roe* analogy its staying power through years of abortion controversy. Milton Sernett, in his explanation of this staying power, dismisses two facile renditions of the analogy. One is the equation of "denial of legal personhood to fetal life with denial of legal personhood to Blacks." According to Sernett, analogies that infer that "the unborn is but 'the latest victim of our propensity for dividing humanity into human and subhuman,' are persuasive only if one assumes that prejudiced-against Blacks and prejudiced-against fetuses belong together under the category, however defined, of legal 'persons.' "[43] However, without a definition of personhood that was accepted and applied to blacks and the unborn in the 1800s as well as to those of today, this historical analogy cannot hold, Sernett logically contends. Moreover, the Fourteenth Amendment, which most conclusively (along with the Civil Rights Act of 1866) rendered the Dred Scott decision moot and granted citizenship to newly emancipated slaves, focuses specifically on "All persons born," not unborn.

The second Scott-related analogy that Sernett dismisses is one based on empathy or identity with the fetus. If a comparison with historical slaves is tenable, the "humanity and/or personhood of the fetus [should be] a matter of fact and not dependent upon our empathic identification." After all, the humanity "of the slave was a matter of fact, in spite of the attitudes and actions of slaveholders."[44] Thus Sernett suggests that the comparison has no historical or logical integrity, only rhetorical appeal. More specifically, the attraction of declaring *Roe v. Wade* to be a contemporary *Dred Scott* lies in the historical fact that "Black slavery has come to symbolize a clear-cut moral blight."[45]

Sernett concludes that the only merit of the *Scott/Roe* analogy lies in the way both abolitionists and pro-lifers construct moral conflict with an irreconcilable, dichotomous worldview based on particular religious tenets.

> The pro-life movement, like the anti-slavery crusade, is motivated by deep religious residuals precisely because an entire system of thought and meaning is symbolically being challenged in the secular, pluralistic state. . . . In retrospect, the abolitionist impulse, which fostered tactics of moral suasion and political action, is seen as having opposed a moral blight gravely threatening to the highest Christian ideals and the social moral order which was to be modeled on them.[46]

Sernett quotes a 1969 article that regards abortion as "a symbolic threat to the moral order espoused by Christians for two millennia" and concludes that *"Roe v. Wade* symbolically represents a victory for the forces of darkness rather than for the children of light."[47] In concluding how limited is the use of the *Roe/Scott* analogy, Sernett both recognizes and employs the same imagery of darkness and light that not only structures the novel *Gideon's Torch* but millennialism itself.

The comparison of the life of a fetus with that of Dred Scott, or the fate of *Scott v. Sandford* with what pro-lifers believe is the ultimate fate of *Roe v. Wade*, does not function as a protest against the injustices inflicted on African Americans. *Gideon's Torch* may decry the evils of lynching and slavery in conjunction with abortion, yet its characterization of African American men is deplorable. Opposing abortion is not tantamount to opposing injustice as suffered by African Americans or by enslaved Africans in America. The rhetorical trope of comparing the fetus with the slave is more than an anti-abortion analogy. It is a historical legacy of opposing slavery without opposing racism or fighting for the rights of African Americans.

Before the Civil War, according to historian David Roediger, some labor leaders rallied against "slavery," which they defined as the economic hardships of white workers, and warned against "indulging sympathies for Blacks in the South."[48] Thus attacking "white slavery" at times meant strongly supporting the slavery of blacks.[49] Christian abolitionists translated fighting "slavery"—which had been shorthand for "white slavery"—to fighting against civil rights for blacks. It should come as no surprise that articulating and forging political relationships between white labor and black slaves involved mobilizing Christian millennialists. "In arguing for the importance of workers in early abolitionism, the antislavery leader Thomas Wentworth Higginson referred, for example, not to freethinkers but to those afire with 'the Second Advent delusion.' "[50] Significantly, the rhetoric of white slavery was most prominent during the 1830s and 1840s, when millennialism was at its nineteenth-century peak.[51] Antebellum discussions of labor and slavery were fraught with millennialist tension and infused American notions of class with racial implications.

Such racial implications forged through millennialism are operating in contemporary abortion-as-slavery discussions. Outrage over the economic institution of black slavery in the South is translated into, and displaced by, fearful charges of white slavery, white genocide, and white persecution. The comparison of *Roe v. Wade* with *Dred Scott* functions in *Gideon's Torch* as it does in pro-life discourse in general. It acts as a rhetorical stepping stone, which pro-lifers use to move from the horror of slavery and its injustice to African Americans to the "horror" of abortion and its perceived injustice to not only the unborn but also white Christians.

Another such stepping stone in *Gideon's Torch* is found in the guerrilla action in which pro-lifers hijack the airwaves to televise the video of a late-term abortion. In the novel, the abortion shown on the video is compared with the Nazis' exterminations of the Jews. More to the point, the pirated video images are explained as an analog to the Holocaust, a notably bloody event. "What you have just witnessed is not footage recovered from the files of Nazi Germany," an anonymous announcer declares, as if it might be mistaken. He continues:

> This *actual video* is currently in use in medical schools across America, equipping doctors to suck the brains from live, unborn babies in ever-expanding numbers. This is what the coming regeneration centers are all about. . . . These deeds of darkness must be exposed to the light. Americans must not allow their so-called freedom of choice to open the door to the greatest Holocaust in human history. We must reject the regeneration centers and turn back this bloody tide before it is too late. (229; emphasis in original)
>
> The imagery of the bloody tide not only adds graphic dimension to the idea of abortion as holocaust, but it resonates with millennialist language that warns of God's wrath, especially as expressed by prophesied floods.

In general, a preoccupation with blood is pervasive in the discourse of millennial movements. Charles Strozier believes that this preoccupation is the result of the historical and interpretive shift from the Sermon on the Mount to the book of Revelation, which for born-again Christians brought a heightened awareness of—and propensity for reveling in—violence, collective destruction, and death. The book of Revelation gives us a moon that is like blood, a great whore who is "drunken with the blood of the saints, and with the blood of the martyrs of Jesus," and blood flowing from all those slain in Armageddon.[52] The multiple references in *Gideon's Torch* to flowing blood—"blood-soaked walls of our nation" (13), "buckets of blood on the Capitol steps" (65), and the "bloody tide" (229)—reflect the apocalyptic language of Revelation. Implicit in the idea in *Gideon's Torch* that pro-lifers can reverse the flow and "turn back this bloody tide" is the understanding that this tide flows from the apocalyptic future. Although there is hope that pro-lifers "can turn back this bloody tide" as part of the "Holocaust Resistance," there is also a sense of something penultimate and imminently approaching. A surge of blood is as sure as a moon-driven tide, as sure as lunar-cycled menstruation, or as sure as millennial purging of the impure, the morally barren, the spiritually ill-conceived. Inevitable and red, this bloody tide will not be a mild or regular flow but the "greatest holocaust in history," because it is the holocaust to end history.

In this way, resistance to the regeneration centers invokes the coming judgment of the last days of mortal humanity as much as the last days of a fetus in the last days of pregnancy terminated by a late-term abortion. This comparison is made explicit during Daniel Seaton's trial when the notion of the regeneration centers and late-term abortion as analogous to the Nazi Holocaust is addressed. Seaton clarifies that his statements about how leaders will be "held to account for their carnage against defenseless human life" do not mean that he or his brother advocates vigilante justice. Instead, Seaton makes statements "all in light of the coming judgment of God" (486), which is shorthand for the end times and Christ's certain return. In *Gideon's Torch* the most sympathetic characters are absolutely certain that the penultimate abortion holocaust will result in the ultimate bloody termination: a cosmic abortion of those judged for "carnage against defenseless human life," a millennialist purging performed by a wrathful God, the Author of Life, whose gift of life humanity has spurned. In symbolic terms, *Gideon's Torch* presents abortion as bloody holocaust and millennialist apocalypse as a bloody, cosmic abortion.

In historical terms, this imagery of the bloody tide is reminiscent of the period of the Red Scare, a time of fear and loathing of the perceived spread of communism, Bolshevism, and Jewishness. In particular and most exactingly, the discussion of the late-term abortion in *Gideon's Torch* re-packages anti-Semitic accounts from the 1920s and 1930s that warned Germans of Jews who "quite literally sap the blood of Gentiles and their children. They do so not for religious reasons, but because their own chaotic blood is in danger of decomposition; it is only in sucking the blood of other peoples that they can preserve their own life."[53] *Gideon's Torch* nearly exactly transforms this standard anti-Semitic view from the Nazi and pre-Nazi eras into pro-life sentiment. Instead of Jews sapping the blood of Gentile children, government-funded doctors are sapping the blood of the unborn in regeneration centers. Instead of Jews "sucking the blood of other peoples" so that they may preserve their own life, government-funded doctors are "suck[ing] the brains from live, unborn babies" so that they may cure the fatal disease of AIDS, thereby preserving the lives of homosexuals. Instead of Jews with blood in danger of decomposition, we have homosexuals who have "contaminated blood" and spill it in public protest for more government funding.

The historical resonance of classic anti-Semitic propaganda thus informs the anti-gay sentiment in *Gideon's Torch*, which portrays homosexuals as agents of the apocalyptic bloody tide. Gay men and lesbians are responsible for "a tidal wave of euphoric public reaction" to the fantastic medical discovery of the "potential effectiveness" of "mature" fetal tissue to cure AIDS—the discovery that leads to the regeneration centers. "Thrilled homosexual groups organized benefits and lobbied Capitol Hill to speed the FDA approvals process." The power of AIDS activists is enormous: "pressure from the homosexual community was so great" that fetal harvesting centers are funded before the technology is ready (50). "The real power base behind the center's creation: key AIDS activists from around the country and a few wealthy supporters" (348).

These wildly ecstatic gay people are portrayed not merely as active in promoting AIDS cures but also as hunting down pro-lifers. A "group of homosexual activists conducted a march outside a Presbyterian church hosting a prayer meeting; later, hundreds of condoms filled with mayonnaise were found scattered throughout the church's Sunday school classrooms" (463). Also, "eight Act-Up protestors had smashed vials of contaminated blood on the door of the Senate Appropriations Committee to protest inadequate funding for the regeneration centers" (180). Because that blood "tested HIV-positive," it is considered a "deadly weapon" (180).

This portrayal fits the logic of *Gideon's Torch*, which converts victims into victimizers and historical persecution of Jews, blacks, and gay people into the ultimate persecution of evangelical Christians, both born and unborn. AIDS is seen as a disease that supplies homosexuals with "deadly weapons." AIDS is seen as an occasion for homosexuals to set up regeneration centers so they can suck the brains and bloods from their enemies. These misrepresentations constitute more than blaming the victim—more than purporting that gay people deserve to be infected with AIDS and associated with the pandemic. These misrepresentations fault the victims of AIDS with the victimization not only of themselves but of others, of born-again Christians. AIDS victims are not, according to *Gideon's Torch*, really victims of AIDS; they are victimizers of Daniel Seaton and all those he represents, born and unborn. This displacement is merely one in a long list of displacements that the narrative of *Gideon's Torch* achieves.

Daniel Seaton's death indicates that these displacements are complete. After his discussion with Gineen, Seaton is killed with a stiletto when he decides to go against the rule of prison life and "get involved" (530). His downfall is trying to protect a young, "borderline retarded" (528) boy from the sexual demands of a doped-up drug king from Washington, D.C., named Shaqqar Redding (529). Here again a black man is ambiguously identified with homosexuality, as Lance Thompson is. The ambiguity lies in the novel's brief explanation that otherwise heterosexual men turn to same-sex activity once incarcerated. The character of Shaqqar Redding consolidates every contagious desire, every indication of cowardice and moral weakness, and every source of godlessness in the novel: homosexuality, nonwhite racial identity, drugs, criminal behavior, and Washington, D.C., the evil urban seat of the federal government.

Thus the novel moves us from Dred Scott to the Holocaust to an evangelical Christian minister in jail, manacled, misunderstood, and martyred. Displacement is complete: instead of Jews or people of color, the white Christian man is being persecuted on racial and religious grounds. His Christianity prevents him from lying in court, and he cannot turn his back on the nearly retarded inmate. Not only is he is killed by a black man but he is convicted by a jury that is predominately black, who are presumed to be prejudiced against whites. "In the District of Columbia the majority of the jurors would be black, probably suspicious of any white suburbanite" (469). There is hope that at least one of the black jurors is a Baptist, but the prosecutor "had done his best to winnow out anyone with religious inclinations. Counsel couldn't ask a juror's religion, of course, but he fished around; one potential juror who admitted listening to WAVA, the Christian radio station, was quickly dropped" (470). In addition to being persecuted on these religious and racial grounds, Seaton also meets his demise because he dares to oppose homosexuality.

Given all this, it is not insignificant that the apocalyptic imagery of the bloody tide, writ small, is re-invoked on Daniel Seaton's last day: "A slender river of blood ran out of his mouth" (531).

Pro-Life Violence as Part of God's Plan

The last days of Daniel Seaton also signal the last godless days of Emily Gineen, who is so moved by her meeting with him that his death comes as the final event necessary to complete her conversion from Episcopalian practice to born-again Christianity. After Seaton's death, Gineen comes to accept the idea that unless you take Christ as the Truth, you either go mad or die. Seaton has explained this belief to her using sailing as a metaphor meant to illustrate how fixed points of reference such as stars, "shining out in the darkness above a spinning world," are necessary for moral "navigation" (518). "Truth has to be fixed in order for us to know how to live. In order for it to be truth. God is real. Certain. Even though we can't see Him, we see the effects of His presence. Like the wind. And one day we *will* see Him. Face to face" (519). This message foreshadows the final scene in the book, in which the U.S. president, J. Whitney Griswold, is sailing with his son and an aide off the shore of Martha's Vineyard.

Like Gineen, Griswold has experienced a profoundly influential death—the suicide of his counsel and longtime friend, Bernie O'Keefe. Unlike Gineen, however, the president has not been born again, has not accepted Christ as the Truth, and consequently he becomes increasingly unglued as the book draws to a close. He becomes, according to Gineen, one of the "bigots" and "zealots" that his public speeches decry (524).[54] By the end of the book, he has gone completely insane, and his mental disintegration is portrayed in terms that recall Seaton's discussion of God's invisible wind-like presence. In the last scene of the book, as Griswold heads out to sea, the wind at first seems to be with him. But then the wind blows his hair "in all directions" and increases in force (550). "Looks like the wind is picking up," says Griswold's son (551). "The water darkened ahead," and a definite "gust" nearly capsizes the boat (550, 551). Both the president's son and the aide grow concerned with Griswold's distraction, his inability to navigate, and his addressing of his dead friend Bernie. Finally, Griswold swears he hears church bells pealing clearly. His aide thinks the president has gone insane.

Through the foreshadowing provided by Daniel Seaton's description, the novel implies that although invisible, the presence of God like the gusting wind is at work on Griswold—and on the country he has been elected to lead. The tolling bells, also foreshadowed earlier in the book, certainly indicate an irony, if not a predestined event, and perhaps the most prophesied event; perhaps the tolling bells signal that this is the "one day we *will* see Him. Face to face." Because Griswold is the president, his insanity represents more than one man's mental decline. It parallels the national chaos that increases toward the end of the novel.

In addition to "random violence" (464), including arson and looting, an earthquake and a "freak storm" wreak havoc on the country. Federal troops patrol the streets. In the nation's capital, a Halloween parade turns deadly as a "gang of teenagers dressed as Hell's Angels started harassing a group dressed as [Nazi] SS officers" (464). The National Guard cannot squelch this upheaval of pagan conflict in the streets. All of these events are arguably signs of the end times, and the born-again assistant attorney general remarks that the preponderance of "national emergencies" is unprecedented: "I can't ever remember a time like these past months" (465). This cannot, it is implied, be too surprising when the country's leader is so unchristian a man.

The character of Griswold represents everything that pro-life Christians are supposed to abhor. He is a privileged, Ivy League–trained lawyer who trusts not in God's but in man's law. Although more paranoid characters consider him a Hitler (65), this view is tempered by others' assessments of him. More sympathetically, he is seen as a dupe of the forces of darkness, especially because he caters to Wall Street and the New York financiers, that is, Jews. "The brave people of Israel will have no greater friend in the world than Whitney Griswold," he tells those attending the United Jewish Appeal banquet in New York (31). And clearly Griswold has his sights on the whole world, possibly a one-world economy if not a one-world government, as the "assured passage" of a "Gatt III Treaty" implies (457).

In short, Griswold symbolizes everything that pro-life politics says it is against, and all this is neatly contained in the insider's joke that is the character's name. Griswold from Connecticut is president of the United States; *Griswold v. Connecticut* is the 1965 Supreme Court decision that paved the way for *Roe v. Wade* by establishing that, on the basis of a right to privacy, states could not restrict the right of married persons to use contraceptives. At the root of all the nation's ills is the idea that one can spurn God's gift of life through contraception or abortion—what is also known as the homosexualization of the procreative act.[55] In this debauchery, America faces the end times. In presenting J. Whitney Griswold as a national symbol of what is wrong with America, *Gideon's Torch* has blended prophecy with politics and has promoted a millennialist take on abortion and pro-life action.

Millennialism is a vibrant and popular prophecy theology that mobilizes mainstream pro-lifers as well as pro-life guerrilla activists and the far right. Even though millennialism may decry violence, violence is not incompatible with millennialism, and in fact violence is necessary for the fulfillment of its prophecy. *Gideon's Torch* lends credence to this view. As Sara Diamond explains, *Gideon's Torch* demonstrates that "like it or not, violence is an integral part of the unfolding events that lead to victory. Violence is a pitfall, but it is part of the prophecy. Read as a sign of the times, *Gideon's Torch* allows the reader to see anti-abortion violence as part of God's plan."[56] Like millennialists with their "ironic ambivalence" toward the suffering of Jews, pro-lifers may react with genuine disdain to violence against Jews, such as that used to murder the Buffalo abortion provider Barnett Slepian, and to killing for life. But they may also see violence as part of God's plan.

Shaped as a millennialist conflict by fiction, films, and political discussions, pro-life ideology is best understood as narrative in form.[57] It is a dramatic narrative about the prophesied culmination of the forces of darkness, of atrocities throughout the ages, from slavery to the Holocaust to abortion. Or more precisely, it is the story of how the historical persecution of blacks, Jews, and homosexuals is displaced by the far more fantastic persecution of white born-again Christians on the basis of their race, religion, and sexuality. It is a story produced and consumed by mainstream pro-lifers who disavow or condemn violence as part of their movement, who see prayer as their only weapon, who do nothing more extreme than sing a hymn outside a clinic—or read a novel at home.

Making Time for America's Armageddon

Bozell's Legacy

Pro-life authors such as Charles Colson and Ellen Vaughn use fiction as a medium for circulating political and religious messages. Pro-life individuals tell stories to witness their faith, negotiate social and cultural roles, and construct their sense of identity.[1] Understanding the way pro-life millennialism functions as narrative involves recognizing as well how pro-life writing transforms consumers of narrative into producers of that narrative. Pro-life writing can transform consumers of millennialist narrative into producers of the story and participants in what they perceive as the biblical time of apocalyptic drama, a holy war.

Once we understand this process, we can see that pro-life militancy—including killing for life—is not merely a matter of inflammatory rhetoric about abortion as murder, which incites vigilantes, as some believe. And it is not a matter of dispossessed individuals asserting their identity by enacting narratives that counter stereotypes of them (although such alienation should be taken into account). It is, rather, a matter of thirty years of uncoordinated yet persistent institutional deployment of a millennialist story that narrates the fight for life as America's Armageddon. To understand this deployment, in addition to understanding how pro-life narratives use millennialist rhetoric to portray violence as part of God's plan, it is important to explore the inherent narrative quality of millennialism itself. It is this narrative quality that can divest apocalypticism of passivity.

In the 1960s and 1970s, the writings and protests of Leo Brent Bozell and his Christian "tribe" inaugurated the strategy of narrating abortion as apocalypse to encourage political action and to make time to fight abortion. Bozell's published material made no effort to hide his odd, millennialist stance, and he publicly lectured on "The Fight for Life: America's Armageddon." This millennialist articulation was unusual for Catholics such as Bozell, and neither Catholic officials nor conservative intellectuals who led right-to-life efforts in the 1960s appreciated Bozell's language or his militant style of protest. Despite their vehement detractors in the 1960s, Bozell's militant writings had a lasting—and largely unacknowledged—political impact. What Francis Schaeffer's work did for evangelicals, Bozell's did for conservative Catholics: it exemplified how to divest apocalyptic thinking of its passivity and resignation.

To recognize the efficacy of pro-life writing and the legacy of Brent Bozell in particular, it is important to review recent scholarship on millennial movements that relates the biblical time of millennialism with the political mobilization of individuals. Professors such as Stephen O'Leary and Catherine Keller are established scholars who analyze writings by influential prophecy believers such as John Nelson Darby of the nineteenth century and Hal Lindsey of the twentieth century. Their commentaries help explain why pro-life rejection of political passivity is tantamount to living according to narrative time, which is to say, "making" time.

Making Time for Pro-Life Action

Prophetic writings situate believers in a scheme of earthly and supernatural happenings. The unfurling of these happenings is sometimes steady, chronological, linear, and historical, and sometimes it is not. Premillennialism, especially, thrives on an interpretation of the Bible that casts believers as going in and out of chronological, historical time. When they are not living according to linear, historical time, they are living according to dispensations, or epochal periods of biblical time.

In the nineteenth century, predictions of the exact date of Christ's return were made, and in time proven false, most famously by the Millerites in the 1840s. As a response to such failed prophecy, John Nelson Darby originated a theory that popularizes the idea of dispensations. By explaining that God deals with humankind epoch by epoch, or dispensation by dispensation, Darby's work suggests that our own epoch, that of the Church Age, will end with the rapture, during which a select group of believers will meet Jesus in the air. The rapture is an actual elevation of true Christians, whose bodies and souls are literally swept up into the sky to meet Christ. This ascension allows them to avoid the hardships of Satan's battle on earth and God's subsequent wrath and retribution. After the rapture, Darby's theory of dispensationalism suggests, Christ's return is imminent.

> Once the prophetic clock starts ticking again with the Rapture, the final sequence of events will unfold with dismaying rapidity for those left behind, beginning with the so-called Tribulation, of which the second half will be sheer hell. The Tribulation will end with the Battle of Armageddon, when Christ, the saints, and the heavenly host return to earth and defeat Antichrist and his army. Next will come the Millennium, Christ's thousand-year rule on earth; a final doomed uprising by Satan; the resurrection of the dead, and history's final event, the Last Judgment.[2]

Before this theory of dispensations, premillennialism had suggested that Christ's return depended on the fulfillment of biblical prophecies; Christ's arrival could not be anticipated by marking days off a calendar but rather by attending to different world events that were to take place before the Second Coming. In slight but significant contrast, dispensationalism espoused a more "futuristic" view of Christ's return, which placed the church "in suspended prophetic time" so that "no prophesied event stood between the present and the rapture. Thus it may occur at any moment."[3] Dispensationalists thus radicalize the already ahistorical bent of premillennialist thought by refusing to determine the precise time of the beginning of the apocalyptic end.

The possibility that the beginning of the end may occur at any moment, this indeterminacy, is a mobilizing force. Instead of rendering some people indifferent to their surroundings and daily lives, this indeterminacy can urge believers to act. Some, of course, may become "passive spectators" in their expectations of the end of the world and the end of time. But others "find that the prediction of the world's End offers not only a cathartic conclusion, but also a role for the believer to play in the cosmic drama," according to Stephen O'Leary.[4] In fact, O'Leary argues, this tendency to see a role for believers in the expected end times drama was promoted in the 1980s by the widely read prophecy writer Hal Lindsey in *The 1980s: Countdown to Armageddon* (1981), which revises Lindsey's own earlier discussion of the coming apocalypse, *The Late Great Planet Earth* (1970).

In the first enormously popular book, Lindsey argues that the world will begin to end "within forty years or so of 1948," which was the year of the unification of the Israeli state after World War II. Thus 1988 became the date to anticipate. But with that date drawing ever nearer, Lindsey made a small yet significant change to his argument and claimed that "this generation is the one that will see the end of the present world." Lindsey's emphasis thereby shifted from a particular year to a particular generation. O'Leary comments on the political ramifications of this new line of reasoning.

Though this shift is ever so slight, it has crucial consequences for the practice of politics. For if, as was the case with the Millerites, the effect of setting a specific date for the End is to turn the audience for apocalyptic rhetoric into passive spectators awaiting the fall of the final curtain on history's drama, then it can readily be seen that proposing a fluid generational timetable, rather than a specific date, opens up a temporal space that may allow the audience to participate as actors in the dramatic finale. A declaration of the End of time in 1843 makes the purely political endeavors of 1842 seem superfluous; an announcement of the End of time "during this generation" diffuses audience expectations by denying them a temporal focus, thereby allowing considerably more latitude for movement, while at the same time forging a generational identity that may endow political acts with sacred significance.[5]

Opening up that "temporal space" in which believers can play their roles as actors in an end times drama is exactly how millennialism mobilizes people as political agents.[6] And because pro-life ideology is best understood as a millennialist narrative, it is an ideology that serves to mobilize people. O'Leary argues that millennialist rhetoric played a large role in transforming previously politically passive Christian evangelicals into voters and activists in the 1980s.

This mobilizing function of pro-life ideology should not be dismissed as the hysteria of an end of a century, millennium, or mortal time. Rather, this mobilizing function is enabled because pro-life ideology operates as a narrative, which is not only descriptive but transformative as well.[7] O'Leary describes this transformation as an opening of temporal space in which people become actors in the course of the drama of millennialism. What O'Leary discusses in terms of millennialism and biblical time, literary theorists discuss in terms of decision making and narrative time, which can resist the steady chronology of the modern world.

The modern world runs like clockwork, and the banality of tick-tock, tick-tock provides a worldwide convention, a sense of normalcy in its daily rhythm of morning, noon, and night—or beginning, middle, and (especially) end. Modern fiction consequently has been characterized by the sense, as Frank Kermode says, of an ending. Kermode, like most modernist literary theorists, believes that modern narrative is profoundly connected to time and that time—like the whole of human history—is a linear progression. Kermode goes so far as to say that modernity is inherently apocalyptic because its narratives adhere to the beginning, middle, and end schemata.[8] Like all narratologists since Aristotle, Kermode thus recognizes that narrative has a special relationship to time. "But [such narratologists] have all thought of time as infinite and homogenous," says literary theorist Wlad Godzich, and this is a mistake.[9] There are dimensions of time, ways of experiencing and classifying time, that provide an alternative to what we perceive as homogenous time, a linear history.

The modern notion of linear, standardized, historical time has developed from earlier conceptions of time, prompting some scholars such as Catherine Keller to ask, "What happened to time? How did we get from the tightening medieval *kairos* of deferrals and eruptions to the banal *chronos* of late capitalism?" Chronological time became the norm because work in a capitalist society demands uniformity. We all need to get to work "on time." Time has been "standardized for production, universalized for global liquidation, transmitted in electronic impulses, and marketed as the technofix."[10]

In contrast to historical time, narrative time is not necessarily homogenous; it is not a regular, steady, standardized tick-tock of modern history.[11] In contrast to Kermode, some literary theorists recognize that the epitome of "high modern" literature actually explores how people experience breaks in that steady, daily time.[12] These breaks are facilitated by memory or social alienation. "Instead of the swift and imperceptible flowing of time," novelist Ralph Ellison explains, "you are aware of its nodes, those points where time stands still or from which it leaps ahead. And you slip into the breaks and look around."[13] An awareness of narrative time can be put to use. As "syncopated temporality," narrative time resists linear, modern time and the homogenous, capitalist modern nation.[14]

To escape norms of conventional time and act in a "temporal dimension free from as many of the constraints of" modern, historical time as possible, we make decisions to act, to reject passivity.[15] Godzich explains that decision making functions in such a way as to "open up a different time, to produce more time where none was otherwise available." Similarly, O'Leary argues that millennialism "opens up a temporal space." Godzich says this process is tantamount to "producing" time. People *make time* in the sense that they cease ruminating over their choices and make a decision to act for effect. One does not stop time in that decision-making moment, nor does one "kill time" with idle chatter or aimless activity.[16] One *produces* time, *makes* time for principled action according to a coherent narrative. Making time is essentially a rejection of passivity and complacency, a refusal to comply with the banal chronology of day-to-day modern living. Making time to kill for life, for example, is a willful production—not only a passive consumption—of millennialist narrative. Once people are situated in the role of abortion warrior and make a decision to kill for life, in a sense they "produce more time" because they transform the millennialist, pro-life "story to history, for the new time is one that can be lived."[17]

This "new time" is not as remote and strange as it sounds. In practical terms, living according to biblical or narrative time does not preclude the quotidian practices of scheduling appointments in date books and keeping those appointments according to wristwatches. Testimony to this effect is the manufacturing and marketing of a rapture watch, on the face of which is the message: "One hour nearer the Lord's return."[18] Regardless of the hour, the watch always situates its wearer in a double temporal existence, inhabiting both the chronological and the millennial. Thus, millennialists are compelled to make decisions and carry out plans according to the ever-present possibility that today may be the beginning of the end, that today may end mortal time and inaugurate the apocalyptic process of the Lord's return to earth. They make the time it takes to do the things that qualify them for salvation and prepare the world for Jesus' return.

Pro-life politicians have been enormously successful in getting evangelical citizens to *make time* to register to vote and to *make time* to call their legislative representatives in droves. To this end, Christian media have been instrumental. In addition to the influence of Hal Lindsey, as O'Leary has argued, and of Francis Schaeffer and C. Everett Koop, as I have argued, millennialist narrative was deployed by Christian media throughout the 1970s, 1980s, and 1990s. It is evident in the mission statement of the Christian Broadcasting Network, which was pioneered by Pat Robertson in the early 1960s and "grew to be a $50-million-a-year operation, with a national audience of five million for the syndicated 700 Club talk show" by 1979.[19]

> CBN's mission is to prepare the United States of America, the nations of the Middle East, the Far East, South America and other nations of the world for the coming of Jesus Christ and the establishment of the kingdom on earth. We are achieving this end through the strategic use of mass communications, especially radio, television and film; the distribution of cassettes, films and literature; and the educational training of students to relate biblical principles to those spheres of human endeavor that play a dominant role in our world. We strive for innovation, excellence and integrity in all that we do. We aim always to glorify God and His Son Jesus Christ.[20]

There is no mistaking the first sentence of this statement as a millennialist effort to promote and politicize the "coming of Jesus Christ and the establishment of the kingdom on earth." CBN's programming proves that the proliferation of millennialist thought and discussions of the last days are a necessary part of the Christian Right's overtly political preparation for the Second Coming.

In May 1995, CBN aired "Signs of the Times: A Special Programming Report by the 700 Club with Pat Robertson," a five-part series that promotes the biblical time of premillennialism. Publicity for the shows appeared on the CBN website:

> Are We Living In The End Times? The book of Revelation describes the end times. It speaks of a one-world government, a godless dictator, total regulation of all business, plagues, crime and rebellion, devastating disasters. . . . To many, it seems like a far-off time. But there are "signs of the times" in today's headlines—signs Jesus said would herald His return. Now, CBN has produced a special programming series which highlights news stories, interviews and thoughtful analysis by Pat Robertson, showing how today's events point to the fulfillment of biblical prophecy. You'll hear

shocking reports on new technologies that could usher in the "mark of the beast." Learn how the occult is infiltrating America. Get facts on crime and the family—and how to take a stand. Discover what science knows about resistant viruses that could become plagues of the future. And look at the Middle East of today—where prophecy will someday unfold in a final battle and Christ's return![21]

This description begins with a question that invites inquiring minds, but the goal of the program is to dispense with the idea that millennial conflict only "seems like a far-off time." "The fulfillment of biblical prophecy," in fact, is prefaced by current events. The program promises to shock people into understanding and action. It fosters a desire—and promotes a way— to "take a stand." In producing millennialist expectation, "Signs of the Times" creates a narrative time and is able to mobilize around it.

For example, Sara Diamond reports that televised evangelical programs, like those on CBN, instruct viewers to call their representatives in Washington to help them "pray." In abundant numbers, viewers do so. Those calls to congressional offices then are tabulated and touted as the voice of the people. This is one way in which "religious broadcasting . . . became the single most important resource in the mobilization of the Christian Right."[22] In this way millennialist narrative can—and has—mobilized millions of voters at the drop of a televangelist's hat. It translates spiritual devotion and millennialist expectation into demonstrable, quantifiable forms of political action.

Pro-life politicians have understood and employed this capacity of millennialist narrative. In 1995, for example, pro-life presidential candidate Phil Gramm sent out a fund-raising letter with a curious conclusion: "I ask you to fight tirelessly and when you are too tired to go on, remember that there is only one person who has ever lived whose values we would be willing to see imposed on America. And when He comes back, He's not going to need government's help to get the job done."[23] Gramm's reference to "when He comes back" is "clearly in the tradition of dispensational premillennialism," according to the *New York Times*. Gramm's letter is a deployment of narrative time, of the time "when He comes back," which (in accordance with dispensationalism) can occur at any moment. Its political function as a fund-raising letter and its success in getting individual citizens to write out a check and send it to Gramm headquarters depend on how it functions as narrative. Narrative opens a different temporal dimension in which Christian politicians and citizens make political decisions and forge political relationships. In doing so, it transforms the reader or viewer from a passive consumer of narrative of Christ's return into a productive actor in that millennialist narrative, a decision maker who makes time to send that check.

Not only does pro-life ideology take the *form* of millennialist narrative, then. It *functions* as narrative by transforming consumers of pro-life millennialism into producers of pro-life, millennialist action—whether that action is to bar the doors of a hospital or clinic, set up pro-life organizations, call up a congressman to help him pray for conservative legislation, or write out a check to a pro-life candidate, such as Phil Gramm, who invokes the coming of Christ. In this way, pro-life ideology narrates individuals as pro-life agents who make decisions according to a biblical time and millennialist expectation. They *make time* for pro-life action.

In its examination of Gramm's invocation of Christ's return, the *New York Times* also noted that Ronald Reagan was successful in using millennialist narrative: "Although premillennialism is a rare doctrine for a political figure to embrace publicly, it has surfaced before in a political forum. In the 1984 campaign, after President Ronald Reagan had speculated about a coming battle of Armageddon, he was criticized by clerics who said such talk gave credence to the idea that the United States was destined for a nuclear clash with the Soviet Union."[24] But Reagan's apocalyptic speculations are certainly not limited to the 1984 campaign. Likewise, millennialist rhetoric—and its deployment of narrative time—is not limited to only Reagan and Gramm.

O'Leary sees Reagan as the New Right's "most eloquent spokesman" whose "diffusion of apocalyptic expectation served as a resource" for the New Right.[25] But Reagan first wielded this mighty deployment of narrative time in "his televised appeal at the close of the 1964 Goldwater campaign, the speech that launched [Reagan's] entry into national politics." In that speech, Reagan quotes Winston Churchill: "There is something going on in time and space, and beyond time and space, which, whether we like it or not, spells duty." Then he proceeds to deliver these famous lines: "You and I have a rendezvous with destiny. We will preserve for our children this, the last best hope of man on earth, or we will sentence them to take the last step into a thousand years of darkness." Riffing on Abraham Lincoln's apocalyptic speech about the last great hope for earth, Reagan blends "political advocacy with the language of apocalypse."[26]

Ronald Reagan was not the only conservative trying to inspire and mobilize the right through millennialist rhetoric in the 1960s. And the phenomenon of deploying narrative time through the manufacture of millennialist expectation for political purposes cannot be seen only as a product of the 1980s and 1990s.

Postmodern and Pro-Life in the 1960s

From their inception, pro-life politics are indebted to conservatives who, consciously or not, deployed narrative time and millennialist rhetoric to spur political mobilization. The exemplar of this practice is L. Brent Bozell, who prefigured the radicalization of conservative, pro-life politics. Bozell and his colleagues made millennialist rhetoric familiar and palatable to Catholics. His magazine, *Triumph*, is filled with apocalyptic expectation that rejects the old right establishment in almost precisely the same ways as—but about ten years before—the New Right would reject it in 1979 with the founding of the American Life League and the Moral Majority. Bozell sought to create a web of pro-life organizations, demanded absolutist opposition to abortion, emphasized spiritual and cultural values over economic goals, and developed a theory and practice of pro-life action that rejected passivity and accommodated militancy. People thought he was crazy.

In particular, biographers of conservative intellectuals explain Bozell's political decisions as manifestations of mental illness. When Bozell left the well-known *National Review* to begin editing *Triumph*, biographical accounts of the shift psychologize the situation as a personal fight with his co-editor and co-author, William F. Buckley. Buckley and Bozell had worked together for years as editors of *National Review* and on books such as *McCarthy and His Enemies*. They became brothers-in-law when Bozell married Buckley's sister, Patricia. Therefore, Buckley biographer John B. Judis examines Bozell's "rejection" of Buckley as a personal, family conflict, concluding that Bozell suffered from "manic depression." This "acute mental illness" exacerbated what Patricia claimed was her husband's feeling of always being cast in the shadow of Buckley, his more famous peer.[27]

Scholarly accounts of the rift, however, specify abortion as key in Bozell's rejection of Buckley and *National Review*–style conservatism. Historian of conservatism Patrick Allitt explains that Buckley's casual attitude toward the abortion law reforms of the mid-1960s was informed by Vatican II and fears of overpopulation. In a *National Review* piece titled "The Birth Rate," Buckley argued that abortion for non-Catholics should be tolerated. This view contrasted sharply with Bozell's ardent opposition to all abortion and contraception. Bozell blasted Buckley in a letter to the editor, which set off a heated exchange between Bozell and a third *National Review* editor. Hardly dismissible as an outbreak of mental illness, Bozell's erudite attacks on Buckley and his staff were couched in the principles of Catholic natural law.[28] This episode at *National Review* was the final one for Bozell; in 1966 he left the magazine to start *Triumph*. Launching *Triumph* was one of many of Bozell's efforts to foster radical Christian, pro-life politics throughout America.

During the midsixties through the seventies, Bozell tried to establish a network of pro-life organizations, including Americans United for Life (or AUL). Founded by a group of Catholics including Charles Rice and Bozell, AUL was considered ecumenical and was meant to appeal to Protestants as well as Catholics. The chair of AUL was George Williams, a professor of theology at Harvard, who fell out of favor with Bozell when Bozell demanded that the group subscribe to an absolutist position against abortion. Williams argued for abortion in cases of rape and incest, adding "we must leave it to the mother in that decidedly small class of cases where her own life is at stake."[29] Bozell expressed alarm at a "continuing erosion of the [AUL] Board's position," which was evidenced, he said, by one board member's letter in the Washington *Evening Star*. It read: "I favor those laws that permit abortion where the life or the physical or mental health of a pregnant woman is seriously threatened."[30] Bozell also insisted that AUL defer the wording of "media advertising or direct mail" to the Society for a Christian Commonwealth, *Triumph*'s "parent organization."[31]

The Society for a Christian Commonwealth (SCC), founded in 1966 by Bozell, early on gave AUL $50,000 as seed money. But the origin of these funds was not always attributed to SCC, and they were never without strings. Sometimes the contributions were said to have been made not by an overseeing organization but "by 50–55 individuals (largely Catholics)."[32] Williams did not want AUL to operate as a front organization for absolutist Catholic opposition to abortion, nor for Bozell, whom he saw as promoting "wars of Christian imperialism and by implication many other uses of force rather than persuasion."[33] When Williams refused to give in to the demands of SCC, Bozell wrote a "hectoring four-page letter against what he saw as [AUL's] half-heartedness," which angered many AUL board members.[34] Effective with this letter, Bozell terminated the relationship between SCC and AUL. In fact, AUL was far less radical in its outlook and less revolutionary in tone than was the SCC. Some of its activities during the early 1970s included filing an amicus curiae brief in the Texas case that would become *Roe v. Wade* and running a three-column ad in the *New York Times* that employed an antiwar metaphor: abortion was a "surgical search and destroy mission within the womb."

In contrast, the SCC had a broader, more radical goal than stopping abortion. The Society for a Christian Commonwealth's mission stated that "the proper object of every social order and every culture is to bring the human condition into harmony with the will of God."[35] This imperative was always put in apocalyptic and militant terms. Bozell's fiery lectures were titled "The Fight for Life: America's Armageddon," and issues of *Triumph* regularly ran articles that monitored so-called Satanism in America, including examinations of popular culture such as the films and books of *The Exorcist* and *Rosemary's Baby*. A 1972 article, "The Rule of Demons," concluded that the "contemporary outbreak of Satanism" was evident in abortion provision:

> Every day the nauseous odor of sacrifice to the demons, who rule man by his own complicity in their aims, rises from the abortion clinics and hospitals of America and most of the other countries of the world. When the wanton sacrifice of innocent life can be allowed and promoted by a society that was once Christian, as a matter of course, can the day be far away when its people will be ready to accept over Satanism as the normal religions of its governing elite?[36]

As in evangelical accounts, *Triumph* depicts abortion as a sign of the rise of Satan and seeks to instill a sense of urgency in its readers. But more than framing abortion or the "fight for life" in the rhetoric of an apocalyptic holy war against Satan, *Triumph* both describes in theoretical terms the way to deploy narrative time for the sake of militant pro-life action and provides concrete examples of that deployment.

The theory of pro-life mobilization was laid out by Bozell in an article written for *Triumph*, titled "The Confessional Tribe," which Bozell referred to as a "self-consciously paridigmatic [*sic*] statement."[37] In it, Bozell grafts millennialist rhetoric that characterized conservative thoughts on ungodly communism in the postwar years onto what he saw as a "life destruction policy which is called 'liberalized abortion' " and an even more encompassing "anti-life campaign that is today being officially prosecuted at the highest levels of government":[38]

> America's war against Christ is variously waged, but two aspects of it are sufficient to the point. One is the country's formal public ag-

nosticism. The Soviet Union is a formally atheistic country, and while some Americans have taken comfort in the difference, they should not. . . . By asserting the power to control and manipulate the production of human life—by usurping authority over what ontologically belongs to the King, because its destiny is in the King—this city has escalated the war against Christ to the highest level.[39]

The "power to control and manipulate" sexual reproduction here refers to what other *Triumph* writers would call the contraceptive mentality. About a year after the "Confessional Tribe" was published, in the wake of the *Rockefeller Commission Report on Population* that recommended reproductive choice without pronatalist pressure, Charles Rice promoted in *Triumph* the idea of a Human Life Society, "an organization [that] would begin with the understanding that, among other things, the contraceptive mentality encourages abortion."[40] Discussions of the contraceptive mentality are couched in apocalyptic terms. "America's war against Christ" is inflamed by the contraceptive mentality and "anti-life policies" such as those the Rockefeller Commission recommends, and its report was touted as "a pagan, Satanic blueprint."[41] Taking the place of ungodly communism, abortion and the contraceptive mentality were signs that the United States "has escalated the war against Christ to the highest level," to America's Armageddon.[42]

Bozell examines the parameters of this apocalyptic battle in relation to the economic, technological, and social changes that characterize the post-war, post-industrial, postmodern world.

> Hardly any serious observer has failed to notice that the social organization of the planet is undergoing a profound change, that the dominant form of organization—the national state, which is the modern mode of the city—is giving way to something else. The less perceptive of these observers, who are not really observers but ideologues, maintain that the movement is toward global unity: that the successor arrangement is to be a world state inhabited by a humankind evolved from diversity to sameness. The more perceptive observers see that the movement is proceeding in a quite different direction: that the dominant social drive is not toward togetherness, but separateness: that the successor arrangement to the national city is not the world city, but the tribe.[43]

Here it is clear that Bozell is engaging contemporary conversations such as Marshall McLuhan's theory of the global village, with an important difference.[44] Both McLuhan and Bozell recognize the impact and promise of electronic media and the dissolving of spatial boundaries in a post-national culture and economy. Bozell's tribe "does not need a geography." But whereas McLuhan examines the way in which youth culture lives according to myth, Bozell suggests—lest Christianity, perhaps, be reduced to myth—that his tribe relies on "symbol and ritual." *Triumph* earlier had blasted the "McLuhanite movement of verbal nihilism" with a piece by Thomas Molnar and in general had exalted the confessional "tribe" as its answer to "modernity's collapse."[45]

Indeed, *Triumph* advertised its Christian Commonwealth Summer Institute as a way to "shape the post-modern world," as a place where "the new Christian tribe is forming." Director of this two-month, $1,050-per-person Institute in El Escorial, Spain, Frederick Wilhelmsen joined Bozell in promoting the confessional tribe. For Wilhelmsen, the relationship to McLuhan's global village theory was explicit: "Wilhelmsen collaborated with Jane Bret on two books, based on Marshall McLuhan's theory of television, about the end of modernity, the 'retribalization' of the world, and the breakdown of nations, literacy, and all the old conventions, out of which this 'Christian tribe' would have to find its own way."[46] The Christian Commonwealth Summer Institute would lead Bozell's tribe into the postmodern era.

Although Bozell's tribe is one of "many semi-autonomous 'tribes' loose in a no-longer Christian culture," it is presented as a "successor arrangement to the national city" or nation-state.[47] More importantly, it is an opportunity to establish a new Christian era.

Is it surprising that the death of modernity should also see the death of its characteristic social form, the city? Is it surprising that postmodernity, recording a new swing of history, should again beckon men into the tribe? . . . But it is less important for those living in a transitional age to understand why history is moving in a particular direction than to recognize that it is doing so, and thus to be in a position to shape the movement along desired lines. If a full understanding of what is happening must be reserved to the future, an openness to what is happening is indispensable to grasping the opportunities of the present. For instance, and depending on God's own plans, the opportunity to help inaugurate the second Christian epoch.[48]

Without a doubt, Bozell's sense of the second Christian epoch is that it is one attainable through Christian politics. As opposed to American politics, which "is a list of proposals, a recipe for solving problems," "Christian politics is a mode of being, a style of life." Moreover, Bozell understands that Christian politics are destined to enable the Gospel life and, inevitably, to "bring it to the ends of the earth."[49]

In this quest to bring the Gospel life to the ends of the earth, to "inaugurate the second Christian epoch," time is all important. Bozell dismisses an "ideological myopia, the inability to see history except in terms of a linear progression" and claims that "the goal of the Christian tribe, like that of the city which Christians could once hope to build, is to establish temporal conditions hospitable to the Gospel life. But first the tribe must be."[50] What Bozell means by these notions of establishing "temporal conditions" and "being" in that time is akin to what Godzich describes as decision making.

Accompanying Bozell's appreciation for the nonlinear nature of time is his desire for "grasping the opportunities of the present." "Being" a Christian demands a concentration of time in which to act, in which to *be* rather than to pontificate. "Decisions are profoundly antithetical to philosophy in this respect. They 'rush' time. What philosophical reflection seeks to defer indefinitely," Godzich explains, "a decision concentrates in a point, the moment, the time of decision."[51] Bozell's discussion of the confessional tribe thus describes in theoretical terms how to *make time* and make political decisions. Bozell had a practice to go with this theory: before establishing the nonlinear "temporal conditions" for a Christian commonwealth, the tribe "must be" in accordance with Christian politics.

Bozell and his tribe—those diligent in the "fight for life" and the establishment of a Christian commonwealth and the second Christian epoch—not only discussed the Christian politics of "establishing the temporal conditions." They also deployed narrative time in order to carry out political decisions. One example of this deployment is a militant protest that led to "the first arrests of the anti-abortion movement" in June 1970.[52]

Prefiguring Operation Rescue's clinic blockades of the 1980s and 1990s, Bozell and members of a Dallas anti-abortion group (which was called the Sons of Thunder and included Bozell's son, Chris) attempted to launch a direct action movement they called Action for Life with an inaugural confrontation at George Washington University Hospital in Washington,

D.C. Sons of Thunder had been successful in occupying a Texas family planning center for six hours until police had intervened with a court order, obtained by Planned Parenthood, and asked the protesters to leave.[53] Action for Life strove in vain to repeat the Texas success. They sought not to close the hospital but to obtain an interview with the hospital administrator, whom they hoped to convince to sign a pledge to cease performing abortions for a day. Other symbolic goals were "to provide facilities for the baptism of infants that are to be killed" and to encourage the "decent and orderly removals of the dead babies to a place of Christian burial."[54] One wonders what in fact they would have done if presented with the actual products of abortion, which are, contrary to pro-life images, most often the form and consistency of jam; no account of the incident mentions any bags or other containers on the ready. Instead, *Triumph* reports that the protest turned violent when police intervened; a plate-glass door was broken, and five demonstrators were roughed up and arrested, including Bozell, who, in handcuffs, made the front pages of the Sunday *Star* and the *Washington Post*.[55]

During the rally of two to three hundred people that had preceded the scuffle, an enraged Wilhelmsen fumed the apocalyptic narrative that would become prevalent years later: "America—land of the scraped womb. You are about to abort your future because you are daggering to death your unborn tomorrow."[56] *Triumph* reported the whole ordeal in a chronicle titled "Present Imperfect." Significantly, the element of time was thus foregrounded in the title of the report and in Wilhelmsen's story of aborting America. The protest may be said to be an attempt to illustrate and enact *Triumph*'s theory of how to "establish the temporal conditions" for a Christian society.

According to "Present Imperfect," the attempt was successful: "three hundred Americans who go to church on Sunday and pay their taxes and mind their own business now shout in a public park in the center of the Nation's Capital—*Viva Cristo Rey!*"[57] Bozell's conservative colleagues at the time found the action embarrassingly similar to leftist protests (such as those held by the Berrigans) and faulted Bozell for his emphasis on Spanish Carlism. Bozell and *Triumph* followers, however, saw the event as more than "Hispanic esoterica" or a "conservative mirror image" of leftist work.[58] "Present Imperfect" heralded a revolutionary beginning; neither the three hundred protesters "nor the city can be unchanged."[59] The tribe's protest at George Washington University Hospital was an attempt to illustrate and enact Bozell's idea to decide to "be" a pro-life and pro-Christian society.

A more explicit example of "establishing the temporal conditions" to inaugurate the new Christian era can be found in a second action by one of Bozell's tribe. Patricia Buckley Bozell, Bozell's wife, made a media splash about a year after the George Washington University incident. When radical feminist Ti-Grace Atkinson spoke at Catholic University in March 1971, Patricia Bozell attended as a reporter for *Triumph*. Upon hearing Atkinson's speech, which according to Bozell "defamed the Mother of God and God Himself in the vilest possible manner," she walked up to the podium and attempted to slap Atkinson across the face. Not just her inflammatory speech but Atkinson's suspected lesbianism and her leaving the less-than-radical National Organization for Women to "push for 'abortion reform'" had offended Patricia Bozell.[60] Her reaction to Atkinson was described and defended in *Triumph* a month later.

Triumph put forth Patricia Bozell's "intolerance of blasphemy" as an example of how to "establish the temporal conditions" in which to act according to biblical time. After describing the scene, an editorial titled "God and Woman at Catholic U." commented on her action as ultimately a moment that spurs on the "day of salvation."

> They wanted to know her views on violence as a means of "social reform." Did she approve of Martin Luther King? Didn't she believe in freedom of speech? Academic freedom? They referred to her famous family, to her family life, to her work. But for Patricia Buckley Bozell these were irrelevant questions. "Miss Atkinson was, in my presence, defaming the Mother of God and God Himself in the vilest possible manner; and I am a Catholic." For this reason, and for this reason alone, when Patricia Bozell understood in her Christian heart what Ti-Grace Atkinson represented, she rose from the reporter's box, went up to the woman, and in the name of women and for the Woman she drew the line. "I cannot let her say that." She slapped her.
>
> For the Greeks, the word *kairos* designated the critical time for a reality to come to be, the critical moment of decision through which a man takes his place in history. For the Christian the *kairos* is the time of salvation, when the outpouring of God's loving grace transforms his life. It may come after a painful preparation; or suddenly; it may come only once; or again and again. It is the moment to *be*—not a moment to think and to argue, but to live, to affirm, to decide, to act.
>
> Blasphemy, the words and *ways of acting* which injure the holi-

ness, majesty and honor of God, His name, His word, His law, even His angels and most certainly His Mother and His bride the Church—blasphemy was the challenge to which this Christian woman reacted from the depths of her being.

She was not alone. The thousands of letters and telegrams confirm it, her solidarity with the Catholic people of the land who applaud the proclamation she made that night, by her act, to all men and women who had hoped the Catholic Church would, at last surrender; to them all and in the name of God, of His eternal Son Jesus Christ, Our King, and of His Virgin Mother, Mary, the Woman, she said, with the Apostle Paul: Now! Now is the moment to act! "Now is the acceptable time! Now is the day of salvation!"[61]

In *Triumph's* portrayal of Patricia Bozell's radical slap, we see not just an apocalyptic rhetoric at work but a Catholic version of deploying narrative time for the sake of pro-life action. The "critical moment of decision through which a man takes his place in history" presents not a progressive linear history but a mode of narrative time that can be concentrated by a political decision and manifested in a political act—a radical slap in the face of feminism (see fig. 7).

The emphasis on *kairos* indicates that revolution rather than reform is the Bozells' goal. As in leftist theologies, *Triumph's* explanation of *kairos* is an "evocation of the time of revolution and revelation, when 'eternity breaks into time.'" *Kairos* can be "beautifully translated into a dissident time, 'admitting the possibility of radical change, radical chaos, radical openness.'"[62] Feminist and liberation theologists alike have embraced *kairos* as a means of resistance and revolution. For example, in South Africa, churches that participated in resistance composed a "Kairos Document" against apartheid.[63] "The *kairos* metaphor caught fire," according to Catherine Keller, "and has leapt through the two-thirds world as a political eschatology of great urgency, an apocalypse not of unconditional doom, but of the dramatic prophetic conditional—that if you change the ways of injustice, then we may all flourish together."[64] *Triumph* magazine, the name of which evokes a victorious, utopian apocalypse rather than a tragic doomsday, exemplifies a right-wing *kairos* based on conservative interpretations of the "ways of injustice."

Whether right wing or left, *kairos* functions less as metaphor than as narrative. Bozell's explanation of *kairos* strongly resembles Godzich's explanation of narrative time as a function of decision making. Godzich says, "we need to recognize that a decision entails that the elements it manages

Fig. 7. Patricia Bozell's slap in the face of feminism is narrated as conservative, Christian kairos, *the time of salvation. Copyright* Washington Post. *Reprinted by permission of the D.C. Public Library.*

and affects exist in a temporal dimension that is incommensurable with the infinite extension of concepts inhabiting an infinite and homogenous time."[65] *Triumph* reports that *kairos* spurs the "time of salvation," which is heterogenous, not uniform, not an infinite flow of time passing. For Bozell, the time of salvation "may come after a painful preparation; or suddenly; it may come only once; or again and again." Godzich says, "decisions are profoundly antithetical to philosophy" and "reflection"; decisions " 'rush' time"; "they produce it."[66] *Triumph* explains that the *kairos* exemplified by Patricia Bozell "is the moment to *be*—not a moment to think and to argue, but to live, to affirm, to decide, to act." Godzich says that it is the narrative quality of decision making that allows for this rupture of standardized, homogenous time: "The function of the story, of its telling within the context of deliberative discourse, is thus to fracture philosophical time, to mobilize its rupture in the service of an alternative, one that will be marked by the sense of a beginning." Bozell's magazine narrates all of the pro-life actions of the Christian tribe as a new beginning, a revolutionary push toward a Christian commonwealth, and a prophesied triumph against "America's war on life."[67]

From the moment Bozell and his wife began living according to narrative time, and in the process working toward the revolutionary establishment of a Christian commonwealth, he fell out of favor with Catholic pro-life leaders.[68] In particular, his protest at George Washington University Hospital, a decidedly revolutionary moment, was seen by others as an obstacle to building pro-life coalitions. Bozell's attempt to organize the first national anti-abortion congress in 1971 was undermined by Father James McHugh, director of the Family Life Division of the U.S. Catholic Conference. Bozell confronted McHugh, who had written a letter to "Right to Life contacts" in every state, encouraging them to snub the event, "since at least some of the supporters of the National Right to Life Congress have already urged violence and a tougher stand."

> Bozell said: "I have never urged violence, Father. Do you have any evidence to the contrary?" The priest triumphantly produced a news service report of the sentencing of Bozell for his role in an anti-abortion demonstration the previous June, and read: "Bozell told reporters after sentencing that he would not let the probation period interfere with his action for life activities."[69]

While Catholic leaders were withdrawing their support from the Bozells because of the couple's public, militant, millennialist activities, conservative leaders were likewise critical. In the face of Bozell's millennialism, the *National Review* ridiculed his repudiation of conservatism, which he had termed "an inadequate substitute for Christian politics." The *Review* complained, "to dismiss even contemporary America as one vast plot against the survival of our eternal souls is Manichean and boring."[70] Both Catholic and conservative leaders, then, may have used apocalyptic rhetoric, but neither group used or recognized and consciously debated the mobilizing power of millennialist narrative as Bozell did at the time.

There is no doubt that Bozell and his tribe were aware of the power of millennialism—its ability to mobilize—and they were sure to put it into Catholic terms. To do this, *Triumph* lambasted the "millennialist" and "gnostic rhetoric" of liberal Protestantism both to denounce it as heretical and to distinguish it from Bozell's conservative formulation of Catholicism. The heresy lies in the "belief that the salvation of man and society can be accomplished on this earth," according to an early essay by Bozell.[71]

The distinction of Bozell's Catholicism from Protestantism is also a distinction from the "moderate, Liberal expression" of gnosticism, which can only, Bozell wrote, conclude as Communism. But for all that distancing and distinction from millennialism, *Triumph* explicitly explored its power and employed its language.

In a two-part article titled "Lincoln's New Frontier: A Rhetoric for Continuing Revolution," Mel Bradford examined for *Triumph* readers the Declaration of Independence, the "Battle Hymn of the Republic," and the Gettysburg Address. In the article, Bradford claims that these exemplary pieces of Americana are essentially millennialist, but "we do not see the gnostic quality" in them "because it is now *our* 'orthodoxy'—even in the most conservative circles."[72] Bradford goes on to delineate the "gnostic" quality of each example.

> Consideration of Julia Howe's politically partisan Jesus—and then of ours—should engender in the rhetorically and theologically literate a deep shudder and should deflate these 'three holy documents' to a status of stratagems. The signers of the Declaration of Independence needed to draw more people into the Revolution and to 'improve its international image'; Lincoln needed to obfuscate the facts surrounding Jefferson's composition in order to 'control' the war effort and justify his 1864 re-election; and Mrs. Howe sensed instinctively that the Union's military spirit in late 1861 needed elevation if it were to be sustained against a vigorous enemy. Gnostic rhetoric was the proper engine for the performance of this business, and perhaps nowhere else has its millennialist impulse been so thoroughly set at liberty as within our own borders.[73]

Bradford clearly is not merely disdainful of gnostic rhetoric but is thoughtfully considering the impact and utility of "its millennialist impulse." He strives to impress upon *Triumph* readers how millennialist language works as political strategy by creating "stratagems" and how anticipation of apocalypse is, as the title announces, tantamount to a "rhetoric for continuing revolution."

Perhaps it was that "continuing" and never-ending quality of millennialism that most disturbed Bradford. American millennialism continually put off, rather than completed, revolution. Bradford's article warned *Triumph* readers against millennialism and "the rhetoric of gnostic hope" as a "politics of discontent."[74] Even though *Triumph* problematizes Protestant millennialism in this way, its pages are rife with millennialist expectation and apocalyptic language. With such a careful and conscious consideration of the "millennialist impulse," *Triumph* disdains the rhetoric of millennialism but employs its language and deploys the narrative time that characterizes millennialism. The "Manichean and boring" formulations of *Triumph* were in fact action-packed narratives that offered an alternative to hell-bent apocalyptic rhetoric that promoted only a "politics of discontent" and doom.

Apocalyptic doomsday rhetoric was in vogue for Catholic conservatives of the late 1960s, as Patrick Allitt explains. But he makes no distinction between *Triumph* and other Catholic, conservative publications.

> Apocalyptic speculation abounded at the end of the 1960s, giving rise to a vast literature of catastrophe, a genre in which Catholic conservatives excelled. In addition to *Triumph*, which was almost wholly written in that idiom, John Lukacs contributed *The Passing of the Modern Age*, Thomas Molnar explained in *The Counter-Revolution* why people of his type were doomed to irrevocable defeat, and Frederick Wilhelmsen [who edited *Triumph* with Bozell] produced *Seeds of Anarchy* (1969), a conservative anthology on the student revolution then in progress at the nation's premier campuses. . . . Wilhelmsen was almost but not yet quite ready to join Bozell in declaring that all was lost for America.[75]

Wilhelmsen used apocalyptic language of mere catastrophe. For example, he claimed that "America—and with her the West—will go down in a Twilight of the Gods from which there will be no recourse."[76] In contrast, Bozell used the language of apocalyptic millennialism, posing the imminent battle as an active fight against Satan and Satanism, an Armageddon that would usher in a Christian utopia, not merely the tragic demise of the West. In fact, as early as 1962, Bozell wrote to dispel the idea that there was no recourse to this apparent decline of the West, in effect rejecting any softer image such as Wilhelmsen's "Twilight of the Gods": "Only when we understand the nature of the enemy: that this is Armageddon, no 'twilight struggle,' then only will the proper battle orders go out."[77] The "proper battle orders" are part of God's plan for the "second Christian epoch," part of the work of Bozell's confessional tribe.

Unfortunately, these profoundly militant, millennialist ideas—of "the fight for life" as "America's Armageddon"—have been overlooked as hysteria attributable to the 1960s if not to Bozell's mental illness. Without a doubt and by his own accounts, Bozell suffered from manic depression. Although dismissed by the conservatives of his day for this reason, Bozell was deliberate in his attempts to describe, circulate, organize, and act on the millennialist narrative of abortion as apocalypse. Although he quotes from the Second Vatican Council to describe how his tribe is a "chosen race, a royal priesthood, a holy nation" and a "messianic people" who are the "sure seed of unity, hope and salvation for the whole human race," the quality of that Catholic messianism so meshes with Protestant millennialism in its deployment of narrative time that, like dispensationalism, it urges a rejection of passivity.[78] It makes time for conservative, pro-life action. It is no wonder that Bozell had a profound impact on right-wing strategists and politicians who became the New Right. In fact, *Triumph*'s legacy to the New Right is precisely that rejection of the sense of resignation from which conservatives of the 1960s suffered.

Bozell's Legacy

In rejecting the "politics of discontent" that it attributed to "the rhetoric of gnostic hope," *Triumph* succeeded in both promoting the pro-life struggle as the millennialist conflict of Armageddon and divesting that millennialism of resignation and passivity. Bozell's tribe and his *Triumph* prefigured a departure from the defeatism that, according to the New Right, plagued the old right.

Seeing the upsurge in liberalism in apocalyptic terms, the conservatives of the 1950s and 1960s became overly pessimistic. They read books such as James Burnham's *Suicide of the West* (which was regularly advertised in *Triumph* as part of the Conservative Book Club) and were convinced that they were in the midst of the catastrophic downfall of the West, America, and conservatism. Buckley's *National Review* reflected this view, according to Paul Weyrich, who, along with Terry Dolan, Howard Phillips, and Richard Viguerie, was a key organizer of the New Right. Weyrich talks about how the New Right took that apocalyptic framing of Western civilization's demise and turned it from a pessimistic, "self-fulfilling prophecy" and "sense of resignation to Fate" into an optimistic sense of overcoming anticonservative forces. "We are not speaking abstractly of the decline of the West," Weyrich explains in contradistinction to the old right, "but concretely about preserving values we know are revered by other middle class Americans."[79] A conservative Catholic himself who read and revered Bozell's work perhaps even more so than Buckley's, Weyrich followed the logic of *Triumph* and saw that the problem was a "politics of discontent" that bred passivity, not action.

Weyrich helped Catholic conservatives switch from a pessimistic, fatalistic, and passive view of the embattled West to a proactive, prioritized, and strategic engagement in that battle. Much has been written about how evangelicals rejected their doomed passivity and came to political action in record numbers between 1976 and 1984, but few have remarked how Catholic conservatives underwent the same transition. Weyrich illustrates this transition with a story about how Buckley himself understood the problem: "In 1978, William Buckley admitted to me that where political action was concerned, *National Review* had been guilty of the theological sin of otherworldliness: the belief that, as long as one's own life was free of sin, one needn't worry about the affairs of this world."[80] This dilemma is exactly the one in which Christian evangelicals found themselves, until Francis Schaeffer and C. Everett Koop (through the *Whatever Happened to the Human Race?* tour) and the New Right pro-life organizations (the Moral Majority and American Life League) began distributing millennialist narrative on a mass scale in 1979.

There is no doubt of the similarity between New Right ideology and that of the Protestant evangelicals. Evangelicals' millennialism was "fully consonant with the ideology of the 'new right,'" which believed that "the United States was created by God to fight the Anti-Christ" of communism and that "the traditional concept of the male-dominated nuclear family is sacrosanct."[81] Under the influence of not just evangelicals but Catholic leaders such as Weyrich, the Antichrist of communism became the Antichrist of abortion and other so-called antifamily, anti-Christian forces. There was a "common ideology—deeply religious and deeply conservative—that the 'new right' leaders shared with the [Protestant] clergymen. It was, after all, Paul Weyrich and not some Baptist preacher who described the conflict over the 'traditional family' as 'really the most significant battle of the age-old conflict between good and evil, between the forces of God and forces against God, that we have seen in our country.'"[82] Weyrich here and elsewhere easily inserts the language of an "age-old conflict between good and evil." This language is less strident than that of Bozell's millennialism, but nonetheless it functions as millennialist narrative, a "common ideology" shared by Protestants and Catholics alike.

Bozell's dismissal of defeatism, his absolutist and militant stance against abortion, and his mobilizing through millennialist narrative prefigured on a small scale those accomplishments of the New Right. Although dismissed by some as a "tiny right-wing Catholic magazine," *Triumph* attracted thirty thousand readers at the height of its popularity.[83] More importantly, *Triumph* was held in high esteem by New Right leaders. It was

Bozell and his magazine, not Buckley and the *National Review*, that received special mention by Weyrich: "*Triumph* magazine, which was founded shortly after 1964 by Brent Bozell, Goldwater's chief speechwriter, deserves mention for keeping the Catholic element politically together because it maintained some thread of continuity between the Catholics who had been Goldwater supporters and current politics."[84] To give Bozell more credit than this would be inconsistent with Weyrich's distinction between the old right as intellectual and "blue blood" and the new right as spiritual and "blue collar." Bozell was both erudite and militant, intellectual and spiritual.

Bozell embodied yet another pair of supposedly paradoxical traits that would become, over the next few decades, characteristic of the militant faction of pro-life politics. Like the so-called extremists who mesh antigovernment and anti-abortion agendas, Bozell "regarded the United States as God's chosen instrument for the preservation of Christendom and the West," yet he then "declared war on his nation as an enemy of religion."[85] In the patriotic anti-Americanism of Brent Bozell as well as in his intellectual spirituality and erudite militancy, some thread of continuity indeed does exist between the Goldwater era and current politics, as Weyrich says.

That Bozell was Goldwater's chief speechwriter indicates how that thread of continuity was stitched into the fabric of contemporary conservatism. Technically, they were Bozell's words, not Goldwater's, that spawned the revitalization of conservatism in the United States. New Right leaders admit as much. Goldwater himself was not the conservative after whom New Right leaders came to model themselves. "The intellectuals behind Goldwater, the Bill Buckleys and Brent Bozells, presented Goldwater as a standard-bearer of truth, a philosopher-politician. That was not the man," Weyrich says.[86] In the first place, Goldwater, like most Republicans in the 1960s, was never anti-abortion. Second, Goldwater believed that "religion has no place in public policy" and in the 1980s attacked New Right institutions such as the Moral Majority. In explaining these attacks, John Lofton, a New Right leader who participated in a series of lectures at the Kennedy School of Government publicized as the New Right at Harvard, makes a distinction between the 1981 Goldwater who attacked the New Right and the 1960 Goldwater, whose defeat in his bid for the presidency is widely acknowledged to be the beginning of the conservatives' renaissance. According to Lofton, "I say the 1981 Goldwater because the 1960 Goldwater who wrote *The Conscience of a Conservative* said that conservatism is based upon the laws of God, that moreover, conservatism looks upon the enhancement of man's spiritual nature as the *primary* concern of political philosophy."[87] But there never was a 1960 Goldwater who wrote *Conscience of a Conservative*. Instead the author was L. Brent Bozell. They were Bozell's words, not Goldwater's, that articulated the conscience of the resurgent right.

Goldwater had so trusted his ghostwriter in 1960 that, by some accounts, he did not even read the manuscript of *Conscience of a Conservative* before it went to press. In fact, Bozell told Allitt that Goldwater did not "know much about conservatism until he read that book" published under his own name.[88] Other conservative leaders and their followers took their cues from the little book. Lee Edwards, a founding member of the conservative Young Americans for Freedom, attests to the importance of Bozell's work: "For us the '60s began not with a bang but with a book, *The Conscience of a Conservative* by Barry Goldwater."[89] Pat Buchanan acknowledged *Conscience of a Conservative* as "our new testament; it contained the core beliefs of our political faith, it told us why we had failed, what we must do."[90]

During what one historian calls the "search for conservative principles" in the late 1950s and early 1960s, *Conscience of a Conservative* claimed for the right the populist idea of the responsible individual against the materialistic masses.[91] It matched Whittaker Chambers's *Witness*, Russell Kirk's *The Conservative Mind*, and even Buckley's *Up from Liberalism* in its apocalyptic binaries and its ability to cast the fight against materialism as a conservative, right-wing, white fight. What Buckley makes implicit when he parallels the title of his book with that of Booker T. Washington's *Up from Slavery*, Bozell makes more explicit.

Echoing populism and republicanism of the nineteenth century, Bozell portrays conservatives as potential slaves in a political system said to honor the material (as opposed to the spiritual) side of man and, under the guise of egalitarianism, to suppress individual talents, ambitions, and abilities. "The Conservative knows that to regard man as part of an undifferentiated mass is to consign him to ultimate slavery," Bozell wrote in *Conscience of a Conservative*.[92] Here liberalism is tantamount to slavery, and the impending plight of Americans enslaved by liberalism displaces the historical plight of African Americans enslaved by whites. Moreover, in comparison with the "ultimate slavery" against which the conservatives are poised, the historical plight of African Americans—who, at the time *Conscience of a Conservative* was written, were organized as never before for equal rights—is grandly diminished.

Conscience of a Conservative thus succeeds in separating a fight against slavery from the fight for civil rights or equal rights. As discussed in chapter 1 of this volume, *Conscience of a Conservative* differentiates the idea of equality from that of an egalitarian society, investing *equality* with a divine character that does not presuppose social or political equity. According to Bozell, the aim of "an egalitarian society [is] an objective that does violence both to the charter of the Republic and the laws of Nature. We are all equal in the eyes of God but we are equal *in no other respect*. Artificial devices for enforcing equality among unequal men must be rejected if we would restore that charter and honor those laws."[93] "Artificial devices for enforcing equality" refers to domestic programs perceived to smack of communism, such as the desegregation of schools that began to be implemented as a result of the 1954 decision in *Brown v. Board of Education*. Another artificial device" is "welfarism," which transforms "the individual from a dignified, industrious, self-reliant *spiritual* being into a dependent animal creature without his knowing it."[94] Equality is a matter for God alone, a matter of nature, nothing "artificial," and everything "spiritual."

Bozell's general emphasis on the spiritual in *Conscience of a Conservative* and *Triumph* paved the way for the New Right's emphasis on morality. Members of the *Triumph* staff, such as William H. Marshner, became architects of cultural conservatism, which differs from old right ideology in its most basic assumption that "traditional values are functional values." Paul Weyrich explains in an essay published in *Cultural Conservatism: Theory and Practice*, a volume edited by Marshner: "Most American conservative thought begins not with culture but with economics: if a nation has a free market economy, all will be well. Cultural conservatives believe in a free market economy, but they do not believe society is economically determined. On the contrary, unless a society's culture is sound—in our case, unless it adheres to traditional Western values—a free market will not work."[95] Privileging culture over economics is the key for Weyrich, who worked with Marshner in numerous capacities. A former journalist for the anti-abortion magazine *The Wanderer* and former assistant editor at *Triumph*, Marshner also edited *The Morality of Political Action: Biblical Foundations*, which was published by the Free Congress Research and Education Foundation, of which Weyrich was president.[96] The emphasis on morality and culture—derived in large part, if we are to take Lofton, Weyrich, Buchanan, and Edwards at their word, from the emphasis on spirituality in *Conscience of a Conservative*—is the right's answer to the left's militant resistance of the 1960s. Buchanan's praise of *Conscience of a Conservative* suggests as much: "We read it, memorized it, quoted it. . . . For those of us wandering in the arid desert of Eisenhower Republicanism, it hit like a rifle shot."[97]

This rifle shot was as politically profound as any that marked the 1960s as a militant time. But both Catholic officials and conservative leaders could not reconcile the rifle-shot impact of Bozell's political writings, which earned him his reputation as a conservative intellectual, with his pro-life militancy, which marred that reputation. Perhaps Bozell lost credibility and influence not only because he suffered from manic depression but because he embodied both the militant protester and the intellectual strategist—an amalgamation that the New Right had to separate in order to distance itself from the blue blood, Ivy League intellectual image of the old right.

What was concentrated in the operations of Brent Bozell became, during the 1970s and 1980s, dispersed among different factions of pro-life politics. As a writer and editor, Bozell possessed the intellectual acuity to shape conservative politics at a national level. As a militant protester, he foreshadowed the emergence of antigovernment disdain from a desire for traditional values and Christian politics. By portraying abortion as America's Armageddon, he deployed a narrative time that freed conservatives from fatalistic defeatism and made pro-life militancy a holy act. These elements of pro-life politics today have been successfully decentralized and dislocated among the New Right, the "radical" right, and the religious right.

Making time for pro-life action is no longer Manichean and boring. Now it is apocalyptic and explosive. And it is, significantly if not entirely, Bozell's legacy.

6

Narrating Enemies

The Jewish Doctor, the Lesbian Nurse, and the
Indeterminacy of Life

Brent Bozell's triumph over conservative apathy indicates that pro-life narrative thrives on the temporal distortions of both millennialism and postmodernism. Encompassing both chronological time and *kairos*, pro-life narrative constructs as well as reflects the decision-making process of individuals in encouraging militants, politicians, churchgoers, and other believers to *make time* for pro-life activity. Pro-life narrative produces a sense of urgency. It produces an ideology against defeatism and passivity. And it produces a formidable, widespread, multiple yet consolidated enemy: a so-called conspiracy against life. How then does it discourage those it has cast as "enemies of life" from responding as a consolidated political entity?

Pro-Life Conspiracy Theories

When it narrates abortion provision as part of a conspiracy, recent pro-life writing runs the risk of being labeled, as Bozell was labeled, paranoid. However, scholars of conspiracist thought now reject the idea that conspiracy theories are merely pathological aberrations of the paranoid mind.[1] They are, rather, manifestations of postmodern society. They are seen as a cultural and political process of identity formation and political expression. Individuals and groups striving to adapt to a world of rapidly changing economic, demographic, and social realities may rely on conspiracy theories to understand their place in society as well as their sense of self. In this way, a conspiracy theory is a narrative that permeates particular subcultures and serves to explain, however erroneously, present social conditions as the result of a conspiring elite.

Posing political conflict in terms of conspiracy theory is usually an "ideological misrecognition of power relations."[2] In the 1960s, the power relations involved in the abortion controversy were posed as a political conflict between the government's regulation of women's fertility (through abortion bans, sterilization abuse, and limited access to humane health care) and women's liberation from such reproductive control. In the 1970s, these power relations were seen as a political debate involving the rights of fetuses versus the rights of women. Since the 1980s, the power relations have been perceived as a cultural or spiritual conflict over values. According to the prevailing pro-life narrative, the conflict is apocalyptic in scope and posed between pro-life individuals, who represent Christian or family values, and antifamily, anti-Christian individuals, who represent an overwhelming satanic force or an entire "culture of death" epitomized (if not launched by) legal abortion. This last articulation of the power relations involved in abortion politics accommodates conspiracist thinking.

Obvious examples of pro-life conspiracist thinking include the Army of God letters that claimed responsibility for the Atlanta and Alabama clinic bombings and decried the New World Order. Another is John Salvi's letter from jail in which he explained his reasons for killing the two women clinic workers. Salvi's letter, rife with conspiracist thinking and encouraged perhaps by Human Life International's writings, talks about an elite, secret order poised against him. Both the Army of God and the Salvi letters are unfortunately easy to dismiss as the products of paranoid minds that have misrecognized the power relations of a political conflict and seen them, instead, as a conspiracy against life.

Such misrecognition of power relations is "articulated to but neither defining nor defined by populism, interpellating believers as 'the people' opposed to a relatively secret, elite 'power bloc.' "[3] Thus those who believe in a conspiracy against life might portray those who kill for life as men heroic enough to act on what they think "the people" really believe—that abortion is murder. Just who comprises that relatively secret elite depends on which particular version of the millennialist pro-life narrative is circulating in a given community. We have already examined several versions of the millennialist pro-life narrative and identified those who comprise the elite enemy of different pro-life communities.

For readers of Brent Bozell's *Triumph*, the secret elite is portrayed as demonic Satan worshipers who provide abortions to wage war against Christ. For readers of *Gideon's Torch*, the elite consists of gay people who convince liberals to fund late-term abortion facilities that will collect fetal tissue to be used in finding a cure for AIDS, and thereby bring about the collapse of American society. Among those who appreciate materials from Life Dynamics Incorporated, the secret elite are those affluent "Quack the Ripper" abortionists who promote an apocalyptic "culture of death" as they exploit, molest, and murder women to satisfy their greed and cover up their medical incompetence. For neo-Nazis, Christian Identity adherents, and Klansmen, the secret elite consists of Jews who have engineered legal abortion in America to destroy the white race. In Norma McCorvey's autobiography (which we examine later in this chapter), the elite consists of foreign-born abortionists who immigrate to America to get rich and simultaneously devalue Christian life. Each of these apocalyptic versions of the pro-life narrative assumes a populist stance in that it "interpellates" those opposed to abortion as "the people," specifically as God's chosen people, who consider themselves to be a persecuted minority.

At the same time, each version of the apocalyptic pro-life narrative "interpellates" certain people as the elite enemies of life. (In the context of pro-life politics, the enemies are "elite" not always in the sense that they comprise a small inner sanctum but in the sense that they hold tyrannical power.) *Interpellation* is an appropriate term to describe how pro-life millennialism narrates its enemies because it carries a sort of indictment. Interpellation is a term used to recognize the interesting process in which authoritative language calls a person into a particular situation, making that person aware of his or her status as someone subject to the law. The famous illustration of this process is a policeman calling "Hey, you!" down the street.[4] You turn around, perhaps feeling a bit guilty or wondering what has happened and if you did anything wrong. You may have done nothing wrong, but in your response to the call, you have been named as someone suspect, as someone under the law.

Another illustration of interpellation might be receiving an overdue bill in the mail, or a form letter that demands a payment you are accused of not having made. The bill or the form letter thus interpellates you as a wrongdoer, as delinquent in your financial responsibilities. Even if you have in fact paid the bill, you feel alarmed by the form letter, your emotions changing from fear that you possibly made a mistake to anger that "they" would send you this notice at all. You feel you do not deserve the notice; you do not deserve being called irresponsible. But the letter, which is authored by no one in particular, has the power to interpellate you as irresponsible or responsible, as being within the law or beyond it, as delinquent and worthy of punishment or innocent and wrongly persecuted.

Pro-life writing that narrates abortion as an apocalyptic conspiracy against life performs this same process of interpellation. Pro-life millennialism has the power to mobilize those who believe in prophecy for the "fight for life" or to indict unbelievers as violators of "God's law." How is it that the millennialist narrative encourages pro-lifers to make time for pro-life action but discourages their "enemies" from making time to oppose them? If apocalyptic culture is so prevalent that millennialism infuses secular institutions and entertainment, what keeps the narrative of abortion politics as America's Armageddon from mobilizing those who believe that abortion is a perfectly safe, sane, and moral way to terminate pregnancy? Do pro-choice advocates ever escape conventional time, slip into narrative time, harness their own sense of *kairos*, and wage an apocalyptic war against pro-life forces? Are there any pro-choice guerrillas? Any pro-choice vigilantes gunning down receptionists at pro-life offices? Any pro-choice snipers picking off parents through the kitchen windows of pro-life homes? Any pro-choice anthrax scares delivered to pro-life lobbying organizations?

These rhetorical questions contain images of terrorism that can challenge the whole idea of the power of apocalyptic narrative. If the story of abortion as apocalypse is so powerful in creating a narrative time, how does it affect those who are interpellated as the enemies of life? How does pro-life writing represent the enemies of life as a consolidated conspiracy without encouraging those people implicated as enemies to act either as New Warriors or as a consolidated political entity?

By interpellating abortion providers or pro-choice advocates as part of a conspiracy against life, pro-life writing manages to narrate the enemies of life as formidable, aggressive, and ubiquitous. At the same time, it discourages those indicted as conspiratorial "enemies" from working together. To demonstrate how this operates, it is important to back up and explore just how prevalent the idea of a "conspiracy of life" is. As I mentioned earlier, it is easy to dismiss writings by the Army of God and John Salvi as products of paranoia. But esteemed religious leaders, such as Pope John Paul II, have also relied on the language of conspiracy to promote pro-life views. What is remarkable about the 1995 papal encyclical *Evangelium Vitae* is not only its apocalyptic conspiracism but its insistence on exalting *life* even while dislocating its meaning across a multitude of theological principles and scriptural references. Life and the sanctity of life are contingently defined, despite being upheld as an absolute value.

The Indeterminacy of Life

Pro-life writing of the 1990s usually does not actually define *life* but instead presents abortion as apocalypse and the "people for life" as victims of a grand conspiracy launched by the "enemies of life." What is portrayed as an absolute value—life itself—survives as a mobilizing force only because it is defined contingently, dislocated from one definition to another in accordance with a profoundly denied relativism. We may ask what the *life* of pro-life politics represents. But this question can only generate discussion and no absolute answers. No singular meaning of life gives pro-life writing coherence or political viability. On the contrary, pro-life politics thrive on the continual displacement of the meaning of *life*. Religious discussions of abortion especially demonstrate this ambiguity.

The idea that all pro-life Christians believe in the sanctity of life, and that Christian opposition to abortion is based on this belief, is questionable. In one explanation, titled "Why Abortion Is a Religious Issue," professor of theology Stanley Hauerwas provides a succinct presentation of several religious ideas that give pro-life discussions a theological richness. This richness is jettisoned, Hauerwas implies, when life becomes the baseline assumption used to present Christians as a cohesive group. In "this secular age," Hauerwas says, religious discussions of abortion may be ignored and displaced by "the assumption that all it really amounts to is that Christians also believe in the value or sacredness of life."[5] This assumption is facile, according to Hauerwas, because

from the perspective of Christian convictions about life as the locus of God's creating and redeeming purpose, claims of life's "value" or "sacredness" are but empty abstractions. The value of life is God's value and our commitment to protect it is a form of our worship of God as a good creator and a trustworthy redeemer. Our question is not "When does life begin?" but "Who is its true sovereign?" The creation and meaningfulness of the term "abortion" gain intelligibility from our conviction that God, not man, is creator and redeemer, and thus, the Lord of life. The Christian respect for life is first of all a statement, not about life, but about God.[6]

According to Hauerwas's logic, Christian convictions and pro-life rhetoric are not necessarily compatible. In particular, reducing a religious stance against abortion to a facile belief "in the value or sacredness of life" involves a displacement of Christian convictions.

Those convictions, according to Hauerwas, include believing not in life but in divine creation, redemption, and dominion. Dominion—or the idea that God is the "true sovereign"—means that God has dominion over human and animal life because God, the so-called author of life, created it. Therefore, Hauerwas explains, "The Christian prohibition against taking life rests not on the assumption that human life has overriding value, but on the conviction that it is not ours to take."[7]

Given that this professor of theology does not believe that the idea "human life has overriding value" is at the base of a Christian anti-abortion stance, how is it that life became such an unquestionable principle? Any criticism of the term

is immediately answered by someone who connects life with right or value or sacredness and, by so doing, evokes six million Jews, or sixty million fetuses, or large numbers of Kurds and Cambodians, or even the rain forests, bugs, and grasses. The four-letter word is meaningless and loaded; it can barely be analyzed, yet it is a declaration of war.[8]

How did the word become so powerful? So unquestioned and unquestionable? How, then, has the idea of the sanctity of life evolved since the 1960s?

Early in the contemporary abortion controversy, the "sanctity of life" was discussed openly as an ethical principle needed to guard against a variety of perceived dangers endemic to the late twentieth century, when medical and military technologies could extend human influence to an unprecedented level in matters of life and death. Key among these dangers were nuclear bombs and genocide. Ethicists, theologians, and bio-medical professionals who had witnessed Hiroshima and the Holocaust were worried about how to avoid such atrocities in the future. The notion of the sanctity of life was discussed as an antidote to Hitler's "valueless life," or *lebensunwertes Leben*, as abortion became an ethical quandary for doctors and a political cause for women, who began publicly to oppose the inhumane circumstances surrounding illegal abortions. At this time, those who favored liberalized abortion laws as well as those who opposed them were discussing the sanctity of life. The stances for or against abortion law reform had not yet become polarized into the pro-life and pro-choice camps, and sanctity of life was not the intellectual or political property of any pro-life movement. In this context, the sanctity of life was discussed openly not as an absolute value but as a means of regulating the many institutions and principles to which *life* referred.

In an essay published in *Updating Life and Death: Essays in Ethics and Medicine*, Daniel Callahan lists concerns that fall under the rubric "sanctity of life." They are "(a) the survival and integrity of the human species, (b) the integrity of family lineages, (c) the integrity of bodily life, (d) the integrity of personal, mental, and emotional individuality, and (e) the integrity of personal bodily individuality."[9] *Life* is variously regarded in terms of species, family lineages, corporeality, and individuality, and the sanctity of those manifestations of life seems to depend on their integrity.

Although the commentaries on Callahan's essay are sophisticated and precise in analyzing the general discussion, none of the commenters disagrees with this list of concerns grouped under the sanctity of life. None disagrees that " 'the sanctity of life' implies a spectrum of values ranging from the preservation of the species to the inviolability of human bodies, from man in the aggregate (present and future) to man as individual (present and future)."[10] Neither Callahan nor his debaters find fault with the sanctity of life as an empty principle defined contingently according to a "spectrum of values."

On the contrary, Callahan, in attempting to establish the sanctity of life in nonreligious terms so as to expand its applicability, understands that such a principle works precisely because it is indeterminate. The sanctity of life works as an ethical principle because it defers any precise, absolute meaning. The sanctity of life "signifies a whole cluster of final meanings, each of which is related to and dependent upon the other to give it sense and significance. In a very real way, then, the principle of the sanctity of life *is* indeterminate and vague, but not meaningless for all that."[11] For Callahan, the meaningfulness of the sanctity of life lies precisely in its ability to defer to makers and evaluators of rules and regulations whatever "final meanings" they deem fit. In this way, the sanctity of life is discussed openly as an ethical principle with a procedural function—making and evaluating rules.[12] Not only does Callahan appreciate that the meaning of the sanctity of life is contingent and relative, but he endorses the indeterminacy of the sanctity of life as a political function. This is not a ploy on Callahan's part; rather, it is an accurate description of how the indeterminacy of language works on the political level—"in a very real way." This is especially true in the way that vagueness of definition allows for greater breadth of coalition.

Since the publication of Callahan's essay and the subsequent liberalization of abortion laws as a result of *Roe v. Wade*, the abortion controversy has been seen as a two-sided, polarized debate, a diametrically opposed clash of absolutes. Defenders of "choice," such as Callahan, would seldom entertain discussions of the sanctity of life because *Roe* defined *life* and *potential life* as that of the fetus, and organized opposition to legalized abortion became institutionalized as *right to life* and *pro-life*. Defenders of life have not been able politically to afford the luxury of acknowledging the indeterminacy of the sanctity of life, as Callahan, and any number of other scholars, did. They have not been so clear as Protestant theologian Paul Ramsey was when he noted that "respect for life" is derived from any number of doctrines—"whether it be the doctrine of creation, the belief that man is made in the image of God, the doctrine of God's covenantal relationship with His people or that of the doctrine of Redemption."[13]

Although in the post-*Roe* era the concept of life has been exalted as something absolute, there are in fact multiple definitions of life, all of which stem from the many different doctrines from which the sanctity of life was derived. In the 1990s, in order to argue for the use of force as a necessary tactic in opposing abortion, pro-life writing defined life in a way that is incongruent with right-to-life rhetoric. As Michael Bray's 1994 manifesto, *A Time to Kill*, makes clear, life is not defined as something human or physical. Instead, Bray criticizes "bad doctrine" and the "non-Christian influences [that] have produced modern pacifism," which have placed "an unbiblical value upon life," "in contrast to the true Life given by God in Christ."[14] Despite his earlier involvement with John O'Keefe's Pro-Life Non-Violent Action Project and the Bowie [Maryland] Right to Life Committee, Bray is adamant in distancing himself from a right-to-life rhetoric.[15] He denounces human rights as a cause that is advanced "in the name of 'ideologies' such as communism and socialism."[16] He bases his ideas, instead, on a religious idea of life: "'Life' in the Christian value system has to do with harmony with God. Christians give up this physical life to gain that Life which never ends. Consider the martyrs and the value they placed on this Life above the life of their bodies."[17] Bray's definition of life is forthright because he wants to defend those he considers martyrs of the pro-life cause. A friend of Paul Hill, Bray was arrested for bombing several clinics in 1985, which at the time was "the biggest anti-abortion bombing case the federal government had ever had, and what made it bigger was the fact that you had someone who had been a leading activist in the movement."[18] Bray's is but one of several definitions of life that permeated the movement throughout the 1980s and 1990s.

Although the definitions of life multiplied because there were many—sometimes conflicting—bases for the sanctity of life, its most common basis is assumed to come from its Catholic roots of divine dominion.[19] But in *Evangelium Vitae* (Gospel of Life), the papal encyclical distributed in 1995, God's dominion is but one of many sources for the sanctity of life. The notion of life thus becomes more indeterminate than ever, and this indeterminacy allows for vastly divergent references yet goes unacknowledged.

Although the press reported that *Evangelium Vitae* broke no new ground, the quantity and theological qualities of the meanings of life multiplied. Scholars saw the encyclical as doing more than "invoking the sanctity-of-life position," which "emphasizes God's dominion." In an unprecedented way, according to James F. Keenan, a professor of moral theology at Weston Jesuit School of Theology, "something terribly distinctive about human life emerges" in *Evangelium Vitae*.[20]

> The Pope has vested "life" with more intrinsic theological authority than ever. But what does he mean by "life"? The term is fluid. More to the point, at times he borders on vitalism, the doctrine that life is the highest good. . . . In the encyclical, because of the variety of scriptural texts invoked, "life" has sometimes a sacramental, a Hebraic, a christological, an eschatological, and even sometimes a very physical meaning. But those many meanings cannot be suddenly conflated, for "life" in these very different instances is nothing more than a homonym.[21]

The "many meanings" that a professor of theology can detect but the mainstream media cannot are not, in fact, "suddenly conflated"; they are constantly dislocated from one scriptural site to another. The encyclical *employs* the indeterminacy of the term *life*.

The encyclical exalts life even as it constantly defers its final meaning across a stunning array of theological principles and scriptural references.

The encyclical defers and dislocates precisely what it represents, and its indeterminate use of the term is not necessarily an indication of the pope's "problematic" and "unsophisticated" use of scripture. Nor does it indicate a papal intention to pull a fast one on an even less sophisticated public by using one word to refer to many ideas.[22] Rather, it is an indication of how pro-life politics generally thrive on the multiple, contingently defined meanings of life.

It also indicates how—in the particular context of the 1990s, when killing for life occurred—that constant displacement works toward a specific articulation of abortion as apocalypse. Although Keenan overlooks the import of *not* defining life in specific terms in the encyclical, he points out how the many references to and meanings of *life* reveal a change in papal articulation that not only is significant theologically but also has political implications.

The move that Keenan detects is a shift toward creation theology, which is a departure from an earlier encyclical, *Humanae Vitae*, in which the sanctity of life is secured to the idea of God's dominion. "Thus," according to Keenan, "in the *Humanae Vitae* text, life is sacred because its owner, God, willed it so; like other objects that God owned and sanctified (the marital bond, the temple), life could not be violated. The sacredness rested not necessarily in anything intrinsic to the marital bond, the temple, or life, but, rather, singularly in the claim of God, who is definitively extrinsic to bonds, temples, and human lives."[23] In fact, Keenan continues, "for the first time since the manualist era, we have reasoned argumentation that places the God's-dominion position into the context of Creation," and specifically into the context of "the Yahwist account of Creation," in which God breathes life into Adam. In this invasive account of creation, life becomes embodied and internal, and not merely bestowed on man. According to Keenan, a ramification of this move is not only that physical, human life is "accorded near sacramental status" but also that this unprecedentedly exalted physical human life is intrinsic, based on the "intrinsic character of human life."[24] The sanctity of life, according to *Evangelium Vitae*, is not, Joseph Boyle agrees, "in extrinsic relationships, such as that of divine dominion."[25] What are the political implications of this shift?

On one hand, this move seems to democratize the dignity and inviolability of life: the encyclical proclaims that "the Gospel of life is for the whole of human society." Life is, as Alan C. Mitchell explains, "not for believers alone." Yet Mitchell is puzzled by the "eschatological" implication of the encyclical's proclamation and concedes, "it is difficult to see how the

Gospel of life can be shared with nonbelievers."[26] The apparent democratization of the inviolability of life is undermined in this turn to creation and eschatology, specifically in what Mitchell sees as the encyclical's emphasis on the "eschatological benefits of becoming a believer." On the other hand, the political implication can be seen as emphasizing creationism and eschatology. Consequently, the encyclical resonates with Protestant millennialism while maintaining its supreme Catholicism. This becomes more apparent as we explore how the encyclical generally is "apocalyptic in tone," as John Conley notes, and how its conclusion is "pointedly drawn only from the Book of Revelation."[27]

More than merely referring to apocalypse or delivering an apocalyptic tone, *Evangelium Vitae* represents abortion as the end times and reinscribes the pro-life fight as a prophetic millennialist conflict. In chapter 4 I analyzed the novel *Gideon's Torch* to define what that pro-life narrative is: a dualist conflict resulting from the powerful forces of darkness arrayed against Christian light and life—a conflict sure to pique God's ultimate, apocalyptic wrath. Like *Gideon's Torch*, *Evangelium Vitae* poses pro-life politics in apocalyptic terms. Despite the fact that *Gideon's Torch* clearly emanates from a premillennialist Protestant mind-set and *Evangelium Vitae* espouses the Roman Catholicism of Pope John Paul II, both texts portray abortion as a sign of the times, which are characterized by an unprecedented struggle between two diametrically opposed forces. Both the novel and the encyclical describe this struggle in terms of willful and well-funded attacks—not only on life but also on what the encyclical calls believers or "the people of life and for life."

The enormity of the enemy, that is, those against the "people of life," is overemphasized in *Evangelium Vitae* and is seen in relation to the end of an era, the end of the twentieth century. Resonating with the fundamentalist *Whatever Happened to the Human Race?* as well as *Gideon's Torch*, the encyclical situates the reader in the future, looking back: "The twentieth century will have been an era of massive attacks on life, an endless series of wars and a continual taking of innocent human life. . . . we are in fact faced by an objective 'conspiracy against life.'"[28] As in *Gideon's Torch*, this conspiracy against life is portrayed by *Evangelium Vitae* in dualist terms of light and darkness. From the encyclical:

> In the early afternoon of Good Friday, "there was darkness over the
> whole land . . . while the sun's light failed; and the curtain of the
> temple was torn in two" (Lk 23:44, 45). This is the symbol of a
> great cosmic disturbance and a massive conflict between the forces

of good and the forces of evil, between life and death. Today we too find ourselves in the midst of a dramatic conflict between the "culture of death" and the "culture of life." (50)

And again, in another place:

This situation, with its lights and shadows, ought to make us all fully aware that we are facing an enormous and dramatic clash between good and evil, death and life, the 'culture of death' and the 'culture of life.' We find ourselves not only 'faced with' but necessarily 'in the midst of' this conflict. (28)

Thus *Evangelium Vitae* and *Gideon's Torch*, both published in 1995, tell basically the same story: Christians are up against a "massive," "cosmic," and "enormous" movement of evil. It is a conflict between a "conspiracy against life" and those few true believers who will not be duped by forces of darkness. Hardly the product of a paranoid individual, the encyclical is an institutional narrative that portrays the conspiracy as an apocalyptic battle.

Scholars assessing this "culture of death versus culture of life" dichotomy as the central theme of the encyclical do not recognize how it contributes to and promotes the idea of abortion as a millennialist conflict. James F. Childress points out that "cultures don't struggle with each other; instead people with certain beliefs, values, norms, and so forth, struggle with each other." Thus Childress is puzzled by how the encyclical's "language suggests a kind of dualistic, almost Manichean, view of cultures and their warfare as objective reality."[29] What marks the encyclical as espousing a specifically millennialist conflict—and not just a Manichean conflict—is the same thing that confirms it as an important anti-abortion tract.

The centrality of abortion to this conflict between the cultures of life and death is clear in the encyclical's discussion of the advent of a new world—as it relates to the first advent of Christ. Veering away from the fundamentalist reading of Revelation that prophesies particular events leading up to a specific thousand-year rule, the encyclical nevertheless relies on Revelation to announce that Christ, as "Life's own Champion, slain, yet lives to reign." *Evangelium Vitae* is otherwise rife with millennial expectation for a " 'new Jerusalem,' that new world towards which human history is travelling," in which "death shall be no more." Mary, as virgin mother of Jesus, is heralded as "bright dawn of the new world," as the one to whom Catholics "entrust the cause of life" (105).

This emphasis on Mary, however, is understood in light of the Gospel of Luke, in which the pregnant virgin visits her elder kinswoman Elizabeth. Despite her old age, Elizabeth, like Mary, is miraculously pregnant. When Mary arrives, Elizabeth feels that the "babe leaped in her womb." Years later that leaping babe, who is John, baptizes Mary's son, Jesus. In the context of abortion, the encyclical uses this interaction between Mary and Elizabeth to demonstrate how they, as women, may only "speak of grace," but it is through their unborn babies, namely, Jesus and John, that grace is "made effective from within." Portraying Jesus and John as just "two children whom [Mary and Elizabeth] are carrying in the womb" shifts this story from being one about Mary or Jesus to a story about the unborn. The encyclical quotes Saint Ambrose to argue that it "is precisely the children who reveal the advent of the Messianic age: in their meeting, the redemptive power of the presence of the Son of God among men first becomes operative" (45). The unborn—not Mary or Elizabeth—are responsible for enabling redemptive grace in relation to the first advent of Christ, the initial advent. To Protestant readers, the encyclical may imply that the unborn enable redemptive grace again as we face a second advent, the second coming of Christ, who, as "Life's own Champion [is] slain, yet lives to reign" (105).

With the story of Mary as the mother of the unborn Messiah and the "bright dawn of the new world," the encyclical appeals to blatantly apocalyptic Catholics in the Marianist subculture, while bridging a gap to Protestant millennialists.[30] In effect, as with Protestant, organizational, and militant pro-life texts, the encyclical promotes a besieged mentality and an absolutist position against abortion based on the idea that abortion is part of an apocalyptic war. In addition, the encyclical emphasizes not only the unprecedented culmination of so-called attacks on life but also a "broad consensus" that puts believers in the minority. "Humanity today offers us a truly alarming spectacle, if we consider not only how extensively attacks on life are spreading but also their unheard-of numerical proportion, and the fact that they receive widespread and powerful support from a broad consensus on the part of society, from widespread legal approval and the involvement of certain sectors of the health-care personnel" (17). The argument that a majority of people are pro-life has lost all effectiveness. Emphasizing that pro-lifers are in the minority is not a concession. It is offered as proof that the world has spun apocalyptically out of control—a situation that is "truly alarming" to true believers.

In employing the indeterminacy of the term *life* and emphasizing apocalyptic concepts, the encyclical multiplies and expands the meanings of life and the applications of the sanctity of life in a way that bridges as many religious differences as possible. The effect, if not the intention, of the encyclical may be to bring as many sheep into the pro-life fold as possible. *Life* has served in this ecumenical capacity before as the object of a new science called biology: "For the academies flourishing during the first decades of the nineteenth century, 'life' was a welcome postulate for overcoming the division of their members among mechanists, vitalists, and materialists."[31] Likewise, *life* functions politically in today's abortion controversy by deferring scriptural and other definitions so that denominational differences can be overcome. Pro-lifers need not agree on what life can mean. In fact it is advantageous to withhold such discussion. For example, at the outset of the Moral Majority, members from many varieties of religious traditions "concluded it is better to argue about denominational differences at another time."[32] This deferral benefited both the New Right, for whom the Moral Majority was an electoral vehicle, and pro-life politics, which grew exponentially with New Right leadership. Settling on one of "many meanings of life" in *Evangelium Vitae* would have depleted the strength of pro-life politics.

Even as it multiplies the meaning of life, the encyclical narrates abortion provision as part of a conspiracy. In this way, the encyclical is "articulated to but neither defining nor defined by populism," as Fenster says, in "interpellating believers as 'the people.' "[33] Insofar as it deploys a narrative of apocalypticism, *Evangelium Vitae* interpellates believers as besieged by enormous, cosmic, anti-life if not outright anti-Christ forces.

But who are those operating the siege? Who are the supposed conspirators against life?

Jews and Lesbians Conspiring

Pro-life millennialism insists that the enemies of, and attacks on, life are multiple and dispersed yet consolidated. They constitute, says the pope, a conspiracy against life. How does pro-life writing represent the enemies and attacks on life as a consolidated whole without encouraging those implicated as enemies to act as a consolidated political entity?

The answer is pro-life writing divides the enemies of life even as it interpellates them as subjects under God's law. Whereas *Evangelium Vitae* discusses only "certain sectors of the health-care personnel" and otherwise leaves the enemies of life unspecified, other pro-life writings precisely name these health care personnel. They are the Jewish doctor and the lesbian nurse.

The presumed Jewishness of abortion doctors is stressed in many pro-life circles. As we saw in chapter 4, a pro-life sniper shot Dr. Barnett Slepian in a way that highlighted his Jewishness as a factor in the crime: Slepian had just returned to his home from synagogue; his picture was found with the words "killer" and "Jew" scrawled on his face. From chapter 1, we also know that some pro-life groups see abortion as the real Holocaust, conducted against "Christian life itself" by a Dr. Herod with stereotypically Semitic features. In addition, a group that calls itself the "largest pro-life organization in the world," Human Life International (HLI), is notorious for arguing that abortionists are predominantly Jews.

HLI's founder, Paul Marx, insists in several publications dating back to the 1970s that opponents of abortion should "note the large number of abortionists . . . and pro-abortion medical professors who are Jewish."[34] In "Pro-Abortion Jews and the New Holocaust," Marx performs an anti-Semitic reversal similar to that seen in *The Real Holocaust*, in which he suggests that Jews are engineering legalized abortion in America.[35] In Marx's first book, *The Death Peddlers*, his anti-Semitism and millennialism are unconcealed. Abortionists are not only predominantly Jewish but they are demonic and apocalyptic: "Much will depend on whether society can be awakened to the nefarious, satanic dishonesties of the death peddlers." He concludes, "it is already late in the day for those who love life."[36] When HLI convened in Minneapolis–St. Paul in 1997, pro-choice activists convinced Archbishop Harry J. Flynn of the Twin Cities to refuse to say mass for the group because of its history of anti-Semitic portrayals of abortion providers.[37]

The Jewish doctor is, in these cases, interpellated as a leading conspirator against life. And he has a partner in his conspiracy: his nurse, assistant, or business associate, who is consistently seen as lesbian. This pairing is an adaptation of what scholar Linda Kintz calls the Jew/dyke. A staple in millennialist conspiracy theories such as those spun by Texe Marrs, the Jew/dyke "produces a terrifyingly monstrous and omnipotent She/He who controls the new world order."[38] Using examples from Marrs's book *Big Sister Is Watching You*, Kintz explains that the Jew/dyke represents "a feminist conspiracy of manly women and unmanly men."[39] Despite variations of the Jew/dyke, this remarkable pairing denaturalizes the categories of man and woman to present a grotesque reversal of the Christian heterosexual reproductive unit. Representing such a reversal, this pairing is not seen as one involving complementary poles of humanity—which man and woman traditionally are presumed to be—but as an omnipotent gender-bender that functions as both anti-humanity and anti-Christ in right-wing millennialism. Although Kintz goes on to link the Jew/dyke ideologically with the "deeply symbolic threat of abortion," she does not discuss how pro-life writing directly recycles the Jew/dyke as doctor and nurse.

Mark Crutcher's Life Dynamics Incorporated (LDI), described in detail in chapter 2, is by far the most prodigious manufacturer of the Jewish doctor/lesbian nurse stereotype. In LDI's first episode of its video magazine *LifeTalk*, the lesbian nurse figures more prominently than does the Jewish doctor. Unlike Texe Marrs's book, however, which only *codes* aggressive women as lesbians, *LifeTalk* freely presents nontraditional women as lesbians—no need to code them. For example, the following dialogue between Dzintra Tuttle, Mark Crutcher's assistant anchor on the video magazine, and Kelly, an undercover "spy" for LDI, clearly paints women working in abortion clinics as lascivious lesbians. Kelly, whose face is hidden and whose voice and gender are disguised, details his/her experiences working in abortion clinics:

DZINTRA: What about, you mentioned in a previous conversation, the attitude of a lot of the lesbian employees?
KELLY: Right. That had a lot of [clinic] staff concerned. Once the patient was unconscious, lying on a table, some of the women would make comments basically on the genitalia area: Um. Nice tattoo. Or: This one looks really nice, what do you think?
DZINTRA: So they were just being generally degrading to the women?
KELLY: Very degrading to the women that were in there.
DZINTRA: And this is while the women were unconscious?
KELLY: Right. While they're unconscious, while they didn't know what was going on.
DZINTRA: So these employees are walking around looking at the patients . . .
KELLY: Right. They were walking around talking to them. There's even been episodes where phone numbers were taken off the charts and people would give them a call weeks down the road to ask them out for drinks. It was not uncommon for women—or men in the clinic—to hit on these women for dates.

This dialogue is so important that it is placed at the end of the interview. It is purposefully edited to leave the viewer with the specter of lascivious lesbians.

Crutcher's *LifeTalk* show is a toned-down video version of the claims he makes in a book titled *Lime 5*. In both the LDI video and publication, he asserts that women are not only "degraded" in abortion clinics but sexually molested. Indeed, he attempts to channel the residual anger and historical residue of any actual mistreatment of women by the medical establishment into pro-life disgust and/or titillation. But the goal of portraying clinic workers as lascivious lesbians is not simply titillation or defamation.

The goal is to interpellate clinic workers as subjects under the law. To this end, the stereotyping becomes part of political strategy to criminalize reproductive health care workers—not for their supposed sexual preferences or ethnic identities but for their conspiratorial attacks on life. In addition to the abortion malpractice suits and proposals for guerrilla legislation that Crutcher details in *Firestorm* (discussed in chap. 2), Crutcher launched a huge campaign to "expose" abortion providers who supposedly were harvesting "body parts" from otherwise "perfectly healthy babies" in women's wombs. Before anyone could sue those lascivious lesbian nurses or Jewish doctors, Life Dynamics first had to interpellate those creatures into existence and establish their crimes against life.

Mirroring precisely the fictional scenario of *Gideon's Torch*, LDI suggested (through a series of reports and interviews during 1999–2000) that selling "baby parts" for profit to researchers of fatal diseases was the "hidden truth behind the 'partial birth' abortion controversy."[40] As one journalist reported, Crutcher posed his own questions only to answer them: "Why do pro-aborts fight so hard to keep them?" he asked, referring to late-term abortions, the banning of which was overturned by the courts. "This is about maximizing profits. First you sell the woman an abortion. Then you turn around and sell the dead baby you take out of her. But you have to take it out whole or you don't have anything to sell."[41] This preposterous scenario captured the imagination of executives at the nighttime news show *20/20*, which ran a supposed exposé of the trafficking in fetal parts the evening before a congressional hearing on the subject in March 2000. The show—which featured an apparently hidden-camera interview with a profit-driven doctor who "harvests" and sells products of abortion—went better than the hearings.

During the hearings the man who had appeared as the doctor in the televised video exposé was not present or identified. However, the supposed eyewitness to the horrors of the abortion "industry," Dean Alberty, "recanted most of his testimony, explaining that he had told [LDI] what they wanted to hear in exchange for money. In addition, the shadowy figure featured in an infamous and widely circulated video known as 'the Kelly tape,' who says she is afraid for her life after witnessing a doctor drown aborted twins in a steel pan (a detail that turned up in Alberty's Congressional testimony), is now thought to be Crutcher's wife."[42]

Alberty's decision not to commit perjury was an enormous blow to LDI's credibility. But the political strategy of outlawing fetal tissue research—and encouraging the criminalization of workers in the reproductive health care field who might directly or indirectly aid in that research—proceeded. Mere days after the congressional hearings, legislation to ban fetal tissue research was introduced into the state legislatures of Missouri, Kansas, Nebraska, and Colorado.[43]

That the Kelly interview is featured on *LifeTalk* and otherwise circulated, ostensibly documenting the lascivious lesbian clinic workers and the money-hungry abortion doctors who supposedly kill for profit, suggests that the pairing is significant. But unlike the lesbians who are blatantly discussed on *LifeTalk*, the abortion doctors must only be coded as Jews—a precaution that results from LDI having been heavily criticized for its portrayal of abortion doctors as stereotypical Jews in their "joke books"—titled *Bottom Feeder* and *Quack the Ripper*—which "lampoon" abortionists. In the first episode of *LifeTalk*, doctors are repeatedly mentioned as getting rich off of "killing babies." Elsewhere, LDI claims that "26% of all doctors who perform abortion[s] are Jewish[:] an assertion that a spokesperson for Planned Parenthood has called ludicrous."[44] Consistent with the populism of pro-life conspiracism, the doctor who appears in the undercover video exposé of "baby-parts marketing" is extraordinarily corpulent and affluent. Instead of appearing Jewish, the man is black.

In fact, the man has a curious resemblance to an African American doctor who, several months later, was indicted on charges related to his practice of providing late-term abortions. James Pendergraft sued the Florida county of Marion, the city of Ocala, and some local officials when they refused to allow him to hire off-duty policemen for added clinic security against persistent protesters. Pendergraft had good reason to increase security because his clinic had encountered enormous opposition from the predominantly pro-life community even before it opened. In fact, the last abortion clinic to serve the vicinity had been "burned to the ground in 1989 and no one was ever charged" with the crime.[45] A meeting to settle Pendergraft's lawsuit, arranged by the county attorney and "surreptitiously taped by the FBI," involved discussing if and how much the county would be willing to pay should Pendergraft concede to the pressure to close his clinic and sell the building. Frustrated with the price offered by the county attorney, which was much too low even to "cover Pendergraft's initial investment in the clinic building," Pendergraft indicated that he would be happy to forego the sale altogether and take the case to trial. "Let the jury decide; the facts are the facts," he said on tape. Then he observed what this might mean financially for local government: "We will bankrupt the county." This phrase caused his demise. He was indicted and convicted for extortion (among other charges) by the federal government, sentenced to four years in jail, and fined $25,000.

In a style epitomized by LDI materials, Pendergraft was interpellated as a kind of "Jewish" doctor: greedy, false, and reprehensible in his ethnic/racial ways. A pro-choice advocate who attended the trial from start to finish recognized that "the prosecution portrayed Pendergraft the way they like to portray abortion providers—as this money-grubbing doctor who doesn't care about women."[46] This portrayal, so consistent with materials distributed by LDI, a so-called clearinghouse of educational materials, was not mere coincidence. LDI itself was probably not behind Pendergraft's prosecution, but local Florida pro-life efforts clearly have thrived because of technical assistance from national pro-life organizations. For one Florida pro-choice attorney, the increased role of national right-wing organizations and foundations in the state during the 1990s was undeniable. It "was so easy for me to see. Bills that were filed in the mid-eighties clearly showed no understanding of the [abortion] procedure, no understanding of women's physiology. They were dumb and easy to challenge. By the mid-nineties, we were seeing boiler plate stuff. That was going on everywhere. They were not only being given tighter language for bills restricting abortion, but [also] they were being given really good talking points."[47] One would presume that such talking points did not include some remarks made during Pendergraft's trial. The key prosecutor "described Pendergraft as having 'shucked and jived' on the witness stand."[48]

By portraying abortion providers as shucking and jiving African Americans or greedy Jews, whose assistants are lascivious lesbians, recent pro-life writing indicts particular groups without bringing them together. In fact, these portrayals may deepen tensions among or within the groups. One example of this infighting is the result of efforts by Janet Folger, a woman who successfully led the campaign to ban late-term abortions in Ohio. Before pro-life groups settled on the term *partial birth* during attempts to ban abortion on the national level, this early pro-life campaign featured the more graphic term *brain suction abortion*. Because of this appellation, the strategy of interpellation worked. Once named, once established through language, any number of late-term procedures could be labeled a crime and doctors could be called criminals. The "brain suction abortion" was named, morally condemned, and legally banned in Ohio.[49]

Likewise, Folger's subsequent campaign highlighted a key term—*ex-gay*—both to indict a particular group and to raise suspicion, not solidarity, among the members. The term, circulated via Folger's 1998 newspaper ad campaign aimed at "ex-gays," was not one Folger had invented. The ads, however, brought unprecedented national attention to a whole "ex-gay movement," comprised of organizations that seek, through Christian "therapy," to convert gay people from their homosexual "lifestyle" to a new heterosexual *life*. Although studies show that these efforts at conversion fail miserably, ex-gays in Folger's ads claimed to have "overcome" homosexuality.[50] The campaign featured statements by the "former lesbian" and current wife and mother Anne Paulk, recording artists Angie and Debbie Winans, Senator Trent Lott, and football star Reggie White. White, who is black and heterosexual, had earlier received media attention for publicly calling homosexuality a sin.

According to Willa J. Taylor, chair of the National Black Lesbian and Gay Leadership Forum, featuring Reggie White in the ex-gay campaign was a tactic intended to divide the black community. "Reggie White's quote saying he has been called a 'nigger' by gay activists seems a despicable attempt to obscure the homophobia in this ad campaign by playing the ultimate race card. Why is the religious right—which is predominantly white—using black stars and spokespersons to spew its antigay rhetoric in the press? This is just the Right's latest outrageous attempt to split the black community along gay and straight lines."[51] Splitting the black community surely may indeed be in the interest of the religious right, as Taylor says.

But the ex-gay campaign cannot be further characterized as the political stratagem of divide and conquer. The religious right, and pro-life ideology in particular, has too much at stake in presenting a multifaceted, enormous conspiracy against life to actually "conquer" any particular community or group. A journalist's description of a 1997 gathering of Washington, D.C., conservatives illustrates how the ex-gay campaign opens up opportunities to promote apocalyptic fears. Among attendees at the conference was Bill Kristol and "a variety of clergy members and therapists who advocated a spiritual and psychoanalytical 'cure' for homosexuals. One speaker, a priest, described homosexuality as a 'history-limiting horizon of a sterile worldview divorced from the promise and peril of successor generations.' Another speaker decried legal contraception and abortion as the 'homosexualization of heterosexual sex,' and bemoaned that nonprocreative trends among white Europeans was leading to 'race death.' "[52] No Klan rally, no Christian Identity militia meeting, no neo-Nazi website, no extremist cell, this gathering demonstrated the same anxiety over the "promise and peril" of white progeny, those Euro-American "successor generations" that the unborn has come to represent to the so-called radical right. According to combined anti-gay and anti-abortion assumptions, gay people are a threat to the Euro-American "race." And they are essentially enemies of life, if we extend the logic articulated in one of Folger's ads: "Calling homosexual behavior sin is not anti-gay, it's pro-life."[53]

Promoting infighting among the so-called enemies of life is, as Taylor says, a matter of a political split. It is divisive politics, but it is not a divide-and-conquer routine. Promoting infighting works hand in hand with promoting a fear about the multiplying attacks on life, as Folger's other work demonstrates. Folger "has traveled to churches and conferences presenting a seminar and slide show on 'the assault against Christians.'" The effect if not the purpose of her work is not to save babies or gays but to capitalize on the fear of a conspiracy against Christian life. She is, as Ralph Reed says, an "ideological entrepreneur."[54]

Folger's two campaigns—the creation and then banning of "brain suction" abortions, and the interpellation and then "curing" of gays—constitute perhaps a paradigmatic entrepreneurship of pro-life ideology, embodying as they do the double whammy of abortion and homosexuality, which causes infighting among opponents of pro-life politics. Nowhere is that double whammy as concentrated as in the pairing of the Jewish doctor and lesbian nurse, a divided doppelganger, a twinned evil concentrated yet split apart.[55]

One lesson to glean from the Jewish doctor/lesbian nurse then is not simply that pro-life writing scapegoats or demonizes non-Christians or gay people (although this is difficult to deny). More precisely, pro-life writing actually constructs the legal subjects it appears only to represent. The "ex-gay" and the "partially born" exist first in pro-life writing. The creation of the term *ex-gay* precedes the existence of those who identify themselves not only as persons with a history of homosexual practice but as "ex-gay" men or women. In the same way, the creation of the term *partial birth abortion* precedes the identification of any medical or legal professional as an opponent of partial birth abortions or as one who wants to indict others as defenders of partial birth. In similar vein, it took two decades of writing about an abortion holocaust before Paul Marx could actually convene "abortion holocaust survivors" in 1992.[56] Likewise, pro-life writing proliferated the idea of the Jewish doctor before Pendergraft could be brought to trial and indicted in the way that he was.

None of this, however, is to deny that there are in fact Jews who perform abortions—Dr. Slepian died because of it. Neither can we deny that there are in fact some unethical providers in the reproductive health care field who should be prosecuted.[57] It would also be a mistake to deny the existence of lesbian employees in clinics that offer abortion. But these facts do not substantiate the wholesale interpellation of abortion providers as blood-lusty, "money-grubbing" villains or of clinic staff as lascivious, molesting perverts who relish their conspiratorial role in spurring the apocalyptic decline of the West, the white race, Christianity, or America.

Norma McCorvey's latest autobiography is our final example of pro-life writing as millennialist narrative that portrays an apocalyptic conspiracy against life. McCorvey, the plaintiff Jane Roe of *Roe v. Wade*, had remained mostly anonymous as the key litigant who had made *Roe v. Wade* arguable. The pro-choice movement had never embraced her as a hero, and she only started to receive publicity in 1989 when she decided to defend "her law" by participating in a pro-choice march on Washington designed as a show of strength against the impending *Webster* decision.

Her first co-authored autobiography, *I Am Roe* (1994), presents the standard pro-choice history of how abortion was legalized, weaving through McCorvey's personal story the social and legal developments that led to the 1973 Supreme Court decision.[58] Her second co-authored autobiography, *Won by Love* (1997), chronicles McCorvey's conversion to born-again Christianity and pro-life ideology.[59] There are few stylistic similarities between the two books, which suggests that the co-authors freely interpreted a dictated tale. *Won by Love* is an exemplary pro-life text that prominently features the Jewish doctor/lesbian nurse—with a twist. It interpellates the doctor as a foreign-born abortionist and the nurse as an ex-lesbian.

Jane Roe, Ex-Lesbian

The lesbian nurse can be converted. This is the moral of the story of *Won by Love*. The questions of just who is a lesbian and what constitutes lesbianism are profoundly begged, however. Instead of simply denouncing McCorvey's lesbian history and pronouncing Jane Roe dead, *Won by Love* converts them. McCorvey becomes Miss Norma, a name provided by Operation Rescue leader Flip Benham, who baptized her as a pro-life Christian in a swimming-pool-media-splash in 1996. The only way Miss Norma retains her identity as Jane Roe is by narrating Jane Roe as an ex-lesbian. Whereas *I Am Roe* conveys McCorvey's troubled journey in accepting her historical identity as Jane Roe, *Won by Love* presents this "sinful" acceptance as a matter of "coming out."

Appropriating the well-known phrase that expresses the often risky process of publicly acknowledging one's gay identity, *Won by Love* characterizes McCorvey's participation in the April 1989 march for reproductive freedom in Washington, D.C., as "Jane Roe Comes Out" (23). In this way, Jane Roe of *Roe v. Wade* is interpellated as homosexual. The female equivalent to John Doe, Jane Roe is a legal pseudonym meant to obscure the plaintiff's identity, in the case of *Roe v. Wade*, but in time Jane Roe came to represent all women who seek abortion. Implicitly, then, all women seeking abortions are homosexual. Saying that "Jane Roe comes out" is congruent with saying that "abortion is the homosexualization of the heterosexual act" because it does not result in procreation. But once Miss Norma is named and baptized, Jane Roe is an ex-lesbian and ex-"icon" of the pro-choice movement. Coming out is redefined as being born again.

The fact that Norma McCorvey has lived with and loved Connie Gonzales since the early 1970s adds depth to this idea of Jane Roe having a lesbian history. In *Won by Love*, McCorvey rejects her lesbianism as well as her support for reproductive freedom: "Some years ago, Connie and I had been lovers, but our relationship had been completely platonic since 1992, though we still shared a home. To be honest, I had grown weary of the homosexual lifestyle. Connie and I had been friends before we ever became lovers, and now that I was 'grown up' and no longer worried about getting pregnant by another man, I simply had no desire to continue a sexual relationship" (10). A fear of pregnancy is later elaborated as the reason for McCorvey's lesbianism. "As I mentioned before, I had ended my lesbian relationship with Connie a couple of years earlier. In fact, the reason I had adopted the lesbian lifestyle was in large part because I had experienced so much trouble with men. It should be obvious to any straight-thinking person that most 'lesbians' don't experience three problem pregnancies, as I had. But the truth is, I finally got so frustrated with men that I thought, *At least with women, I can't get pregnant*" (133). Thus, lesbianism (not unlike abortion, as pro-life ideology sees it) is presented as an immature, inadequate, and sinful response to the challenges of heterosexuality and its potential consequences for women, that is, motherhood. But McCorvey never denounces her love for Connie, and they live together still. One could argue that McCorvey is ambiguous or disingenuous in this denunciation of the "homosexual lifestyle" but not the same-sex love that she and Gonzales evidently share.

More to the point, it is important to see *Won by Love* as another text in the canon of pro-life writing that perpetuates the theme of the Jewish doctor and lesbian nurse, and variations thereof. McCorvey, no longer committed to lesbian sexuality (the love between McCorvey and Gonzales notwithstanding) or abortion rights, in *Won by Love* presents Jane Roe as an ex-lesbian and attests to the depravity of the lascivious lesbian committed to abortion rights. McCorvey also provides an insider's story of the so-called abortion industry, which although autobiographical, conforms to the conventions of millennialist narratives and interpellates the enemies of life as lesbians, Jews, people of color, and foreigners.

Details of the coming out of Jane Roe as an ex-lesbian and former enemy of life are almost self-consciously consistent with the stock plots of apocalyptic and millennialist popular fiction. *Won by Love* juggles the elements of realism and the supernatural in a way that invokes popular apocalyptic fiction as well as the classic conversion narrative. This no doubt would appeal to readers of other titles published by the same press, the Christian publishing house of Thomas Nelson Publishers, which has also produced millennialist novels such as Larry Burkett's *The Illuminati* (1991) and, through its Word Publishing division, *Gideon's Torch*. Mark Fenster succinctly articulates the problem faced by Burkett's novel and similar fiction when he asks, "How can realistic naturalism, human agency, and narrative closure—so central to the structure of popular fiction—be achieved within a narrative structured around an apocalyptic belief in the supremacy of the spiritual, a belief that denies the possibility of realism, humanism, and human triumph?"[60] *Won by Love* faces a similar problem as Miss Norma undergoes her conversion. How can the supernatural be incorporated into the tale of Jane Roe if it is to be seen as a realistic autobiography and a plausible insider's exposé of the abortion "industry"?

The answer is to invoke the supernatural as something familiar to us all, because it is part of popular culture. Thus, as Miss Norma confronts the supernatural spirituality of what she only heretofore has seen "on those late-night religious television shows," her narrative cites familiar novels.

At the end of the service, the pastor called for people to come forward to receive prayer. I watched a middle-aged gentleman go forward, fall to the ground, and start twitching like he was having cardiac arrest. . . . *He's gonna die!* I shouted to myself. *He's gonna die, right here in church!* But nobody around him moved. Everybody acted like this was normal, so I suddenly felt abnormal for being so alarmed.

I couldn't take it anymore. "I gotta get out of here," I whispered to Flip, then bolted out the back door.

I didn't stop until I reached a tree that was a block away. It was not enough just to be out of the church; I wanted off the property! At the time, I was addicted to Dean Koontz and Stephen King horror novels, and every plot came sailing back into my mind. (131)

Later Miss Norma nervously goes to church again, this time searching the skies for fire and preparing for the apocalyptic events featured in popular culture: "We sat down in chairs. *Okay, when is the ceiling coming down? I thought. When will the walls start to crumble? The glass is going to start shooting out any second now. I just know it*" (158).

Instead of these events, she experiences the supernatural spirituality that, by comparison, seems real. The pastor's "words burned their way into [her] soul" and, at the suggestion that she approach the altar to meet Jesus, "Time seemed to stop." At this point, she sees the Spirit of God and feels "something 'swooshy' inside, like something flew right through me." The guilt she feels for her "role in legalizing abortion" becomes overwhelming and she tells herself, "*Okay, Norma, this is your judgment day*" (160). Thus, Miss Norma internalizes the end times within her own body, and *Won by Love* transfers the apocalyptic images of popular culture to the realm of "real" supernatural happenings, that is, those produced through born-again Christianity.

Before she is born again, Miss Norma can explain the supernatural only as dementia—that is, paranoia induced by the so-called horrors of working in the abortion clinic. She hears the mysterious sounds of children running and laughing when no children are present; she dismisses the sounds as evidence that she is losing her mind. This prevalent theme—of clinic workers besieged by mental illness because of the "horrifying" nature of their work as abortion providers—is a staple in LDI's *LifeTalk* series. *Won by Love* repeatedly states that clinic workers are driven to drink, drugs, and gallows humor in order "to cope with what everyone intuitively knew were inhumane conditions" (122). It turns populist in its indictment of the reproductive health care professions as it zeros in on the abortion doctor.

The abortion provider in *Won by Love*, named Arnie, is not only foreign born but decidedly un-American, unfaithful to his wife, greedy, cowardly, and inconsiderate of his staff. "Though Arnie made a very good living, the money was not passed down, believe me," says Miss Norma, who takes offense at his salary when she is paid only six dollars an hour (112). Moreover, this populist characterization of the abortion provider is fused with anti-immigrant sentiment: "Arnie is a small man of foreign descent. It's a closely guarded fact," purports *Won by Love*, "that a disproportionate number of abortion doctors are actually from other countries—foreigners who perceive that our lax abortion laws create a tremendous moneymaking opportunity." Arnie symbolizes the idea of abortion providers as the "bottom-feeders" of society. "Foreign-born abortionists don't have to worry about acquiring bedside manners. They don't even have to talk to the patients if they don't want to, so it's a practice ready-made for someone who simply wants to show up, do his dirty work, and go home with a fistful of cash" (7). Finally, we are given a physical description, one that suggests he is unhealthy and unhygienic: "Arnie is five feet three inches tall, with a good paunch. He always goes barefoot, even when he's operating. He has green eyes and carefully cropped hair, and he speaks with a strong accent" (7).

Won by Love presents dialogue spoken by Arnie as broken English: "You want abortion? . . . You sign here, I give abortion" (55). In actuality, Arnie is Dr. Jasbir Ahluwalia, who owns A Choice for Women clinic, and who was asked by his staff, McCorvey's friends, to examine her when she sank into a depression in mid-1994 after she was fired from one Dallas abortion clinic for being "abusive" on the job. A *Village Voice* article on McCorvey's baptism does not duplicate the broken English dialect found in *Won by Love* and otherwise characterizes the doctor as competent and compassionate. According to Ahluwalia, as quoted by the *Voice*, McCorvey "looked like she was 60 years old! Run-down, depressed, crying, suicidal. I told her what an honor it was to meet her and that I'd treat her at no charge. I told her to come to A Choice for Women later that evening so I could give hormones I had in stock there. She came, looked around my clinic, and said, 'You have such a beautiful place! Can I have a job?' 'I feel really privileged,' I said. 'You're hired.' "[61]

When Operation Rescue moved next door to Dr. Ahluwalia's clinic, a team of pro-lifers, including Flip Benham and a mother whose daughter is touted as "the precious little girl whose love changed [McCorvey's] life," commenced to love-bomb McCorvey. It worked. But how did the rest of the employees of A Choice for Women respond to Operation Rescue as neighbors? According to *Won by Love*, Arnie had fierce disdain for Benham and was panicked about Operation Rescue's proximity and potential influence. In fact, however, Ahluwalia "paid McCorvey's plane fare in early summer of [1995] so she could appear with Benham on *Good Morning Today* and 'dialogue' about common ground in the abortion controversy."[62] This act flies in the face of portraying the doctor as obsessed with money and fearful of Benham and Operation Rescue.

Won by Love persists in its negative portrayal of the doctor. Miss Norma eventually tells him off: "You're not a man, you're just a little cardboard cutout. You should do something. It's a circus out there, but you leave it all to the women. You're always hiding behind a woman's skirts" (111). Like stereotypes of Jews, Arnie is portrayed as parasitic, unclean, unmanly, un-American, and motivated by greed. Arnie tells Miss Norma to lie to a client and tell her that her pregnancy is more advanced than it actually is because "the difference between an abortion at ten weeks and twelve weeks was a hundred dollars" (61). The only aspect of classic anti-Semitism missing in this description is the supposed link to the media.

In this regard, the portrayal of pro-choice litigator Gloria Allred takes up the slack. She is a "Yiddish mamma" and "media junkie" who "knows how to do seventy-two hours worth of media in a twenty-four hour day" (33, 36). The point that she drives a Mercedes and travels a lot attests to her affluence, implicitly gained by "using" people like Miss Norma. The detail of her listening to reggae music by Bob Marley suggests an affinity with people of color. Enemies of life are all connected.

The racism in *Won by Love* is coded but not subtle. The description of two "ugly lugs" hired to harass Operation Rescue protesters outside a clinic heavily implies African American men who prey on white women; the myth of the black rapist persists. "The two men played loud rap music so our clients could not hear the Christians' pleas, but they quickly cut the music when no clients were in sight and then whispered their juiciest obscenities at the most pious-looking women they could find. Sometimes they would even lean over and say, 'You know, some evening, I'm gonna get you alone and I'm going to . . .' " (120–21). As with the mention of reggae, rap here is a musical code for anti-Christian, non-white values and hedonistic behavior.

At one point, the idea of not only turning white but also being white is posed in contradistinction to Arnie's inhumanity and foreignness. Miss Norma believes she has seen a "head float by" (62) in a bag in the "Parts Room" of the clinic, where supposedly "babies were stacked like cordwood" (6). Consequently she vomits all over Arnie, who "complains" and asks if she can continue her work. " 'You cannot do this?' he asked. I was white. I thought I might throw up again. And he was asking me if I was sure I couldn't do this?" The phrase "I was white" is certainly not intended to denote racial identity; in fact *Won by Love* mentions that McCorvey is part Cajun and part Cherokee, although in less detail than it is discussed in *I Am Roe*. But neither is the phrase merely a declaration of her physical illness. It is a sign of being morally and physically—that is, essentially—unable to do the work that lesser people like Arnie can do. The message is clear: Miss Norma's whiteness is incompatible with providing abortion services.

In another race-related incident in *Won by Love*, we find that as a born-again Christian, Miss Norma is now open to attacks by people of color. Going public with her new pro-life stance, McCorvey barely escapes an animalistic "herd of reporters" only to run into a studio worker. The "Asian woman looked at me and said, 'What are you doing?' 'I'm going to be on *Nightline*.' 'Oh,' she said, disgust in her tone, 'I know who you are.' 'Well, don't be biased or anything!' I said. She responded with a snort and a sneer" (182). Accusing the woman of color of being biased is congruent with the populist, anti-immigrant, and white supremacist trope of portraying white Christians as persecuted by racial minorities. Although McCorvey herself in no way deserves to be labeled a white supremacist, the pro-life narrative perpetuated through her autobiography no doubt resonates with white supremacist language. This may explain why McCorvey was a featured speaker at a 1998 gathering called the Jubilation, which is an annual event organized by the newspaper *The Jubilee*.

The Jubilee is rife with theories about how the United Nations is conspiring to assert global control. This feared New World Order is in cosmic combat with the "descendants of the Israelites of scripture," purported to be "the Anglo-Saxon, Scandinavian, Celtic, Germanic and European people with whom God has made His covenant." Claiming white people to be the real Jews, *The Jubilee*'s message is consistent with that of Christian Identity. "Those who refer to themselves as Jews," explains the newspaper's website, "are NOT but are of the synagogue of Satan (the adversary)." In the May/June 1998 issue of *The Jubilee*, the editor of the paper is pictured sitting with his arm around Norma McCorvey.[63] Does this photograph demonstrate a conspiracy among pro-life and Christian Identity adherents? No. It demonstrates that what Miss Norma represents—the ex-lesbian, ex-clinic worker who reveals the so-called horrors of reproductive health care, including its parasitic, un-American, anti-Christian doctor—resonates cleanly with more overtly anti-Semitic, white supremacist language.

Interpellated as an ex-lesbian, Miss Norma is "Roe No More." Jane Roe has not been conquered; she has been converted. Norma McCorvey and Connie Gonzales have not renounced their love for one another; they have only displaced it with an allegiance to a "higher" love of God. *Won by Love* is not only the personal tale of Norma McCorvey's conversion to born-again Christianity; it is a narrative that follows the conventions of popular millennialist fiction. It narrates the enemies of life as an enormous, cosmic, conspiratorial threat that nevertheless is destined to be defeated, to be brought under God's law by a minority of defiant, vigilant pro-lifers.

Pro-life writing can interpellate its enemies not only because it is apocalyptic—not because it presents a melodramatic, dichotomous allegory in which people can identify their role in political conflict. Rather, pro-life writing, characterized as it is by millennial narrative, accomplishes the interpellation of its enemies because narrative is an articulatory practice of social assignment. *Won by Love* does not just illustrate the process by which Norma McCorvey herself came to identify as born again and pro-life. It is also the means by which Jane Roe is narrated as ex-lesbian. It is not telling a story about McCorvey as much as it is interpellating the enemies of life—and, in the process, attempting to re-create Jane Roe—that pseudonym that refers to every fertile woman—as an ex-lesbian, as a subject of God's law and no longer a subject of man's law, namely, *Roe v. Wade*. Janet Folger's partial birth, ex-gay campaigns are no less narrative productions than is the tale of Jane Roe's pro-life, ex-lesbian conversion. Couched in compassion and charity, both are narrative love bombs lobbed to offset the apocalyptic anti-Christian forces, the conspiracy against life. In the 1990s, pro-life writing enacted the political inscription that scholars say operates in conspiracy theories. But pro-life narrative is not merely a conspiratorial framework, worldview, or context. It is political strategy that produces new abortion warriors as righteous subjects under God's law and the enemies of life as criminals.

Pro-life writing of the 1990s went beyond stereotyping and demonizing people who provide or obtain abortions as selfish, irresponsible, or hedonistic. More than an escalation of vitriolic rhetoric, pro-life apocalypticism of the 1990s was consistent and persistent in narrating the "enemies of life" as Jews, lesbians, people of color, and immigrants—and in a way that prevented their solidarity. Because pro-life writing inscribes Jews, lesbians, people of color, and immigrants as the conspirators against life, we might be tempted to conclude that life, therefore, is meant to refer to life that is exclusively white, Christian, and heterosexual. But as we have seen, narrating abortion as part of an apocalyptic conspiracy demands that life be defined contingently and relatively, especially by those who exalt life as an absolute value. No phenomenon better illuminates this profoundly denied relativism than killing for life.

Conclusion

No New Embryos

If pro-life murders, fatal pro-life bombings, and pro-life advocates of capital punishment were not enough to demonstrate the untenable, multiple meanings of *life*, President George W. Bush's decision to fund stem cell research may be. For many pro-life groups, this decision violated the sanctity of life, and Bush lost his credibility as a pro-life president. Many of the dissenters were those most invested in the apocalyptic narrative of abortion. American Life League immediately posted a scathing analysis of the president's speech on its website and listed nine other groups that were critical of the decision, including the U.S. Conference of Catholic Bishops, Human Life International, Flip Benham's Operation Save America, and the Republican National Coalition for Life.[1] The *New York Times* reported that Charles Colson's Prison Fellowship ministry also expressed disappointment with the decision.[2] Despite the fact that the National Right to Life Committee commended the president, which gave the media license to report that the largest anti-abortion group in the United States was happy with Bush, most of the other overtly organized pro-life Americans were displeased. For those covert activists—the vigilantes, the Phineas Priests, the guerrilla snipers, the leaderless resistance, the Army of God—who had never trusted the Feds in the first place, Bush's decision doubtless solidified their apocalyptic vision.

Evidence of this is Paul de Parrie's reaction to the decision, which he fused profoundly with his response to the terrorist attacks of September 11, 2001. De Parrie spoke at Mount Hood Community College with a group of pro-life students as well as other students who had attended the publicly advertised meeting wearing pro-choice T-shirts in silent protest. After showing the movie *The Hard Truth*, de Parrie talked passionately about why the apathetic Church and Christians were to blame for the continuing legal status of abortion. In what some students described as "a convoluted story about cornhusks falling for three days from the skies of Wichita, Kansas," de Parrie suggested that divine communication in the form of these cornhusks had rained down on a section of town whose center was a church that supported Dr. George Tiller and pro-choice efforts. He then made an observation about other projectiles from the sky, drawing a parallel between the cornhusks and the planes that had brought down the World Trade Center towers and damaged the Pentagon. According to the student newspaper, de Parrie "blatantly spoke of the 'coincidence' of the 9-11 attacks on America having happened only three days after President Bush made his statement in support of stem cell research." Students understood de Parrie's narrative as "echoing the Reverend Jerry Falwell's infamous statements concerning the unspeakable terrorist acts on the American people."[3]

Falwell's statements, made on the television program *The 700 Club*, were indeed infamous but hardly surprising, given his 1999 announcement that the Antichrist is alive and Jewish. His remarks on *The 700 Club* included, "I really believe that the pagans, and the abortionists, and the feminists, and the gays and the lesbians who are actively trying to make that an alternative lifestyle, the ACLU, People for the American Way, all of them who have tried to secularize America. I point the finger in their face and say 'you helped this happen.' " As in 1999, he later issued an explanation that clarified his millennialist stance so as to appear less hostile. Gays and abortionists were not directly responsible for the terrorist attacks, only indirectly. They had "created an environment which possibly caused God to lift the veil of protection which has allowed no one to attack America on our soil since 1812," he said.[4]

This idea that acts of destruction are permitted by a God whose restraint is wearing thin was echoed by Neal Horsley when he said he thought it was a miracle that more bombs did not destroy abortion clinics, implying that without God's grace, pro-life warfare would be rampant.[5] This sentiment is no doubt echoed by scores of other Americans who are not notorious public pro-lifers but who appreciate and duplicate the apocalyptic pro-life narrative in their own communities. According to National Public Radio reporter Andy Bowers, who visited Springfield, Missouri, to ask residents what they thought of the war against terrorism, one woman, knowing that "the Reverend Jerry Falwell was criticized for saying so," nevertheless "agrees that God allowed the September 11 attacks in order to get America's attention." This woman identified abortion and homosexuality in particular as the sorts of things that need to be stopped if "God is going to help the country win the war on terrorism."[6] Bowers's woman-in-the-street interview indicates that portraying abortion as apocalyptic is not the narrative practice of only highly paid or high-profile pro-lifers.

Nevertheless, it is important to recognize that although this shared narrative practice may solidify pro-life ideology and millennialist expectation, it does not dictate responses to what is seen as God's warning signs. As much as de Parrie's, Falwell's, Horsley's, and the Springfield resident's comments attest to a shared understanding, their responses to particular events or strategies may vary greatly. For example, Falwell actually commended Bush's stem cell decision, but de Parrie lambasted Bush's tolerance for "cutting up little babies and making them into medicine for adults."[7] Obviously there is plenty of room for interpretation within pro-life millennialism and many opportunities to create a variety of alliances. For those such as de Parrie, who blame the likes of Falwell, the Church, and the government for not properly reacting to God's warnings, the events of September 11 may have solidified an antigovernment view as well as apocalyptic expectation. The swell of patriotism that emerged after the attacks, however, has complicated antigovernment sentiment in pro-life writing.

With the impending trial of James Kopp, the alleged assassin of Dr. Barnett Slepian who was apprehended in France in 2001, Life Dynamics, Inc., sought to fan the flames of antigovernment sentiment with a report apparently exposing the FBI's misconduct in the Kopp case.[8] Like Gore Vidal's examination in *Vanity Fair* of Timothy McVeigh's trial and execution, Mark Crutcher's report on the Kopp case taps into the growing fear that federal agencies abuse their power at the expense of a citizen's right to privacy and a fair trial.[9] High-profile cases such as Kopp's, which has already been compared with the disastrous FBI encounters with the falsely accused Richard Jewell in Atlanta and the wrongly torched Branch Davidians in Waco, have the capacity to call into question the abuses of the United States government. Indeed the concern with governmental abuse of power has grown enormously since hundreds of legal immigrants and citizens were detained after September 11, 2001. Adhering to the apocalyptic narrative that has operated through pro-life writing since the 1960s, groups such as Life Dynamics do everything in their power to narrate people such as Kopp, the pro-life white, Christian male, as the ultimate—if not the sole—victim of such abuses.

Narrating the new abortion warrior as besieged, outnumbered, and victimized, pro-life writing makes the white, Christian, heterosexual (and working- or middle-class) male a hero above all others. Despite the fact that people, regardless of their race, gender, sexuality, religion, class, or ethnicity, may deplore abortion and fashion sophisticated reasons to prohibit it, pro-life ideology habitually and consistently defines its hero as male, straight, Christian, and white. If this is not an intention of pro-life writers, surely it is an effect of their writing, of narrating abortion as apocalypse.

We can see, for example, that the new abortion warrior is narrated absolutely as masculine when we consider gender as feminist narratologists have. They "focus on gender not as a predetermined condition of the production of texts, but as a textual effect."[10] The apocalyptic narrative of pro-life writings defines the warrior according to gender and sexual difference. For example, the baby held aloft on the memorial to the unborn in *Whatever Happened to the Human Race?* has a penis, that visible marker of sexual difference. In *Gideon's Torch*, Daniel Seaton dies because he is a heterosexual who will not allow a black man to ravish a retarded boy. Members of the Army of God seek not to be "vaginally defeated."[11] Michael Bray condemns the "testosterone deficiency" of the emasculated church.[12] All of these images and phrases are examples of how the abortion warrior is gendered male; they do not detract from the fact that some pro-life organizations are headed by women or that at least one woman, Shelley Shannon, shot a doctor.

The new abortion warrior is also, in effect if not by intention, white—not merely because everyone who has killed for life has been, to the best of my knowledge, Caucasian, but because pro-life writing represents its heroes in terms of racial difference. Daniel Seaton and his brother from *Gideon's Torch* are the most obvious examples, juxtaposed as they are against the foil characters of Shaqqar Redding and Lance Thompson. The novel's fetus-as-slave and abortion-as-holocaust analogies do not relieve this tendency to narrate the pro-lifers in contrast to racialized Others. Likewise, the semiotics of whiteness in *Whatever Happened to the Human Race?* override the book's token gestures to depict some victims of abortion as unborn babies of color. Understanding the new abortion warrior as white is not to deny that some people of color are pro-life; Alan Keyes and Mildred Jefferson are African American leaders of the cause.[13] Nor do I suggest that pro-choice organizations are devoid of institutional racism or that pro-choice individuals cannot be bigots. But these situations do not obscure the way the apocalyptic narrative of pro-life politics consistently racializes the unborn as white and abortion warriors in terms of racial difference.

So it is not quite accurate to suggest that the apocalyptic, pro-life narrative ultimately represses social differences—even if it describes a social order that many find oppressive. On the contrary, the narrative creates differences in order to manage them. Perhaps this is true because the pro-life apocalyptic narrative is not based on chronology or linearity. Some narrative theory suggests that eschatology is a system bound by narrative linearity, which "is in itself a form which represses difference."[14] But the eschatology of pro-life millennialism seems to me to reject linearity and does not embrace time as infinite or homogenous. Because it situates pro-lifers in a double temporal condition that is not a perpetual timeline but a "mode of existence," to quote Bozell, pro-life millennialism is not a narrative linearity and is not, therefore, necessarily a form that represses difference. In fact, although it has form (and we have examined some of its formal elements, such as racial metaphors and blood imagery), the apocalyptic narrative of pro-life ideology is not "a form" at all.

Instead, the apocalyptic narrative is an articulatory practice that seeks to narrate, through a production of differences, some particular people as pro-life warriors and others as conspiratorial enemies of life. This narration (or articulation or interpellation) is not, therefore, dismissible as the imaginary, the simulacra, or "the dream life of political violence."[15] The apocalyptic pro-life narrative is, even with its fantastic elements, profoundly real. Narratives such as this are not "inventions of the mind but political and ideological practices as much a part of the material texture of reality as bombs and factories, wars and revolutions."[16]

Therefore, when the president announced that he would allow limited funding of stem cell research, his narrative—that of thwarting the mad scientist in a "culture that devalues life"—was not an invention of the mind of George W. Bush. Nor was it a new idea from his speechwriters. It was instead the old apocalyptic pro-life narrative, which is far more powerful than anti-abortion rhetoric. Bush did not even mention abortion or speak of a right to life to explain his decision.

Instead, his speech addressed and reinforced people's fears that a disregard for life is saturating the world, recalling the dystopian vision of a famous piece of science fiction:

> We have arrived at that brave new world that seemed so distant in 1932 when Aldous Huxley wrote about human beings created in test tubes in what he called a hatchery. There are many things which could be done but should never be done, regardless of the alleged beneficial outcome. In recent weeks, we learned that scientists have created human embryos in test tubes solely to experiment on them. This is deeply troubling and a warning sign that should prompt all of us to think through these issues very carefully.[17]

For both secular and religious America, the "warning sign" of stem cell research set an apocalyptic tone. Bush's decision was articulated as one that acknowledges the sign of the end times of sexual reproduction if not the end times of the mortal world itself. Bush's (and his speechwriters') language perpetuates the apocalypticism that has shaped pro-life politics. It even referenced the most potent "enemy of life": the doctor, recast as mad scientist.

With the image of the mad scientist, Bush tapped simultaneously into all of the referents that make the image so rich for secular as well as spiritual America. It recalled the red-scare politics from Huxley's novel, which equated communism with fascism as an enterprise that eliminates individuality. It recalled from history the eugenic experimentation of the Nazis. It resonated with every version of Dr. Frankenstein from Mary Shelley to Mel Brooks. Not least of all, the image also has the power to invoke, in the minds of those who have been primed to see it, the harrowing idea of the foreign, black, or Jewish abortion doctor harvesting fetal tissue for disease research. Anyone who has read Colson's *Gideon's Torch*, or watched LDI's *LifeTalk*, or caught the *20/20* "exposé" on "baby parts" marketing, or attended the congressional hearings the day after that program aired, saw a similar scenario in the stem cell decision—with the important exception that test tubes, not abortions, were the source of the embryos.

Bush thus invoked the potential horror of secular science but then sought to mitigate it with godly, pro-life devotion: "I also believe human life is a sacred gift from our creator." More than simple, passive piety, Bush's position resonated directly with the idea of actively confronting and globally defeating a "culture of death" and the "conspiracy against life." He said, "I worry about a culture that devalues life, and believe as your president I have an important obligation to foster and encourage respect for life in America and throughout the world."[18] Using key phrases and engaging the narrative of apocalypticism, the speech clearly sought to reassure pro-life voters that stem cell research was not another attack on life. Like his father, notorious for his broken promise of "no new taxes," George W. Bush promised that the federally funded stem cell research would involve no new embryos, only existing cell lines. No new embryos are necessary for the narrative perpetuation of pro-life politics as an apocalyptic battle.

The embryo, the fetus, the unborn have served as proxy victims of the psychological and political abuses some men believe they have experienced in the wake of social change since the 1960s. Apocalyptic pro-life writing evolved as a history-making narrative, the effects of which may be repressive, destructive, and absolutist, but the operation of which is profoundly productive, creative, and relativistic. Narrating abortion as America's Armageddon since the 1960s, pro-life ideology has produced multiple meanings of *life* and created new warriors. Created first in writing and then in society, these warriors cast away their embryonic proxies and threw themselves into the fray of fantastic evil, making time to kill for the American life they felt they deserved. As a political manifestation of religious and personal retribution, killing for life exemplifies the material reality of narrative practice and indicates that paramilitary pro-life culture is strong enough to flaunt its relativism.

Notes

Introduction

1. *Soldiers in the Army of God*, directed by Marc Levin and Daphne Pinkerson, is part of the Home Box Office Undercover Series of television films. It was broadcast in spring 2001 on the Home Box Office cable network (HBO).

2. Ibid. This phrase is HBO's.

3. Much of the scholarship on pro-life activists has focused on discounting stereotypes, which helps to illuminate the wide variety of pro-life individuals; see James R. Kelly, "Beyond the Stereotypes: Interviews with Right-to-Life Pioneers," *Commonweal*, November 1981, 653–57; Kristin Luker, *Abortion and the Politics of Motherhood* (Berkeley: University of California Press, 1984); and Faye D. Ginsburg, *Contested Lives* (Berkeley: University of California Press, 1989). In contrast to Luker's delineation of the different

worldviews that characterize pro-life and pro-choice individuals, Ginsburg articulates and dismisses stereotypes by examining individual "life stories" from ethnographic interviews she conducted in Fargo, North Dakota. She found that pro-choice advocates "were extremely sensitive" to the "stereotype" of being "opposed to marriage, family, and children" (153), whereas pro-lifers revealed themselves to be "much more complex than the stereotype that portrays pro-life women as reactionary housewives and mothers passed by in the sweep of social change" (193). Still, according to Ginsburg, battling stereotypes is but one aspect of the "paradigmatically American" "process of self-definition through social action" (221) in which pro-life and pro-choice activists are engaged. Ginsburg concludes that "pro-life and pro-choice stances, like all genuine dialectical oppositions, have a number of elements in common," including the desire "to alleviate the unequal conditions faced by women in American culture" (226). Although this conclusion seems to minimize the political differences between the two camps, Ginsburg's later work recognizes the particularities of pro-life political aims and rhetoric; see Ginsburg, "Rescuing the Nation: Operation Rescue and the Rise of Anti-Abortion Militance," in *Abortion Wars: A Half Century of Struggle, 1950–2000*, ed. Rickie Solinger (Berkeley: University of California Press, 1998). Nevertheless, Jeffrey Kaplan's indictment of Ginsburg's work in particular as especially "egregious" in ignoring pro-life writing seems valid; see Kaplan, "America's Last Prophetic Witness: The Literature of the Rescue Movement," *Terrorism and Political Violence* 5, 3 (autumn 1993): 58–77. For a discussion of the disciplinary assumptions evident in Ginsburg's and other feminist anthropologists' work on reproductive politics, see Carol Mason, "Fundamental Opposition: Feminism, Narrative, and the Abortion Debate" (Ph.D. diss., University of Minnesota, 1996), esp. chap. 1, "Against Ethnography: Reproductive Politics and Narrative Analysis."

4. Horsley's website is accessed at ⟨http://www.christiangallery.com⟩. The Nuremberg Files, where Horsley lists abortion providers' names and crosses them out when those providers are killed, is available at ⟨http://www.christian gallery.com/atrocity/⟩.

5. For documentation of ongoing harassment and threats to abortion providers, their families, and patients, see Patricia Baird-Windle and Eleanor J. Bader, *Targets of Hatred: Anti-Abortion Terrorism* (New York: Palgrave, 2001).

6. Instead of claiming that, generally speaking, narrative is a social process by which pro-life activists negotiate gender roles and forge their identities, I show that a particular millennialist narrative has been deployed by a variety of pro-life institutions in a persistent but uncoordinated fashion since at least 1979. My examination of pro-life writing as millennialist narrative encompasses more than suggesting that individual pro-life activists are motivated in relation to a cognitive schemata, cultural template, or discursive frame through which they assess a situation and determine their course of action. In

addressing both the form of pro-life narrative and its articulatory function, I draw from poststructuralism.

For poststructuralist scholars of language, the relationship between narrative and discourse is an important problem:

How does narrative differ from what poststructuralism describes as "discourse," "écriture," "textuality," "the symbolic," and so forth? Since in one way or another each of these concepts incorporates and yet suppresses the vital element of narrative, we are not interested in defining narrative as a distinct object of inquiry within this panoply of terms. Our project sets out to demonstrate, among other things, that one cannot account for the rise of writing unless and until one acknowledges the narrative component of poststructuralist conceptions of language. (Leonard Tennenhouse and Nancy Armstrong, "History, Poststructuralism, and the Problem of Narrative," *Narrative* 1, 1 [1993]: 46–47)

Armstrong and Tennenhouse's project privileges narrative as an inherent part of the "rise of writing," just as I privilege narrative as an inherent part of the historical development of pro-life writing. My reasons for focusing on narrative and writing are to question how the history of the pro-life movement has been written, to fill in the gaps in documentation, and to pressure some of the trends in scholarship on the abortion conflict.

7. For the original theory of interpellation, see Louis Althusser, *Lenin and Philosophy* (London: New Left Books, 1971). For an account of interpellation in the context of narratology, see Mark Currie, *Postmodern Narrative Theory* (New York: St. Martin's Press, 1998), 28–29.

8. Examining pro-life ideology is necessary because the cherished ideal of life is so entrenched and intact on both sides of the debate that nothing seems to call it into question. Life is the common ground upon which two formidable foes battle over abortion in America, whether we call that battle an opposition between the life of the child and the life of the mother, or between the life of the fetus and the life of the woman. The pro-life faction integrated this ideal of life into the name of its appeal, although the pro-choice endeavor is nonetheless concerned with life, and pro-choicers lament the way their opposition claimed the name first. Pro-choicers and pro-lifers both fight for the sake of life itself. The individual lives of babies are at stake, pro-lifers claim. The individual lives of women are at stake, pro-choicers claim. The state has a compelling interest in the potential life of the unborn and can protect that interest by regulating abortion. The state has no right to limit the potential of a woman's life by denying her an abortion if she chooses it. Legal abortion permits the murder of the unborn. Outlawed abortion results in women dying. Life is as dear as it is unquestioned on both sides of the debate.

In choosing the term *ideology* to describe pro-life writing, I am following Slavoj Žižek's conception of it. He makes a distinction between what he calls a dialectico-materialist opposition and an idealist-ideological opposition, explaining that the latter already contains within it the sought-after third term, the common ground, the naturalized, idealized assumption that holds the two poles in complementary position. When I assume life to be the common ground that holds the two poles together, I understand pro-life ideology not as an explicit, imposed doctrine of belief or a "homogeneous mechanism that guarantees social reproduction" (Slavoj Žižek, Introduction, in *Mapping Ideology*, ed. S. Žižek [London and New York: Verso, 1994], 14). Rather, I conceive it as ideology in the sense of a contingent operation of assumptions at work— unexamined assumptions that constantly defer rather than define what *life* means. I hope this notion will allow us to articulate better the important political differences at stake, instead of succumbing to sound bites and rhetorical roundabouts. If we remain satisfied with the dialectical approach to analyzing abortion politics, it "can easily ensnare us in historicist [or political] relativism" by neutralizing two sides of debate and regarding each side's ideology as "a mere expression of social circumstances" (9).

1. New Abortion Warrior

1. John Warwick Montgomery, "The Fetus and Personhood," *Human Life Review* 1, 2 (summer 1975): 46.

2. Paul de Parrie, *Haunt of Jackals* (Wheaton, Ill.: Crossway Books, 1991), 31.

3. Even pro-life doctors agree that women are not traumatized by abortion. C. Everett Koop, the pro-life surgeon general in Ronald Reagan's cabinet, oversaw a study that did not conclude that women suffer psychologically after terminating their pregnancies (Koop, "Postabortion Syndrome: Myth or Reality?" *Health Matrix* 7 [summer 1989]: 42–44). Bernard Nathanson, an abortionist who cofounded the National Association to Repeal Abortion Laws before he turned pro-life and narrated *The Silent Scream*, concedes that "psychiatric scare tactics" used by anti-abortionists have no bases in fact. His book, *Aborting America*, acknowledges that "abortion may produce feelings of regret, perhaps even remorse, but this is not a clinical syndrome of psychopathology. Sadness is not sickness. Guilt reactions do relate to the care of the individual patient, and in some cases may provide a clinical reason not to abort. But in the professional literature of the '60s and '70s in the United States, there is no solid evidence that psychopathology is either induced or appreciably worsened in the general run of cases" (Nathanson, *Aborting America* [Garden City, N.Y.: Doubleday, 1979], 185–86). He goes on to quote a 1978 study that summarizes, "Post-abortion psychiatric complications are not common. There are no unequivocal psychiatric contraindications for termination on a psychiatric basis. The risk of exacerbation or precipitation or a major psychiatric illness is small and unpredictable." Nathanson then concludes that "All these points

should be borne in mind in diagnosis and care of the individual patient; they are not the basis upon which society should limit abortion" (186). More recent studies that indicate abortion entails no psychological damage include Nada Stotland, "The Myth of the Abortion Trauma Syndrome," *Journal of the American Medical Association* 268, 15 (October 21, 1992): 2078–79; and Nancy Adler et al., "Psychological Factors in Abortion: A Review," *American Psychologist* 47, 10 (October 1992): 1194–1204. Contrary to claims that feminist and pro-choice groups disregard women's feelings of ambivalence during or after an unplanned pregnancy, see K. Kaufmann, "Taking Care of Yourself," in *The Abortion Resource Handbook* (New York: Simon and Schuster, 1997).

4. Barry Goldwater with Jack Casserly, *Goldwater* (New York: Doubleday, 1988), 236.

5. James William Gibson, *Warrior Dreams: Paramilitary Culture in Post-Vietnam America* (New York: Hill and Wang, 1994), 28.

6. Gibson's analysis is based largely on Richard Slotkin's understanding of regenerative violence, detailed in Slotkin, *Regeneration through Violence: The Myth of the American Frontier, 1600–1860* (Middletown, Conn.: Wesleyan University Press, 1973); and idem, *Gunfighter Nation: The Myth of the Frontier in Twentieth-Century America* (New York: Maxwell Macmillan, 1992). For discussions of Rambo as exemplar of regenerative violence, see Adi Wimmer, "*Rambo:* American Adam, Anarchist, and Archetypal Frontier Hero," in *Vietnam Images: War and Representation*, ed. James Aulich and Jeffrey Walsh (New York: St. Martin's Press, 1989); Harold Schechter and Jonna Semeiks, "Leatherstocking in 'Nam': *Rambo, Platoon*, and the American Frontier Myth," *Journal of Popular Culture* 24, 4 (spring 1991): 17–25.

7. James Risen and Judy L. Thomas, *Wrath of Angels: The American Abortion War* (New York: Basic Books, 1998), 44–77.

8. Ibid., 55; emphasis added.

9. Ibid., 43.

10. Ibid., 54.

11. Ibid., chap. 3.

12. Susan Jeffords, *The Remasculinization of America: Gender and the Vietnam War* (Bloomington: University of Indiana Press, 1989).

13. De Parrie, *Haunt of Jackals*, chap. 7.

14. Gregory Waller, "*Rambo*: Getting to Win This Time," in *From Hanoi to Hollywood: The Vietnam War in American Film*, ed. Linda Dittmar and Gene Michaud (New Brunswick, N.J.: Rutgers University Press, 1990).

15. William B. Hixson, *Search for the American Right Wing: An Analysis of the Social Science Record, 1955–1987* (Princeton, N.J.: Princeton University Press, 1992); Jerome Himmelstein, *To the Right: The Transformation of American Conservatism* (Berkeley: University of California Press, 1990); Chip Berlet and Matthew N. Lyons, *Right-Wing Populism in America: Too Close for Comfort* (New York: Guilford Press, 2000); Michelle McKeegan, *Abortion Politics:*

Mutiny in the Ranks of the Right (New York: Free Press, 1992); and Sara Diamond, *Roads to Dominion: Right-Wing Movements and Political Power in the United States* (New York: Guilford Press, 1995).

16. Rosalind Petchesky, *Abortion and Woman's Choice: The State, Sexuality, and Reproductive Freedom* (Boston: Northeastern University Press, 1984).

17. Diamond, *Roads to Dominion*, 170.

18. Ibid.; Connie Paige, *The Right-to-Lifers: Who They Are, How They Operate, Where They Get Their Money* (New York: Summit Books, 1983); Andrew Merton, *Enemies of Choice* (Boston: Beacon Press, 1981).

19. For an interesting summation of contradictory analyses of the evangelicals' voting patterns during the 1980 election, see Berlet and Lyons, *Right-Wing Populism in America*, 223.

20. Richard Viguerie, *The New Right: We're Ready to Lead* (Falls Church, Va.: Viguerie Company, 1980), 33.

21. Berlet and Lyons, *Right-Wing Populism in America*, 223.

22. Andrew Sullivan, "Going Down Screaming," *New York Times Magazine*, October 11, 1998, 50.

23. National Right to Life Committee, "When Does Life Begin? Abortion and Human Rights," pamphlet, 1993.

24. Fritz K. Beller and Gail P. Zlatnik, "Medical Aspects of the Beginning of Individual Lives," in *The Beginning of Human Life*, ed. F. K. Beller and R. F. Weir (Dordrecht, the Netherlands: Kluwer Academic Publishers, 1993), 3–17.

25. Although actually ghostwritten (by Brent Bozell, as discussed in chap. 5 of this volume), *Conscience of a Conservative* (Shepherdsville, Ky.: Victor Publishing, 1960), a bestseller, is widely regarded as Goldwater's thinking and is generally believed to have given unprecedented coherence to conservative thought. The influence of Goldwater on the New Right and their connection to abortion are substantial. Michelle McKeegan begins her book by attesting: "The story of how a dedicated corps of right-wingers turned abortion into a household word at the Republican National Committee begins with the 1964 presidential bid of conservative Barry Goldwater" (*Abortion Politics*, 1).

26. Goldwater, *Conscience of a Conservative*, 62.

27. Diamond, *Roads to Dominion*, 170.

28. National Right to Life Committee, "When Does Life Begin?"

29. American Life League, *Celebrate Life* 17, 6 (November/December 1995), inside cover.

30. Nathanson, *Aborting America*, 205.

31. Lauren Berlant, *The Queen of America Goes to Washington City: Essays on Sex and Citizenship* (Durham, N.C.: Duke University Press, 1997), 121. Feminist scholarship has examined the nexus of apocalypticism, extraterrestrialism, nationalism, and abortion in pro-life videos, medical imaging, popular culture, and the public sphere. On abortion and apocalypticism, see Berlant, *Queen of*

America; Petchesky, *Abortion and Woman's Choice;* and Faye Ginsburg, "Rescuing the Nation: Operation Rescue and the Rise of Anti-Abortion Militance," in *Abortion Wars: A Half Century of Struggle, 1950–2000,* ed. Rickie Solinger (Berkeley: University of California Press, 1998). On abortion and extraterrestrialism, see Zoe Sofia, "Exterminating Fetuses: Abortion, Disarmament, and the Sexo-Semiotics of Extraterrestrialism," *Diacritics* 14, 2 (1984): 47–59. On abortion and medical imaging, see Carole Stabile, "Shooting the Mother: Fetal Photography and the Politics of Disappearance," *Camera Obscura* 28 (January 1992): 179–205; Lisa Cartwright, *Screening the Body: Tracing Medicine's Visual Culture* (Minneapolis: University of Minnesota Press, 1995); Lynn M. Morgan and Meredith W. Michaels, eds., *Fetal Subjects, Feminist Positions* (Philadelphia: University of Pennsylvania Press, 1999); Alice Adams, *Reproducing the Womb: Images of Childbirth in Science, Feminist Theory, and Literature* (Ithaca, N.Y.: Cornell University Press, 1994); Valerie Hartouni, "Fetal Exposures: Abortion Politics and the Optics of Allusion," *Camera Obscura* 29 (1993): 131–49. On abortion and the public sphere, see Barbara Duden, *Disembodying Women: Perspectives on Pregnancy and the Unborn* (Cambridge: Harvard University Press, 1993); Janelle Taylor, "The Public Fetus and the Family Car: From Abortion Politics to a Volvo Advertisment," *Public Culture* 4, 2 (spring 1992): 67–80; Rosalind Petchesky, "Foetal Images: The Power of Visual Culture in the Politics of Reproduction," in *Reproductive Technologies: Gender, Motherhood, and Medicine,* ed. Michelle Stanworth (Minneapolis: University of Minnesota Press, 1987).

32. Michael W. Cuneo, "Life Battles: The Rise of Catholic Militancy within the American Pro-Life Movement," in *Being Right: Conservative Catholics in America,* ed. Mary Jo Weaver and R. Scott Appleby (Bloomington: Indiana University Press, 1995), 284–85.

33. Duden, *Disembodying Women,* 2.

34. Stanley Hauerwas, "Why Abortion Is a Religious Issue," in *The Ethics of Abortion: Pro-Life vs. Pro-Choice,* ed. Robert M. Baird and Stuart E. Rosenbaum (Buffalo, N.Y.: Prometheus Books, 1993), 162.

35. Gibson, *Warrior Dreams,* 102.

36. Ibid., 102–3.

37. Several *Army of God* manuals were unearthed from the backyard of Rachelle "Shelley" Shannon, who in 1993 was arrested for shooting abortion provider Dr. George Tiller of Wichita, Kansas. According to Risen and Thomas, "federal law enforcement officials believe" that the manual "first surfaced within activist circles during the 'Summer of Mercy' in Wichita" in 1991 (*Wrath of Angels,* 351). I obtained an overly xeroxed copy of the "revised and expanded" *Army of God* manual from the archives of Political Research Associates, Somerville, Mass. As a result of the quality of my copy, some page numbers are missing or illegible.

38. This description was given by the head of the Atlanta office of the Bu-

reau of Alcohol, Tobacco, and Firearms and quoted by Ron Martz and Kathy Scruggs, "Bomb Probe Looks Harder at Army of God: Web Page, Manual May Show Connection between Bombings in Atlanta and Birmingham," *Atlanta Journal-Constitution*, February 4, 1998, A9.

39. Mark Potok is quoted in Christina Nifong, "Anti-Abortion Violence Defines 'Army of God,'" *Christian Science Monitor*, February 4, 1998 (http://www.csmonitor.com).

40. *Army of God* manual, 48.

41. Sandi DuBowski, "Storming Wombs and Waco: How the Anti-Abortion and Militia Movements Converge," *Front Lines Research* 2, 2 (October 1996): 2. Fairness and Accuracy in Reporting (FAIR) investigated the reluctance to cover evidence of links between militia and pro-life groups. Most interesting in this investigation is that NBC refused to broadcast a segment of the program *TV Nation* that featured pro-life activists advocating homicide. The show aired on the BBC in Britain, but not in the United States. See Laura Flanders, "Far-Right Militias and Anti-Abortion Violence: When Will the Media See the Connection?" *Extra!* July 1995, 11-12.

42. The economic devastation to farmers since the 1970s is well documented and described with much feeling in Joel Dyer, *Harvest of Rage: Why Oklahoma City Is Only the Beginning* (New York: Westview, 1997). Other sources that acknowledge economic devastation as an element in the development of the militia movement and other forms of right-wing resistance include Kenneth Stern, *A Force upon the Plain: The American Militia Movement and the Politics of Hate* (New York: Simon and Schuster, 1996); Richard Abanes, *American Militias: Rebellion, Racism, and Religion* (Downers Grove, Ill.: InterVarsity Press, 1996); and Morris Dees and James Corcoran, *Gathering Storm* (New York: HarperCollins Publishers, 1996).

43. DuBowski, "Storming Wombs and Waco," 2.

44. Joseph Scheidler, *Closed: 99 Ways to Stop Abortion* (Toronto and Lewiston, N.Y.: Life Cycle Books, 1985), chap. 17.

45. Linda Kintz, *Between Jesus and the Market: The Emotions That Matter in Right-Wing America* (Durham, N.C., and London: Duke University Press, 1997), 256.

46. Ibid.

47. John Brockhoeft as quoted in Jeffrey Kaplan, "Absolute Rescue: Absolutism, Defensive Action and the Resort to Force," in *Millennialism and Violence*, ed. Michael Barkun (London and Portland, Ore.: Frank Cass, 1996), 147.

48. Kintz, *Between Jesus and the Market*, 265.

49. Kintz attributes this idea to Sigmund Freud; ibid., 264.

50. Kintz attributes this idea to Julia Kristeva; ibid.

51. Ibid., 264-65.

52. Rey Chow, *Ethics after Idealism: Theory, Culture, Ethnicity, Reading* (Bloomington: Indiana University Press, 1998), 21.

53. Ibid.

54. Nifong, "Anti-Abortion Violence Defines 'Army of God.' "

55. Reuters News Service, Internet wire, February 3, 1998. The Reuters office in Atlanta was one of two news media to receive the letter. The other was the *Atlanta Journal-Constitution*. June Preston, "FBI Sees Possible Serial Bomber in Southern Blasts."

56. Tony Horwitz, "Run, Rudolph, Run: How the Fugitive Became a Folk Hero," *The New Yorker*, March 15, 1999, 46–52.

57. North Carolina Militia Corps, from the Command of Southeastern States Alliance, approval from Gen. Beauregard per John W. Hassey, Chief of Staff, Warning, at 2235 hrs 13 February 1998; verification 334-567-7032.

58. DuBowski, "Storming Wombs and Waco," 4.

59. Michael Grunwald, "Militia Leader Will Try to Persuade Clinic Bombing Suspect to Give Up," *Washington Post*, August 11, 1998, A2.

60. Ibid.

61. Susan Jeffords and Claudia Springer, "Masculinity as Excess in Vietnam Films: The Father/Son Dynamic of American Culture," *Genre* 21, 4 (winter 1988): 487–522.

62. Kathy Scruggs and John Harmon, "The Rudolph Family: Talented, Tragic, Mysterious," *Atlanta Journal-Constitution*, March 22, 1998, C6.

63. Lewis Kamb, "Putting the Puzzle Together: Profile as Elusive as Rudolph Himself," *Birmingham Post-Herald*, March 21, 1998; "Grand Jury Investigates Clinic Blast," *Birmingham News*, March 13, 1998; Victoria Agnew, "Rudolph Message," *Post and Courier* (Charleston, S.C.), March 12, 1998.

64. Scruggs and Harmon, "Rudolph Family."

65. The *Birmingham News* is quoting Mark Potok of the Southern Poverty Law Center; "Grand Jury Investigates Clinic Blast," *Birmingham News*, March 13, 1998.

66. Scruggs and Harmon, "Rudolph Family."

67. Kamb, "Putting the Puzzle Together."

68. This message was in response to a discussion about the "FBI chasing their tale," distributed by Deja News on the Internet, and posted on March 19, 1998.

69. James Ridgeway, *Blood in the Face: The Ku Klux Klan, Aryan Nations, Nazi Skinheads, and the Rise of a New White Culture* (New York: Thunder's Mouth Press, 1990), 113.

70. Nick Patterson, "Experts See Links in Attacks: Abortion Clinic Bombing," *Birmingham Post-Herald*, February 16, 1998.

71. Dave Parks and John Archibald, "Northpoint Teams Chief Says Rudolph Not Linked to His North Carolina Group," *Birmingham News*, February 14, 1998; Scruggs and Harmon, "Rudolph Family."

72. Kevin Sack, "Suspect in Southern Bombings Is Enigma," *New York Times*, February 28, 1998, A1.

73. Aryan Nations recruiting pamphlet, collected by Political Research Associates, Somerville, Mass.

74. "Profile Focuses on Family and Early Years of Man Sought in Bombing," Associated Press, Murphy, N.C., February 24, 1998.

75. Deborah Rudolph, ex-wife of Eric Rudolph's brother, made these claims in an interview featured on "CNN Presents: The Hunt for Eric Rudolph," a Cable News Network program hosted by Art Harris, broadcast July 29, 2001, to mark the fifth anniversary of the bombing of Centennial Park in Atlanta.

76. Martin A. Lee, *The Beast Reawakens* (Boston: Little, Brown, 1997), 345.

77. "Christian Identity," Center for New Community, Oak Park, Ill., 1996.

78. Sally Avery Bermanzohn, *KKK and Domestic Terrorism* (Boulder, Colo. : Lynne Rienner, forthcoming).

79. Ridgeway, *Blood in the Face*, 79; Berlet and Lyons, *Right-Wing Populism in America*, 271.

80. Lee, *Beast Reawakens*, 335.

81. Ridgeway, *Blood in the Face*, 100.

82. Henry Ford, the automobile entrepreneur, first distributed an anti-Semitic essay on the "International Jew" to his workers in the 1920s. Like the *Protocols of the Elders of Zion*, a forgery meant to serve as evidence of a Jewish conspiracy to rule the world in the first part of the twentieth century, it is considered to be a classic text of anti-Semitic propaganda.

83. "Ku Klux Klan Pickets Aware Woman," *Body Politic*, October 1994, 3–6.

84. Ridgeway, *Blood in the Face*, 15, 23.

85. This transcript was printed in the *Body Politic*, October 1994, 7.

86. Bermanzohn, *KKK and Domestic Terrorism*.

87. Angela Davis, "Racism, Birth Control and Reproductive Rights," in *From Abortion to Reproductive Freedom*, ed. Marlene Fried (Boston: South End Press, 1990); Carole McCann, *Birth Control Politics in the United States, 1916–1945* (Ithaca, N.Y.: Cornell University Press, 1994); Linda Gordon, *Woman's Body, Woman's Right: A Social History of Birth Control in America* (New York: Grossman, 1976); Dorothy Roberts, *Killing the Black Body: Race, Reproduction, and the Meaning of Liberty* (New York: Pantheon, 1997), chap. 2. On the intersection between nineteenth-century white women's campaigns for voluntary motherhood and imperialist fears of race suicide, see Stephanie Athey, "Eugenic Feminisms in Late Nineteenth-Century America," *Genders* 31 (2000).

88. Loretta Ross, "White Supremacy in the 1990s," in *Eyes Right! Challenging the Right Wing Backlash*, ed. Chip Berlet (Boston: South End Press, 1995).

89. Scheidler, *99 Ways to Stop Abortion*, chap. 48.

90. Tom Burghardt, *Dialectics of Terror: A National Directory of the Direct Action Anti-Abortion Movement and Their Allies* (San Francisco: Bay Area Coalition for Our Reproductive Rights, 1995).

91. Ida B. Wells-Barnett, *Selected Works* (New York: Oxford University

Press, 1991); Robyn Wiegman, *American Anatomies: Theorizing Race and Gender* (Durham, N.C., and London: Duke University Press, 1995); Joel Williamson, *A Rage for Order: Black/White Relations in the American South since Emancipation* (New York: Oxford University Press, 1986).

92. *Army of God* manual, 2.

93. For psychoanalytic discussion of abortion, see Drucilla Cornell, *The Imaginary Domain: Abortion, Pornography, and Sexual Harassment* (New York: Routledge, 1995). Cornell combines Lacanian analysis with traditional literary ideas about reading for "wholeness" and unity to argue that "it is the woman, not the state, that should have the narrative power over her decision. The narrative power is as important for her personhood as the decision itself since the chance to become a person is dependent on the imagined projection of one's self as whole" (35). Drawing from writings of Judith Butler, Cornell contends that this coherency and wholeness are necessary for women to receive governmental protection for and legal recognition as a "body that matters." Instead of asserting women's right to bodily integrity as the rationale behind abortion rights, some feminist theorists advocate a disembodied notion of personhood to argue for reproductive freedom. See Patricia Mann, "Cyborgean Motherhood and Abortion," in *Micro-Politics: Agency in a Postfeminist Era* (Minneapolis: University of Minnesota Press, 1994); and Mary Poovey, "The Abortion Question and the Death of Man," in *Feminists Theorize the Political*, ed. Joan W. Scott and Judith Butler (New York: Routledge, 1992).

94. Ross, "White Supremacy in the 1990s"; Michael Novick, "Women's Right: Target for Racist Terror: Neo-Nazi Involvement in the Anti-Abortion Movement," in *White Lies, White Power* (Monroe, Maine: Common Courage Press, 1995); Karen Houppert, "John Burt's Holy War," *Village Voice*, April 6, 1993, 27–31.

95. Risen and Thomas, *Wrath of Angels*, 199.

96. Jerry Reiter, *Live from the Gates of Hell: An Insider's Look at the Antiabortion Underground* (Amherst, N.Y.: Prometheus Books, 2000), 103.

97. Joan Andrews was the pro-life activist who "was offended when she first visited [Burt] and saw anti-Catholic literature in his home." See Risen and Thomas, *Wrath of Angels*, 195.

98. Kathleen Blee, *Women of the Klan: Racism and Gender in the 1920s* (Berkeley: University of California Press, 1991), 89.

99. Ibid.

100. Ibid., 87.

101. Ross, "White Supremacy in the 1990s," 24.

102. Tom Burghardt, "Neo-Nazis Salute the Anti-Abortion Zealots," *CovertAction*, spring 1995, 27.

103. Lee, *Beast Reawakens*, 337.

104. "The Tragedy of the White Race," *Aryan Nations Church of Jesus Christ Christian Newsletter*, no. 39, 3–4.

105. The cover illustration appears in Burghardt, "Neo-Nazis Salute the Anti-Abortion Zealots," *Covert Action Quarterly* 52 (spring 1995) : 27.

106. Lin Collette, "Encountering Holocaust Denial," in *Eyes Right!* 246–65.

107. Roberts, *Killing the Black Body*, esp. 98–103; Loretta J. Ross, "African-American Women and Abortion: 1800–1970," in *Theorizing Black Feminisms*, ed. Stanlie James and Abena Busia (New York: Routledge, 1993), 149; Robert G. Weisbord, *Genocide? Birth Control and the Black American* (Westport, Conn.: Greenwood Press, 1975); Manning Marable, *The Question of Genocide* (Dayton, Ohio: Black Research Associates, 1982); Thomas Shapiro, *Population Control Politics: Women, Sterilization, and Reproductive Choice* (Philadelphia: Temple University Press, 1985); Betsy Hartmann, *Reproductive Rights and Wrongs: The Global Politics of Population Control and Contraceptive Choice* (New York: Harper and Row, 1987); Susan E. Davis, *Women under Attack: Victories, Backlash and the Fight for Reproductive Freedom* (Boston: South End Press, 1988); Toni Cade, "The Pill: Genocide or Liberation? in *The Black Woman, an Anthology*, ed. Toni Cade (New York: Signet Books, 1970), 162–69; Marsha Coleman, "Are Abortions for Black Women Racist?" *The Militant*, January 21, 1972, 19; "New York City Passed New Abortion Law," *Black Panther*, July 4, 1970, 2.

108. The Center for Bio-Ethical Reform website (http://www.cbrinfo.org/gap) lists the colleges and universities.

109. "The Eighth Promise," *Life Advocate*, November/December 1997, 17.

110. Ibid.

111. Center for Bio-Ethical Reform website.

112. Answers to frequently asked question 9, "Why are you calling this the Genocide Awareness Program? Abortion isn't genocide," at the Center for Bio-Ethical Reform website.

113. Gregg Cunningham, "Why Abortion Is Genocide," Center for Bio-Ethical Reform website. The legal scholar who coined the word *genocide* "stumbled on the idea while reading Plato, who used the Greek word genos to describe a clan or ethnic group," according to Barbara Crossette, "Salute to a Rights Campaigner Who Gave Genocide Its Name," *New York Times*, June 13, 2001.

114. Robert Thompson, "It's Genocide," February 24, 1998, American Dissident Voices Online Radio. Associated with the National Alliance based in Hillsboro, W.V. (http:///www.natall.com/radio/radio.html).

115. Center for Bio-Ethical Reform website.

116. "Eighth Promise."

117. Joe Conason, Alfred Ross, and Lee Cokorinos, "The Promise Keepers Are Coming: The Third Wave of the Religious Right," *The Nation*, October 7, 1996, 16.

118. Ibid., 14.

119. "The Eighth Promise."

120. However, when faced with his daughter's unplanned pregnancy by his star quarterback, McCartney "said he would back her if she chose to have an abortion." See Conason, Ross, and Cokorinos, "Promise Keepers Are Coming," 14.

121. Ibid., 12.

122. Kintz, *Between Jesus and the Market*, chap. 4.

123. As Martin E. Marty made clear in an Op-Ed piece in the *New York Times*, the Promise Keepers are "not the first Protestants to organize in an effort to advance some version of the male cause. A century ago, their ancestors invented 'muscular Christianity,' a set of initiatives intended to fight cultural degeneration" (Marty, "The Promise Keepers, in Perspective," *New York Times*, October 3, 1997, A15). Marty goes on to discuss similarities and differences among the Promise Keepers and the YMCA, the Boy Scouts, and other Christian men's organizations. A history of masculinity in America is germane to understanding how contemporary notions of manliness have evolved in relation to Christianity, capitalism, and sexuality. For a history of the emergence of manhood as an individual attribute needed to survive a market economy, see E. Anthony Rotundo, *American Manhood* (New York: Basic Books, 1993), chap. 1. For examinations of the more recent "crisis" faced by American men and the contested nature and social construction of "masculinity," compare Susan Faludi, *Stiffed* (New York: William Morrow, 1999), and Judith Halberstam, *Female Masculinity* (Durham, N.C.: Duke University Press, 1998).

124. Michael Bray, *A Time to Kill* (Portland, Ore.: Advocates for Life Publications, 1994), 156.

125. See, for example, Archibald E. Roberts, *The Republic: Decline and Future Promise* (Fort Collins, Colo.: Betsy Ross Press, 1975).

126. According to Sara Diamond, "Klan membership was at an all time low of about 1,500" by 1974 (*Roads to Dominion*, 152). James Ridgeway makes the comment about Duke's transformation of the Klan (*Blood in the Face*, 146).

2. From Protest to Retribution

1. On de Parrie, see Mark O'Keefe, "Anarchy in the Name of God," *Oregonian*, January 24, 1999. On Bray, see James Risen and Judy L. Thomas, *Wrath of Angels: The American Abortion War* (New York: Basic Books, 1998), chap. 4.

2. Risen and Thomas, *Wrath of Angels*, 347.

3. Ibid., 370.

4. Mark Crutcher, *Firestorm: A Guerrilla Strategy for a Pro-Life America* (Denton, Tex.: Life Dynamics, 1992). This manual is archived in the library of Political Research Associates of Somerville, Mass. Thanks to Jean Hardisty

and Chip Berlet for their help. Subsequent page numbers for quotations from *Firestorm* appear parenthetically in the text.

5. For a Texas Press Association award-winning exposé on the questionable financial workings of Crutcher's organizations, see Donna Fielder, "Sticks and Stones," *Denton Record-Chronicle*, September 13, 1998.

6. Mark Ballard, "The New Abortion Front," *Texas Lawyer*, April 22, 1996.

7. See Risen and Thomas, *Wrath of Angels;* Jeffrey Kaplan, "Absolute Rescue: Absolutism, Defensive Action and the Resort to Force," in *Millennialism and Violence*, ed. Michael Barkun (London and Portland, Ore.: Frank Cass, 1996); Faye Ginsburg, "Rescuing the Nation: Operation Rescue and the Rise of Anti-Abortion Militance," in *Abortion Wars: A Half Century of Struggle, 1950–2000*, ed. Rickie Solinger (Berkeley: University of California Press, 1998).

8. Risen and Thomas, *Wrath of Angels*, 340.

9. "French Court Recommends Extradition of Kopp," USAToday.com, June 28, 2001; available at ⟨http://www.usatoday.com/news/world/june01/2001-06-28-kopp.html⟩.

10. Christina Nifong, "Bomb Signals New Strategy," *Christian Science Monitor*, February 2, 1998.

11. Karen Foerstel and Andy Soltis, "6 Injured in Abort-Clinic Bomb Blasts," *New York Post*, January 17, 1997. See also the June 9, 1997, FBI press release, which reads, "there were secondary bombs designed to explode after law enforcement personnel arrived on the scene." These articles pertain to three bombs detonated in and around Atlanta, Ga., in 1997 and 1996.

12. See the Abortion Rights Activist website for chronologies of pro-life violence, including butyric acid attacks ⟨http://www.cais.com/agm/main/ytd98.htm⟩.

13. "Anthrax Scare," *Body Politic*, November 5, 1998.

14. " 'Pro-Life' Murder: Charleston Clinic Threat," *Charleston Gazette*, February 26, 1999.

15. Frederick Clarkson, "FBI: High Priority to Anti-Abortion Anthrax Mail," Women's Enews Internet news service ⟨http://www.womensenews.org⟩, November 8, 2001. Also available on the website of Political Research Associates ⟨http://www.publiceye.org/frontpage/911/clarkson1.html⟩. Virginia Dare, according to Clarkson, was the "first white child born in the New World in 1557."

16. Ibid.

17. Ibid. Clarkson is quoting Tracy Sefl of the University of Illinois.

18. "Clinic security experts say they doubt that Horsley was actually taken hostage by Waagner," according to Frederick Clarkson, "Abortion Terrorism Intrigue," Salon Internet news service ⟨http://salon.com/news/feature/2001/11/28/waagner/index_np.html⟩, November 11, 2001.

19. Bray is quoted by Bill Berkowitz, "Unfinished Business," Working for

Change news service (http://www.workingforchange.com/index.cfm), February 7, 2002. Bray's discussion of Waagner appeared on Neal Horsley's website, January 14, 2002.

20. In the 1980s the number of abortion providers in the United States began to decline. Between 1992 and 1996, the "number of abortion providers fell 14%, to 2,042, with the greatest decline among hospitals and physicians' offices rather than clinics. Eighty-six percent of counties had no known abortion provider, and 32% of women aged 15–44 lived in these counties" (Stanley K. Henshaw, "Abortion Incidence and Services in the United States, 1995–1996," *Family Planning Perspectives* 30, 6: 263–70, 287; available on the Internet at [http://www.gutmacher.org/pubs/journals/3026398.html]).

21. These figures are from Sharon Lerner, "Blight to Life," *Village Voice*, October 28–November 3, 1998.

22. The *Army of God* manual, which has no publication date or author listed, discusses "babies rescued through the increased cost of killing."

23. Joseph Scheidler, *Closed: 99 Ways to Stop Abortion* (Lewiston, N.Y.: Life Cycle Books, 1985), details legal ways to interfere in abortion provision; it is a more moderate version of the anonymous, underground *Army of God* manual, which delineates how to make bombs and other weapons of destruction for pro-life purposes. In a similar way, Crutcher has publicly circulated more openly a few, selected, toned-down ideas from *Firestorm* as *Lime 5: Exploited by Choice* (Denton, Tex.: Life Dynamics, 1996).

24. Ballard, "New Abortion Front."

25. Ibid.

26. Louis Beam, a former Grand Dragon in David Duke's Texas Klan and then a member of Aryan Nations, delivered in 1992 the finer points of leaderless resistance to 150 participants at a militia meeting in Estes Park, Colo. See Martin A. Lee, *The Beast Reawakens* (Boston: Little, Brown, 1997), 348.

27. Quoted in Waveney Ann Moore, "Man's Views Change Radically: A Man Once Part of Operation Rescue Became an FBI Informant and Now Calls Himself a Humanist," *St. Petersburg Times*, January 6, 2001. The quotation is gleaned from Jerry Reiter, *Live from the Gates of Hell: An Insider's Look at the Antiabortion Underground* (Amherst, N.Y.: Prometheus Books, 2000).

28. Scheidler, *Closed*, 151.

29. The trend in feminist academic accounts of abortion politics is to synthesize the pro-life and pro-choice movements, to analyze them comparatively, to find common ground, and then to depict the whole "debate" as a paradigmatic American phenomenon. This ten-year-old approach is exemplified in Faye Ginsburg, *Contested Lives: The Abortion Debate in an American Community* (Berkeley: University of California Press, 1989). The trend in media accounts of anti-abortion violence is to tell the perpetrator's life history in an attempt to uncover the psychological motive behind the crime. This trend informs Risen and Thomas, *Wrath of Angels*, which attempts to answer why the

anti-abortion movement turned violent. In contrast, the richly detailed Baird-Windle and Bader volume, *Targets of Hatred: Anti-Abortion Terrorism* (New York: Palgrave, 2001), documents the psychological and political effects of anti-abortion violence in a way that underscores the immense difference between pro-choice and pro-life politics. I know about the policy to not publicize threats from firsthand experience as a former employee of the largest Planned Parenthood affiliate in the country.

30. Vivienne Walt, "Group Offers Case in a Kit; New Tactic vs. Abortion Docs," *Newsday*, September 6, 1993.

31. Ballard, "New Abortion Front."

32. Letter to National Abortion Federation members from Feminist Women's Health Center, Chico, Calif., March 17, 1998.

33. Ballard, "New Abortion Front."

34. Dr. Steir's message was posted on the website (http://www.steirs defense.org).

35. Phyllida Burlingame, *Unfair Prosecution of Abortion Providers: Bias by the Medical Board of California* (San Francisco, Calif.: American Civil Liberties Union of Northern California, 2000). The report is available on line at (http://www.aclunc.org/reproductive-rights/medical-bias.report.html).

36. Ibid.

37. These quotations are from the Alan Guttmacher Institute. For additional compelling information on the safety and frequency of abortion in America, visit their website (http://www.agi-usa.org). See also Joseph Berger, "Abortion Access Drops for Poor after Slayings," *New York Times*, November 3, 1998, A28.

38. On the criminalization of abortion in the United States, see the following: Carroll Smith-Rosenberg, *Disorderly Conduct: Visions of Gender in Victorian America* (New York: Oxford University Press, 1985); James C. Mohr, *Abortion in America: The Origins and Evolution of National Policy, 1800–1900* (New York: Oxford University Press, 1978); Ginsburg, *Contested Lives;* and Kristen Luker, *Abortion and the Politics of Motherhood* (Berkeley: University of California Press, 1984).

39. For a history of Jane, the illegal abortion service, especially with regard to the self-help movement, see Ninia Baehr, *Abortion without Apology: A Radical History for the 1990s* (Boston: South End Press, 1990). See also Laura Kaplan, *The Story of Jane: The Legendary Underground Feminist Abortion Service* (New York: Pantheon, 1996).

40. Nell Bernstein, "Law Creates a New Class of Children: Isolated, Illegal," *San Jose Mercury News*, July 19, 1998.

41. Sharon Lerner, "The 'Partial' Ploy: How the Anti-Choice Campaign against a Nonexistent Procedure Threatens *Roe*," *Village Voice*, September 23–29, 1998.

42. Katheryn Katz, "The Pregnant Child's Right to Self-Determination," *Albany Law Review* 62, 3 (1999): 1123.

43. American Life League letter, in *Defending Reproductive Rights: An Activist Resource Kit* (Somerville, Mass.: Political Research Associates, 2000), 72.

44. Ilaina Jonas, "Girl, 12, in Incest Case Has Abortion," *Pittsburgh Post-Gazette*, August 1, 1998.

45. Tamar Lewin, "Nebraska Abortion Case: The Issue Is Interference," *New York Times*, September 25, 1995, 1, 6.

46. Ibid., 6.

47. When it was realized that the girl was twenty-seven weeks pregnant, she and her family decided not to abort the pregnancy. "Four years later the girl's family settled the lawsuit they had filed against the ex-boyfriend's family and local officials for interfering with the family's decision concerning the pregnancy" (Katz, "Pregnant Child's Right to Self-Determination," 1124).

48. The pamphlet was printed and distributed by Pro-Life Action Ministries, St. Paul, Minn.

49. See *The Facts Speak Louder*, Planned Parenthood's response to the film. See also Lauren Berlant, *The Queen of America Goes to Washington City: Essays on Sex and Citizenship* (Durham, N.C.: Duke University Press, 1997), 116–24.

50. DeNeen L. Brown, "Deborah's Choice," *Washington Post*, September 27, 1998.

51. Alison Fitzgerald, "Woman Sues Abortion Clinic for 'Wrongful Birth,' " *Charlotte Observer*, September 1, 1998; Brian MacQuarrie, " 'Wrongful Birth' Suit Raises Fears for Children," *Boston Globe*, September 5, 1998.

52. "Clinic Workers Get 'Chilling' Mailing," *Boston Herald*, February 28, 1997.

53. For an image of the poster, see the Life Dynamics, Inc., website (http://www.lifedynamics.net/Products/index.dfm?fuseaction=Product&id =18). For a list of subjects that clinic employees are compelled to consider, go to (http://www.clinicworkers.com/TOC.htm).

54. Charles E. Rice, "Can the Killing of Abortionists Be Justified?" *Wanderer*, September 1, 1994, reprinted on the Internet at (http://www.trosch. org); Frederick Clarkson, *Eternal Hostility: The Struggle between Theocracy and Democracy* (Monroe, Maine: Common Courage Press, 1997), 151.

55. For an earlier discussion of retribution and "retributive justice" with regard to both capital punishment and "respect for life" as manifested in anti-abortion campaigns, see Thomas J. Higgins, "Why the Death Penalty?" *Triumph*, February 1973, 20–23. The article appeared in this Catholic magazine just a month after the Supreme Court handed down its decision of *Roe v. Wade*. According to Patrick Allitt, Rice was one of the conservative Catholics who deplored social changes such as widespread approval of oral contraception. Rice and companions such as Michael Lawrence and Brent Bozell "were among the first groups to publicize evidence that contraceptive pills could

have adverse health consequences for longtime users; and supported black leaders who denounced proposals that 'welfare mothers' should be compelled to use contraceptives" (Allitt, *Catholic Intellectuals and Conservative Politics in America, 1950–1985* [Ithaca, N.Y.: Cornell University Press, 1993], 173). Rice's early works included key texts, *The Vanishing Right to Live* (Garden City, N.Y.: Doubleday, 1969), and *Authority and Rebellion: The Case for Orthodoxy in the Catholic Church* (Garden City, N.Y.: Doubleday, 1971).

56. Rice, "Can the Killing of Abortionists Be Justified?"

57. Charles E. Rice, "The Death Penalty Dilemma," *New American*, April 4, 1994, 23–24.

58. Elizabeth Mensch and Alan Freeman, *The Politics of Virtue: Is Abortion Debatable?* (Durham, N.C.: Duke University Press, 1993), 35.

59. Jacques Derrida, "Force of Law: The 'Mystical Foundation of Authority,'" in *Deconstruction and the Possibility of Justice*, ed. Drucilla Cornell, Michel Rosenfeld, and David Gray Carlson (New York: Routledge, 1992), 32.

60. Rice, "Death Penalty Dilemma," 23.

61. Ibid., 24.

62. Ibid.

63. Mensch and Freeman discuss natural law and the Catholic tradition with regard to anti-abortion arguments (*Politics of Virtue*, 31).

64. Michael Bray, *A Time to Kill* (Portland, Ore.: Advocates for Life Publications, 1994), 110. In addition to being influenced by Rice, Bray acknowledges another source for his thinking on the legality of killing for life, which Frederick Clarkson discusses in detail in *Eternal Hostility* (144–51). Bray's influence was attorney Michael Hirsh's article, "Use of Force in Defense of Another: An Argument for Michael Griffin," *Regent University Law Review*, spring 1994. (Griffin was the first man convicted of killing an abortion provider, Dr. David Gunn.) When Paul Hill killed John Britton, Michael Hirsh, a former director of Operation Rescue in Atlanta and a lawyer with Pat Robertson's American Center for Law and Justice, had been defending Hill against charges of disruption and trespassing on clinic property; after the killing, Hirsch withdrew his article from circulation. The suppressed article is dedicated to Bray and argues that killing Dr. Gunn was legally justifiable and "consistent with Biblical Truth" (Clarkson, *Eternal Hostility*, 145). In *A Time to Kill*, Bray acknowledges that "his lay legal argument was based in part on Michael Hirsh's Regent University thesis" (Clarkson, *Eternal Hostility*, 149).

65. Chip Berlet, "John Salvi, Abortion Clinic Violence, and Catholic Right Conspiracism," Political Research Associates, March 19, 1996. In addition to Rice's article, Salvi kept materials from Human Life International and the *Fatima Crusader* in his apartment. These are not available "at the corner newsstand. They are circulated mainly within a distinctly right-wing conspiracist subculture." See Chip Berlet and Matthew N. Lyons, "John Salvi: God's Pa-

triot," in *Right-Wing Populism in America: Too Close for Comfort* (New York: Guilford Press, 2000), 297–99.

66. Clarkson, *Eternal Hostility*, 150.

67. Berlet and Lyons, *Right-Wing Populism*, 297.

68. The ultimate objective of retribution, such as capital punishment, is to restore a particular order rather than to punish a particular individual. See Walter Benjamin, "Critique of Violence," in *Reflections: Essays, Aphorisms, Autobiographical Writings* (New York: Schocken Books, 1986), 277–300.

69. See Moore, "Man's Views Change Radically," 6.

70. David J. Garrow, "Abortion Before and After *Roe v. Wade*: An Historical Perspective," *Albany Law Review* 62, 3 (1999): 833–52.

71. Ibid., 851.

72. Ibid.

73. Ibid., 852.

3. Protection from and for the Fetal Citizen

1. Michael Barkun, introduction to *Millennialism and Violence* (London and Portland, Ore.: Frank Cass, 1996), 2.

2. This Gallup poll is quoted in Didi Herman, *The Antigay Agenda: Orthodox Vision and the Christian Right* (Chicago: University of Chicago Press, 1997), 19.

3. Paul Boyer, *When Time Shall Be No More: Prophecy Belief in Modern American Culture* (Cambridge: Harvard University Press, 1992).

4. Lee Quinby, *Anti-Apocalypse: Exercises in Genealogical Criticism* (Minneapolis: University of Minnesota Press, 1994), xii.

5. Ibid.

6. On the tragic and comic aspects of apocalyptic narrative, see Stephen O'Leary, *Arguing the Apocalypse: A Theory of Millennial Rhetoric* (Oxford: Oxford University Press, 1998).

7. Michael Barkun, *Religion and the Racist Right: The Origins of the Christian Identity Movement* (Chapel Hill: University of North Carolina Press, 1994).

8. The 1999 PBS program "Apocalypse!" makes the same point as Chip Berlet and Matthew Lyons: "The government's failure to comprehend the Davidian's apocalyptic millennialist worldview set the stage for the deadly miscalculations by government agents, which cost the lives of 80 Branch Davidians (including 21 children) and four federal agents in April 1993" (Berlet and Lyons, *Right-Wing Populism in America: Too Close for Comfort* [New York: Guilford Press, 2000], 290–91).

9. Jerry Reiter, *Live from the Gates of Hell: An Insider's Look at the Antiabortion Underground* (Amherst, N.Y.: Prometheus Books, 2000), 152.

10. Jeffrey Kaplan, "America's Last Prophetic Witness: The Literature of the Rescue Movement," *Terrorism and Political Violence* 5, 3 (autumn 1993): 67.

11. Reiter, *Live from the Gates of Hell*, 71, 75.

12. Ibid., 106.

13. Ibid., 34.

14. Ibid., 188.

15. Hill is quoted in Jeffrey Kaplan, "Absolute Rescue: Absolutism, Defensive Action and the Resort to Force," in *Millennialism and Violence*, ed. Michael Barkun (London and Portland, Ore.: Frank Cass, 1996), 155.

16. Ibid.

17. James Ridgeway, *Blood in the Face: The Ku Klux Klan, Aryan Nations, Nazi Skinheads, and the Rise of a New White Culture* (New York: Thunder's Mouth Press, 1990), 111–12.

18. Berlet and Lyons, *Right-Wing Populism in America*, 249.

19. Kaplan, "Absolute Rescue," 155.

20. Berlet and Lyons, *Right-Wing Populism in America*, 250.

21. As Jeffrey Kaplan notes, "Identity theology is in a state of constant flux" but "does generally hold to a set of beliefs which do translate to . . . an orthodox which is subjected to a constant process of review and refinement" (Kaplan, *Radical Religion in America* [Syracuse, N.Y.: Syracuse University Press, 1997], 47).

22. Ridgeway, *Blood in the Face*, 113.

23. "Terrorists in the Name of God and Race: Phineas Priests Use Religious Arguments to Justify Their Violent Crimes," *Body Politic*, April 1997, 17–21. Reprinted from Klanwatch Intelligence Report published by the Southern Poverty Law Center.

24. Ibid., 20.

25. Ibid., 18.

26. Ibid., 20.

27. Kaplan, "Absolute Rescue," 154–55. For a discussion of "blood guiltiness," see James Risen and Judy L. Thomas, *Wrath of Angels: The American Abortion War* (New York: Basic Books, 1998), chap. 10.

28. According to Frederick Clarkson, "Hill told journalist Judy Thomas that he rejects the racism of the Phineas Priesthood." Clarkson's report on the links between white supremacist and anti-abortion ideology, "Anti-Abortion Extremism: Anti-Abortion Extremists, 'Patriots' and Racists Converge," *Intelligence Report* (Southern Poverty Law Center), summer 1998, 8–16.

29. *I Witness*, Attie and Goldwater Productions, 2000.

30. In this sense, Hill is postmillennialist. I address the different types of millennialism in chap. 4.

31. Kaplan, "Absolute Rescue," 152.

32. According to pro-choice advocates, "the term 'partial-birth' abortion cannot be found in any medical dictionary because anti-choice advocates made

it up as part of their ongoing public relations campaign to stigmatize abortion." See collected papers and sources compiled as *Project Stop the Abortion Ban: A Message on So-Called 'Partial-Birth' Abortion Bans*, sponsored and distributed to pro-choice organizations by Fifty Plus One, the Feminist Majority Foundation, and Pro-Choice Resource Center, March 1998. See also Sharon Lerner, "The Partial Ploy: How the Anti-Choice Campaign against a Nonexistent Procedure Threatens *Roe*," *Village Voice*, September 23–29, 1998. I use the term not in reference to actual late-term abortion procedures but instead to the neological, fantastic abortion procedure fabricated by pro-life strategists.

33. For an interesting discussion of how feminists theorize the fetal subject, and how fetal protection laws and abortion restrictions define women in relation to fetuses, see Lynn M. Morgan, "Fetal Relationality in Feminist Philosophy: An Anthropological Critique," *Hypatia* 11, 3 (summer 1996): 47–70.

34. U.S. House of Representatives Bill No. 1833, Partial-Birth Abortion Ban Act of 1995.

35. Charles Canady, *Report from the Committee on the Judiciary to the 104th Congress*, 1st sess., House Report 104–267: Partial-Birth Abortion Act of 1995 (Washington, D.C.: Government Printing Office, 1995), 3. This report, which includes the cost estimate of the Congressional Budget Office, together with dissenting views, was intended to accompany H.R. 1883.

36. Ibid., 4.

37. Ibid., 2.

38. Ibid., 23.

39. U.S. Senate Republican Policy Committee Legislative Notice no. 15, H.R. 1122—Partial-Birth Abortion Ban Act of 1997, May 13, 1997. Text available at (http://www.senate.gov/~rpc/releases/1997/15-pba.htm).

40. The AMA brief is quoted in the dissenting opinion written by Justice Kennedy in *Stenberg v. Carhart*. Available on line at (http://supct.law.cornell.edu/supct/html/99-830.ZD3.html), section II B.

41. Janet Benshoof, quoted in Ruth Padawer, " 'Partial-Birth' Abortion Ban Struck Down," *Record* (Bergen, N.J.), June 29, 2000.

42. David Garrow, "Abortion before and after *Roe v. Wade*," *Albany Law Review* 62, 3 (1999): 845.

43. Benshoof, quoted in Padawer, " 'Partial-Birth' Abortion Ban Struck Down."

44. *Stenberg v. Carhart*, Kennedy's dissenting opinion, sec. 3.

45. This image was sent anonymously from Boston in response to a direct mail campaign by Planned Parenthood of New York City. I thank Vivian Saldana for sharing this material with me.

46. According to one journalist, "what is really important in this cartoon is that the pregnant woman has been turned into a headless, hollow torso" (see Verlyn Klinkenborg, "Violent Certainties," *Harper's*, January 1995, 48).

47. Karen Newman, *Fetal Positions: Individualism, Science, Visuality* (Stanford, Calif.: Stanford University Press, 1996), 21–23.

48. According to Katha Pollitt, focusing on "third-trimester medical tragedies" was partially a response to an "onslaught of propaganda" surrounding a revelation by Ron Fitzsimmons. Fitzsimmons, the executive director of the National Coalition of Abortion Providers and not himself an abortion provider, dramatically stated that he had "lied through his teeth" about the number of late-term abortions performed annually in the United States. See Pollitt, "Secrets and Lies," *The Nation*, March 31, 1997, 9.

49. Dave Ranney, "Tiller: Abortion Bill an Insult to Women," *Wichita Eagle*, April 11, 1998.

50. Colleen McCain and Dave Ranney, "Five Kansas Families Share Deeply Personal Stories," *Wichita Eagle*, April 19, 1998.

51. Alexander Sanger, "Good Reasons for Partial-Birth Abortion," letter to the editor, *Wall Street Journal*, October 2, 1996.

52. Alexander Sanger, "Battle over Partial Birth Abortions: Don't Curb Women's Rights," *New York Daily News*, September 24, 1996.

53. The Utah ban was enacted in 1996 (Utah, UC 1953 76–7-310.5). The text is available from the Abortion Law website homepage.

54. U.S. Senate Republican Policy Committee Legislative Notice no. 15.

55. This statement is a quotation from the *Washington Post* (September 17, 1996), as cited in "Reasons for Partial-Birth Abortion" (ibid.).

56. See Dorothy Roberts, *Killing the Black Body: Race, Reproduction, and the Meaning of Liberty* (New York: Pantheon Books, 1997); and Lynn M. Paltrow, "Punishing Women for Their Behavior during Pregnancy," in *Drug Addiction Research and the Health of Women* (Rockville, Md.: National Institute on Drug Abuse, 1998), 467–501.

57. Petition for a Writ of Certiorari to the South Carolina Supreme Court from the U.S. Supreme Court, in re *Cornelia Whitner v. State of South Carolina* and *Malissa Ann Crawley v. Michael Moore* (as director of the South Carolina Department of Corrections), October term 1997, 2.

58. Ellen Goodman, "Prosecuting Pregnant Women: Court Victory May Be Shortlived," *Sarasota* [Fla.] *Herald-Tribune*, March 28, 2001.

59. Stephen R. Kandall, *Substance and Shadow: Women and Addiction in the United States* (Cambridge: Harvard University Press, 1996), 6.

60. Both Deborah A. Frank and Barry S. Zuckerman ("Children Exposed to Cocaine Prenatally: Pieces of the Puzzle, *Neurotoxicology and Teratology* 15 [1993]: 299) and Mike Gray (*Drug Crazy: How We Got into This Mess and How We Can Get Out* [New York: Random House, 1998], 108) use this quotation, which the former attributes to the *Rolling Stone* article.

61. Gray, *Drug Crazy*, 108.

62. Roberts, *Killing the Black Body*, 21.

63. Charles Molony Condon, "Bureaucrats Stopped Crack-Baby Prevention Program," *Greenville News*, May 28, 1995, 3.

64. Gray, *Drug Crazy*, 108–9.

65. Kathy Fackelmann, "The Crack-Baby Myth," *Washington City Paper*, December 11, 1991.

66. Lynn Paltrow, letter to executives at CBS, May 28, 1998.

67. For a comprehensive list of methodological flaws of early research on pregnant cocaine users and a summation of evidence that "points to the lack of quality prenatal care and the use of alcohol and tobacco as primary factors in poor fetal development among pregnant cocaine users," see *Cocaine and Pregnancy* (New York: Lindesmith Center, a Project of the Open Society Institute, 1997).

68. Gray, *Drug Crazy*, 110.

69. Condon, "Bureaucrats Stopped Crack-Baby Prevention Program," 3.

70. Charles Molony Condon, *Statement by the Attorney General of South Carolina before the U.S. House Committee on Government Reform and Oversight Subcommittee on National Security, International Affairs, and Criminal Justice*, Federal Information Systems Corporation, Federal News Service, July 23, 1998.

71. Rick Bragg, "Defender of God, South and Unborn," *New York Times*, January 13, 1998, A10.

72. Ibid.

73. See "C.R.A.C.K. Uses Unethical Tactics to Stop Women with Substance Abuse Problems from Becoming Pregnant," *Fight for Reproductive Freedom: A Newsletter for Student Activists* 14, 1 (fall 1999): 6. See also Ellen H. Chen and Charon Asetoyer, "Ethical Concerns," excerpted from "A Review of the Use and Effects of Depo-Provera on Native American Women within Indian Health Services and Other Federal Agencies," in *Defending Reproductive Rights: An Activist Resource Kit* (Somerville, Mass.: Political Research Associates, 2000), 105–12.

74. Letter to C.R.A.C.K. founder Barbara Harris from the Committee on Women, Population, and the Environment, *Fight for Reproductive Freedom: A Newsletter for Student Activists* 14, 1 (fall 1999): 7. The newsletter is produced by the Population and Development Program, Hampshire College.

75. "The USA became the first nation in the world to permit mass sterilization as part of an effort to 'purify the race.' By the mid-1930s, about 20,000 people had been sterilized against their will and twenty-one states had passed eugenics laws," according to Dianne Jntl Forte and Karen Judd ("The South within the North: Reproductive Choice in Three U.S. Communities," in *Negotiating Reproductive Rights*, ed. Rosalind Petchesky and Karen Judd [New York: ZED Books, 1998], 269). See also Thomas Shapiro, *Population Control Politics: Women, Sterilization, and Reproductive Choice* (Philadelphia: Temple

University Press, 1985); and Betsy Hartmann, *Reproductive Rights and Wrongs: The Global Politics of Population Control and Contraceptive Choice* (New York: Harper and Row, 1987).

76. "Mothers Paid to Stop Having Children," *Marie Claire*, December 1998, as quoted in "C.R.A.C.K. Uses Unethical Tactics to Stop Women with Substance Abuse Problems from Becoming Pregnant."

77. See "C.R.A.C.K. Uses Unethical Tactics to Stop Women with Substance Abuse Problems from Becoming Pregnant," 6.

78. Louisiana Coalition Against Racism and Nazism, "Duke's Louisiana Government Record: Duke's Sterilization Plan," July 1991 (http://www.stopduke.org).

79. The Louisiana Coalition Against Racism and Nazism gleaned archived audio recordings from Tulane University's special collection.

80. "C.R.A.C.K. Uses Unethical Tactics to Stop Women with Substance Abuse Problems from Becoming Pregnant."

81. For a discussion of the impact of drugs on prenatal development that is devoid of crack baby mythology, consider Linda Ferrill Annis, *The Child before Birth* (Ithaca, N.Y.: Cornell University Press, 1978).

82. Alan Mozes, "Poverty Has Greater Impact Than Cocaine on Young Brain," Reuters Health, citing Hallum Hurt et al., "Problem-Solving Ability of Inner-City Children with and without in Utero Cocaine Exposure," *Journal of Developmental and Behavioral Pediatrics* (1999): 418–19. Quoted in Lynn Paltrow, David S. Cohen, and Corinne A. Carey, *Year 2000 Overview: Governmental Responses to Pregnant Women Who Use Alcohol or Other Drugs* (Philadelphia and New York: Women's Law Project and National Advocates for Pregnant Women, 2000).

83. Paltrow, Cohen, and Carey, *Year 2000 Overview*, 1.

84. *Ferguson et al. v. City of Charleston et al.*, 121 S. Ct. 1281 (2001).

85. Goodman, "Prosecuting Pregnant Women."

86. Sue Anne Pressley, "S.C. Verdict Fuels Debate over Rights of the Unborn," *Washington Post*, May 27, 2001.

87. Linda Kintz comments on Stephen O'Leary's formulation of apocalyptic narratives as comedy and tragedy, in the introduction to *Between Jesus and the Market: The Emotions That Matter in Right-Wing America* (Durham, N.C., and London: Duke University Press, 1997), 9.

4. The Gideon Story

1. The cartoon was penned by "MacNelly—*Richmond News Leader*" and copyrighted by the *Chicago Tribune* in 1974. It appears in Charles Colson, *Born Again* (Old Tappan, N.J.: Chosen Books, 1976).

2. For a detailed account of the changes in leadership from Randall Terry

to Keith Tucci, and the subsequent splintering of Operation Rescue into Operation Rescue National, see James Risen and Judy L. Thomas, *Wrath of Angels: The American Abortion War* (New York: Basic Books, 1998), chap. 13.

3. To reflect this shift and to create distance from the law-breaking "rescues" that made Operation Rescue famous, Benham changed the official name of the organization from Operation Rescue National to Operation Save America. This name change occurred in conjunction with the action in 1999, as is evident in Benham signing off as "Director ORN" on promotional literature for the event, which I obtained there. Because Benham's organization was both Operation Rescue National *and* Operation Save America during the Buffalo action—depending on which available pamphlets you read, who you spoke with, and when you spoke with them—I am using the name Operation Rescue for simplicity.

4. Eric Goodman, "On the 19th of April . . . ," *Self*, April 1999, 111.

5. Risen and Thomas, *Wrath of Angels*, 333.

6. Katie Roiphe, "Abstract Hate, Real Victim," *Jerusalem Report*, December 21, 1998, 55.

7. Ibid.

8. Adrian Humphrey, "Bizarre Threats to Doctor; Police Protect Local Obstetrician," *Spectator*, December 12, 1997; idem, "Is Threat to Abortion MD Work of Sniper?" *Spectator*, December 13, 1997.

9. Goodman, "On the 19th of April," 111.

10. According to Andrew Gow, Falwell is repeating a myth that goes back to the advent of the printing press near the end of the Middle Ages. "One of the first books ever printed (around 1450) was 'The Book of Antichrist.'" According to this myth, the Antichrist is a Jew who will convene Jews in Jerusalem under false pretenses of world peace, will rebuild the Jewish Temple there, and will commence with world domination—sometimes described as a one-world government—which is a precursor to Armageddon. Inherent, historically, in this myth is the premise that the Antichrist is the love child of a Jewish whore and Satan. In some cases, Satan is also the whore's father, which adds an element of incest to the mix of wickedness and lasciviousness that characterizes the Antichrist. The historical residue of this myth may result not only in distrust of actual Jews but in passive tolerance or active instigation of anti-Semitism. Falwell's claim that the Antichrist is alive and Jewish is dangerous for this reason. As Gow says, "The danger in this case is that large numbers of Christians will believe this hateful myth because Falwell has repeated it." See Gow's Internet essay, "The Myth of the Jewish Antichrist: Falwell Stumbles Badly," a position paper from the Center for Millennial Studies at Boston University (www.mille.org). Gow has also written *The Red Jews: Anti-semitism in an Apocalyptic Age, 1200–1600* (Boston: E. J. Brill, 1994).

Falwell is certainly not the only one suggesting that the Antichrist will ascend to power soon. In William T. James, ed., *Foreshocks of Antichrist* (Eugene,

Ore.: Harvest House Publishers, 1997), contributors assume that if not Benjamin Netanyahu, Israel's former prime minister, then some other Jewish leader will dupe Jews into assembling a New World Order. "One day, perhaps quite soon, a leader will step from the ranks of his contemporaries, and through guile, persuasion, and diplomatic acumen unparalleled in the world's long, war-torn history, he will convince even the most skeptical Israeli hardliner to trust him to ensure Israel's security" (8).

11. Paul Boyer, *When Time Shall Be No More: Prophecy Belief in Modern American Culture* (Cambridge: Harvard University Press, 1992), 219.

12. Ibid., 217.

13. Charles Strozier, *Apocalypse: On the Psychology of Fundamentalism in America* (Boston: Beacon Press, 1995).

14. Michael Barkun, "Racist Apocalypse: Millennialism on the Far Right," in *The Year 2000: Essays on the End*, ed. Charles Strozier and Michael Flynn, 190–205 (New York: New York University Press, 1997), 201.

15. See Lee Quinby, "Coercive Purity: The Dangerous Promise of Apocalyptic Masculinity," in Strozier and Flynn, *The Year 2000*, 154–165.

16. Risen and Thomas, *Wrath of Angels*, 220.

17. On the important theme of light versus darkness, see Norman Cohn, *Cosmos, Chaos and the World to Come: The Ancient Roots of Apocalyptic Faith* (New Haven: Yale University Press, 1993).

18. In particular, Risen and Thomas have looked at this debate as it relates to the historical trajectory of the pro-life movement. They argue that a particular kind of millennialism—premillennial dispensationalism—"kept Protestant fundamentalists out of the anti-abortion movement" (ibid., 81) and that not until Francis Schaeffer came along were they able to "break . . . free from the premillennial trap." The trap, as Risen and Thomas portray it, lies in the idea that premillennialists are complacent because they believe Christ will inaugurate the millennium of peace and justice. "Christians thus should not stand in the way of chaos, because it was a necessary precursor to Christ's return" (81).

Risen and Thomas are accurate in portraying this problem, and accurate, too, in pointing to Schaeffer as a key person in helping to argue that evangelicals should not be politically complacent. However, Schaeffer's theological argument and the subsequent mobilization of multitudes of evangelical Christians into the U.S. political process are no indication that premillennialism has been "discarded" in the pro-life movement or in U.S. evangelical circles in general. This is true, too, for dispensationalism and rapture theory—two elements that mark premillennialism as "a mystical eschatology," as Risen and Thomas call it.

At the heart of their misunderstanding is the authors' preconception that premillennial dispensationalism is a "pseudotheology" (81). On the contrary, it is a major theology in American history and culture that is endemic to a wide variety of evangelical and fundamentalist religions. For the widely divergent developments of fundamentalism and evangelicalism, see Donald W. Dayton and Robert K. Johnston, eds., *The Variety of American Evangelicalism* (Knoxville: University of Tennessee Press, 1991).

19. Charles Colson with Ellen Santili Vaughn, *Kingdoms in Conflict* (Grand Rapids, Mich.: Zondervan Publishing, 1987), 89.

20. Ibid., 46.

21. Ibid., 278.

22. Risen and Thomas, *Wrath of Angels*, 123.

23. Sara Diamond, *Roads to Dominion: Right-Wing Movements and Political Power in the United States* (New York: Guilford Press, 1995), 209.

24. Risen and Thomas, *Wrath of Angels*, 130.

25. Charles Colson and Ellen Vaughn, *Gideon's Torch* (Dallas, Tex.: Word Publishers, 1995), 180, 516. Hereafter, page references for the novel appear parenthetically in the text.

26. At least one reviewer of the novel has seized on its encouragement of guerrilla warfare. Comparing *Gideon's Torch* with William Pierce's (aka Andrew MacDonald) *The Turner Diaries* (New York: Barricade Books, 1978), pro-choice activist Debra Sweet delineates the ways in which the novel can be seen as "both a how-to manual and a justification for explicit anti-abortion violence." Sweet's was possibly the first review to bring *Gideon's Torch* to the attention of some in leftist circles. According to Sweet, who advocates discussion, not censorship, the novel "deserves to be read, critiqued, exposed and opposed by those who are concerned with the right-wing onslaught against women's rights and reproductive choice." See her book review, dated December 23, 1995, on the Refuse and Resist website (http://www.refuseandresist.org/ab/colsonreview.html).

Although descriptions of the guerrilla actions in the novel are vividly detailed and can be read as instructional, *Gideon's Torch* is not intended to motivate people to action as is the *Turner Diaries*, which was said to be the blueprint for the 1995 Oklahoma City bombing. Unlike *Gideon's Torch*, which could be classified as popular fiction, *Turner Diaries* conforms more readily to the genre of revolutionary fiction in which the movement itself becomes the protagonist. In general, scholarship on revolutionary fiction takes leftist writings as its focus, but fiction from the far right is part of the genre too. Pro-life fiction that resembles the *Turner Diaries* more than *Gideon's Torch* is usually published by a vanity press or distributed through the Internet. Two examples are Gabriel Daniel Farenheit, *Xinnis: Confessions of a Clinic Bomber* (available through Life Enterprises Unlimited), and David Maccabee, *Rescue Platoon* (posted on Life Enterprises Unlimited website [http://www.trosch.org]).

27. Dallas Blanchard and Terry J. Prewitt, *Religious Violence and Abortion: The Gideon Project* (Gainesville: University Press of Florida, 1993), 170.

28. Ibid., 171.

29. Connie Paige, *The Right-to-Lifers: Who They Are, How They Operate, Where They Get Their Money* (New York: Summit Books, 1983), 100.

30. Ibid., 101.

31. The reason the abortion-as-slavery argument flourished after *Roe v. Wade* may be because the state's arguments against the plaintiff Roe were centered on the idea that the fetus is a person and therefore protected under the Fourteenth Amendment, which granted citizenship to newly emancipated slaves. The word and idea of *protection* are grafted from the phrasing of the Fourteenth Amendment and may be the origin of the term *fetal protection*. The Court, however, rejected this claim outright and stated explicitly that the fetus is not a person.

In a dissenting opinion, Justice Rehnquist said that rejecting the argument that a fetus is a person was tantamount to withdrawing the states' right to legislate this matter because at the time the Fourteenth Amendment was created, twenty-six states had laws restricting abortion. Thus, Rehnquist's logic went, if at the time of its passage the Fourteenth Amendment did not eliminate the states' right to restrict abortion, then how could the Supreme Court in 1973 eliminate that right in *Roe v. Wade*?

In his dissent, Rehnquist is not necessarily defending the argument that a fetus is a person; instead he is forging a different argument: that the state, not the federal government, has jurisdiction in determining whether abortion is restricted. For a discussion of Rehnquist's dissent, see John M. Riddle, *Eve's Herbs: A History of Contraception and Abortion in the West* (Cambridge: Harvard University Press, 1997), 6.

32. Risen and Thomas, *Wrath of Angels*, 125.

33. Ibid., 127.

34. Among those who explore the relationship between secular and biblical apocalypticism are Lee Quinby, *Anti-Apocalypse* (Minneapolis: University of Minnesota Press, 1995), and Boyer, *When Time Shall Be No More*.

35. Francis Schaeffer and C. Everett Koop, *Whatever Happened to the Human Race?* (Old Tappan, N.J.: Fleming H. Revell Co., 1979). In addition, Gospel Films distributed an entire "video curriculum" based on the film and the book. The package of three videotapes contained all five episodes of the film plus a study guide prepared by Jeremy C. Jackson. The video curriculum was an FSV Production directed by Frankie Schaeffer V and produced by Jim Buchfuehrer.

36. Risen and Thomas, *Wrath of Angels*, 127, 219.

37. Ibid., 232.

38. Schaeffer and Koop, *Whatever Happened to the Human Race?* 110, 195.

39. See Richard Dyer, *White* (New York: Routledge, 1999).

40. For discussions of these allegations and their legitimacy, see Robert G. Weisbord, *Genocide? Birth Control and the Black American* (Westport, Conn.: Greenwood Press, 1975); and Dorothy Roberts, *Killing the Black Body: Race, Reproduction and the Meaning of Liberty* (New York: Pantheon, 1997), esp. 98–103.

41. Milton C. Sernett, "The Efficacy of Religious Participation in the National Debates over Abolitionism and Abortion," *Journal of Religion* 64, 2 (April 1984): 212. Sernett is quoting Justice Taney's infamous opinion in the Dred Scott decision.

42. Milton C. Sernett, "The Rights of Personhood: The Dred Scott Case and the Question of Abortion," *Religion in Life* 49 (winter 1980): 470.

43. Ibid., 463.

44. Ibid., 464.

45. Ibid., 472.

46. Ibid., 474.

47. Ibid.

48. David Roediger, *The Wages of Whiteness: Race and the Making of the American Working Class* (London: Verso, 1991), 75.

49. Ibid., 74.

50. Ibid., 86.

51. Ibid., 81.

52. Strozier and Flynn, Introduction, in *Year 2000*, 3.

53. Klaus Theweleit, *Male Fantasies*, vol. 1, *Women, Floods, Bodies, History*, trans. Stephen Conway (Minneapolis: University of Minnesota Press, 1987), 12.

54. This same trope of the term *bigot* is used in Pierce, *Turner Diaries*, where the white supremacists are called "bigots" and "racists," just as the evangelical Christians are called "bigots" and "zealots" in *Gideon's Torch*. The trope comes from the fact that only the unsympathetic characters and unreliable narrators in each novel use the term, so the critique of them as racists, bigots, and zealots is undercut narratively.

55. Andrew Sullivan observes how conservatives view abortion and contraception as "the homosexualization of heterosexual sex" and link them to "nonprocreative trends among white Europeans . . . leading to a 'race death.' " See Sullivan, "Going Down Screaming," *New York Times Magazine*, October 11, 1998, 46.

56. Sara Diamond, *Not by Politics Alone: The Enduring Influence of the Christian Right* (New York: Guilford Press, 2000), 54.

57. For a discussion of how ideology is best understood as narrative in form, see Michael Denning, *Mechanic Accents: Dime Novels and Working-Class Culture in America* (London: Verso, 1987).

5. Making Time for America's Armageddon

1. See Faye Ginsburg, *Contested Lives: The Abortion Debate in an American Community* (Berkeley: University of California Press, 1989).

2. Paul Boyer, *When Time Shall Be No More: Prophecy Belief in Modern American Culture* (Cambridge: Harvard University Press, 1992), 88.

3. Timothy Weber, "Premillennialism and the Branches of Evangelical-

ism," in *The Variety of American Evangelicalism,* ed. Donald W. Dayton and Robert K. Johnson (Knoxville: University of Tennessee Press, 1991), 10.

4. Stephen O'Leary, *Arguing the Apocalypse: A Theory of Millennial Rhetoric* (New York: Oxford University Press, 1994), 178.

5. Ibid.

6. For an explanation of this phenomenon in terms of psychology, see Charles Strozier, *Apocalypse: On the Psychology of Fundamentalism in America* (Boston: Beacon Press, 1995); and Robert Robins and Jerrold Post, *Political Paranoia* (New Haven: Yale University Press, 1997).

7. For a discussion of narrative's descriptive and transformative qualities, see Tzvetan Todorov, *Genres in Discourse* (Cambridge: Cambridge University Press, 1990). Todorov, who coined the term *narratology* in 1969, aimed to "lift all of literary and cultural studies to the dignity of science," according to Wlad Godzich, *The Culture of Literacy* (Cambridge: Harvard University Press, 1994), 123. This structuralism of narratology was later challenged both by poststructuralist theories of narrative and by postclassical narratology. See David Herman, ed., *Narratologies: New Perspectives on Narrative Analysis* (Columbus: Ohio State University Press, 1999).

8. See Frank Kermode, *The Sense of an Ending: Studies in the Theory of Fiction* (Oxford: Oxford University Press, 1996); and idem, "Apocalypse and the Moderns," in *Visions of Apocalypse: End or Rebirth?* ed. Saul Friedlande, Gerald Holton, Leo Marx, and Eugene Skolnikoff (New York: Holmes and Meier, 1985), 84–108.

9. Godzich, *Culture of Literacy,* 130–31.

10. Catherine Keller, *Apocalypse Now and Then* (Boston: Beacon Press, 1996), 116.

11. For the sake of brevity and focus, I have grossly oversimplified the relationship among narrative, time, and history, which whole schools of criticism have debated. My analysis is influenced by what Mark Currie identifies as a "certain direction in criticism—a path back to history but concerned to displace historicism with the temporal aporias of narrative time, a certain mix between historical writing and a psychoanalysis of exclusion in the construction of identity, a self-conscious textuality in which material processes are transposed into stories and metaphors." See Currie, *Postmodern Narrative Theory* (New York: St. Martins, 1998), 94. For those engaged by such criticism, it would be more precise for me to discuss historicist—rather than historical—time as something juxtaposed to narrative time.

12. Frederic Jameson, as quoted in Paul Gilroy, *The Black Atlantic: Modernity and Double Consciousness* (Cambridge: Harvard University Press, 1993), 196. See also Jameson, *The Political Unconscious: Narrative as a Socially Symbolic Act* (London: Methuen, 1980). For an interesting discussion of how Jameson's work—as well as Hayden White's *Metahistory: The Historical Imagination of Nineteenth-Century Europe* (Baltimore: Johns Hopkins University Press,

1978)—assumes that narrative is part of a "realm of sub- or pretextuality," see Nancy Armstrong and Leonard Tennenhouse, "History, Poststructuralism, and the Problem of Narrative," *Narrative* 1, 1 (1993): 50–52.

13. Ralph Ellison, as quoted in Gilroy, *Black Atlantic*, 202.

14. Paul Gilroy refers to Homi Bhabha to make this point. Narrative time is a "double-time," as Homi Bhabha calls it, which characterizes the modern nation and narrates its people both as "historical objects of a nationalist pedagogy" and as political subjects who conform to or reject that nationalism (ibid.). See also Homi Bhabha, "DissemiNation: Time, Narrative and the Margins of the Modern Nation," in *Nation and Narration*, ed. Homi K. Bhabha (London and New York: Routledge, 1990), 291–322.

15. Godzich, *Culture of Literacy*, 132.

16. Godzich explains that decision making does not stop time but "rushes time" (ibid.). Keller, *Apocalypse Now and Then*, 85, discusses killing time.

17. Godzich, *Culture of Literacy*, 132.

18. Boyer, *When Time Shall Be No More*, plate.

19. Sara Diamond, *Spiritual Warfare: The Politics of the Christian Right* (Boston: South End Press, 1989), 163.

20. This is CBN's mission statement as it appeared on its website in 1995. Today the statement includes "the Internet and New Media" in the list of communications. See (http://www.cbn.org/about/).

21. This description of the "Signs of the Times" series was listed on the website for Christian Broadcasting Network (http://www.cbn.com) in 1995. The program was broadcast on television during the week of May 8 through 12, 1995, and subsequently.

22. Sara Diamond, *Roads to Dominion: Right-Wing Movements and Political Power in the United States* (New York: Guilford Press, 1995), 98.

23. Gustav Niebuhr, "Stumping Gramm Invokes Second Coming of Christ," *New York Times*, September 23, 1995, 9.

24. Ibid.

25. O'Leary, *Arguing the Apocalypse*, 179.

26. Ibid., 180.

27. John B. Judis, *William F. Buckley: Patron Saint of the Right* (New York: Simon and Schuster, 1988), 320.

28. Patrick Allitt, *Catholic Intellectuals and Conservative Politics in America, 1950–1985* (Ithaca, N.Y.: Cornell University Press, 1995), 140–41.

29. This wording appears in a letter from George H. Williams to Dr. John F. Hillabrand, dated September 2, 1972. George Huntston Williams Collection, bMS 438 and bMS 404. Andover-Harvard Theological Library, Harvard Divinity School. All George H. Williams letters quoted in this chapter can be found in this collection.

30. Bozell quotes the letter in his letter to John F. Hillabrand, dated March 3, 1972 (George H. Williams collection).

31. Allitt, *Catholic Intellectuals and Conservative Politics*, 144. Bozell makes this stipulation clear in his letter to Hillabrand, March 3, 1972 (George H. Williams collection).

32. A letter from Joseph Stanton, M.D., president of the Value of Life Committee based in Boston, represents the inception of AUL without mention of the Society for a Christian Commonwealth (George H. Williams collection).

33. This description, a summary of Brent Bozell, "The Confessional Tribe" (*Triumph*, July 1970, 11–15), appears in the letter by Williams, to John F. Hillabrand, September 2, 1972.

34. Allitt, *Catholic Intellectuals and Conservative Politics*, 187.

35. This wording is attributed to one of the founders of the Society for a Christian Commonwealth who wrote to Williams during the controversy over its relationship with Americans United for Life (George H. Williams Collection).

36. Robert A. Miller, "The Rule of Demons," *Triumph*, February 1972, 16.

37. Letter to George H. Williams, August 27, 1971 (George H. Williams Collection).

38. For discussion on apocalyptic belief and anticommunist rhetoric, see Boyer, *When Time Shall Be No More*. In her examination of the antiabortion movement and the apocalyptic framework of the New Right, Rosalind Petchesky notes that "feminists are the 'communists' of the 1970s and 1980s" (*Abortion and Woman's Choice* [Boston: Northwestern University Press, 1984], 246).

39. Bozell, "Confessional Tribe," 11.

40. Charles Rice, "The Population Commission Report: New Mandate for the Pro-Life Movement," *Triumph*, May 1972, 11–15. Michael Cuneo discusses the "contraceptive-mentality thesis," arguing that "Joseph Scheidler and other Catholic conservatives became increasingly more convinced that contraception (of all things) was significantly to blame" when "America's abortion rate continued to escalate throughout the late seventies" (Cuneo, *Smoke of Satan: Conservative and Traditionalist Dissent in Contemporary American Catholicism* [New York: Oxford University Press, 1997], 61). *Triumph* demonstrates that the contraceptive mentality idea was prominent among Catholic conservatives in the early 1970s too.

41. Rice, "Population Commission Report," 15.

42. Bozell, "Confessional Tribe," 12.

43. Ibid., 14.

44. Other early pro-life writers engaged McLuhan's notions without disparaging them. Donald De Marco wrote about McLuhan's idea of the mechanical bride in relation to abortion, and he had McLuhan write a brief forward to his book *Abortion in Perspective: The Rose Palace or the Fiery Dragon* (Cincinnati, Ohio: Hiltz and Hayes Publishing, 1974). The book also acknowledges editors of *Triumph* magazine, Paul Marx, and of course Dr. J. C. Willke, owner of Hayes Publishing.

45. Allitt, *Catholic Intellectuals and Conservative Politics*, 156.

46. Ibid.

47. Ibid.

48. Bozell, "Confessional Tribe," 14.

49. Ibid., 12.

50. Ibid., 14–15.

51. Godzich, *Culture of Literacy*, 131.

52. James Risen and Judy L. Thomas, *Wrath of Angels: The American Abortion War* (New York: Basic Books, 1998), 21.

53. Ibid.

54. Michael Lawrence, "Present Imperfect," *Triumph*, July 1970, 8.

55. Ibid., 42.

56. Ibid., 9.

57. Ibid., 10.

58. Allitt, *Catholic Intellectuals and Conservative Politics*, 144, 157.

59. Lawrence, "Present Imperfect," 10.

60. "God and Woman at Catholic U," *Triumph*, April 1971, 21.

61. Ibid., 22.

62. Keller, *Apocalypse Now and Then*, 136; Keller is quoting Rebecca Chopp, *The Power to Speak: Feminism, Language, God* (New York: Crossroad, 1989), which puts forth a feminist theology.

63. Keller, *Apocalypse Now and Then*, 39.

64. Ibid., 314 n. 6.

65. Godzich, *Culture of Literacy*, 131.

66. Ibid., 131–32.

67. "America's War on Life" was the title of *Triumph*'s discussion of *Roe v. Wade*, March 1973, 17–32.

68. In his desire to build a Christian commonwealth, Bozell was militant and revolutionary in his thinking, but he did not actually believe revolution was within his reach. In "On Going to Jail," reflections written after an anti-abortion rally, Bozell wrote:

> The issue, be it noted, is not revolution. The necessity and wisdom of revolution are questions that do not properly arise unless you are in a position to make a revolution. Consideration of such questions at the present time may be entertaining and eventually instructive, even as it may be agonizing at another time; but for so far as we can see into the future the questions are academic.
>
> But the question of jail is not academic. It is not possible in America today to think seriously about being a Christian, much less about carrying out a public Christian apostolate, without also thinking about the possibility of jail or other discouragements, whether of lesser or greater sternness, which the state may throw up to serious Christianity.

(Bozell, "On Going to Jail," in *Mustard Seeds: A Conservative Becomes a Catholic* [Manassas, Va.: Trinity Communications, 1986], 183.)

69. "Catholic Abortion," *Triumph*, April 1971, 11.

70. Judis, *William F. Buckley*, 320.

71. L. Brent Bozell, "To Magnify the West," *National Review*, April 24, 1962; this article was reprinted in Bozell's autobiography, *Mustard Seeds*.

72. Mel Bradford, "Lincoln's New Frontier: A Rhetoric for Continuing Revolution, Part II," *Triumph*, June 1971, 17.

73. Ibid.

74. Ibid.

75. Allitt, *Catholic Intellectuals and Conservative Politics*, 161.

76. Ibid.

77. Bozell, "To Magnify the West," in *Mustard Seeds*, 20.

78. Bozell quotes the Second Vatican in his essay "On Going to Jail," written during January–April 1972, in *Mustard Seeds*, 190.

79. Paul Weyrich, "Blue Collar or Blue Blood? The New Right Compared with the Old Right," in *The New Right Papers*, ed. Robert W. Whitaker (New York: St. Martin's Press, 1982), 54–55, 57.

80. Ibid., 50.

81. William B. Hixson Jr., *Search for the America Right Wing: An Analysis of the Social Science Record, 1955–1987* (Princeton, N.J.: Princeton University Press, 1992), 230.

82. Ibid., 231.

83. Risen and Thomas, *Wrath of Angels*, 21; Allitt, *Catholic Intellectuals and Conservative Politics*, 158.

84. Weyrich, "Blue Collar or Blue Blood?" 51.

85. Allitt, *Catholic Intellectuals and Conservative Politics*, 155.

86. Weyrich, "Blue Collar or Blue Blood?" 51.

87. John Lofton, "The Media Attack on the Religious Right," in *The New Right at Harvard*, ed. Howard Phillips (Vienna, Va.: Conservative Caucus, Inc., 1983), 83.

88. Allitt, *Catholic Intellectuals and Conservative Politics*, 142.

89. John A. Andrew III, *The Other Side of the Sixties: Young Americans for Freedom and the Rise of Conservative Politics* (New Brunswick, N.J.: Rutgers University Press, 1997), 17.

90. Robert Alan Goldberg, *Barry Goldwater* (New Haven: Yale University Press, 1995), 139.

91. Andrew, *Other Side of the Sixties*.

92. Barry Goldwater, *The Conscience of a Conservative* (Shepherdsville, Ky.: Victor Publishing, 1960), 12.

93. Ibid., 62.

94. Ibid., 73.

95. Paul Weyrich, "Cultural Conservatism and the Conservative Movement," in *Cultural Conservatism: Theory and Practice*, ed. William S. Lind and

William H. Marshner (Washington, D.C.: Free Congress Research and Education Foundation, Inc., 1991), 20.

96. References to Spanish Carlists indicate that the memory of Bozell's early militancy is fresh. William S. Lind and William H. Marshner, *Cultural Conservatism: Toward a New National Agenda* (Institute for Cultural Conservatives, 1987); Marshner was senior scholar at the institute.

97. Quoted in Goldberg, *Barry Goldwater*, 139.

6. Narrating Enemies

1. Jodi Dean, *Aliens in America: Conspiracy Cultures from Outerspace to Cyberspace* (Ithaca, N.Y.: Cornell University Press, 1998); Robert S. Robins and Jerrold M. Post, M.D., *Political Paranoia: The Psychopolitics of Hatred* (New Haven: Yale University Press, 1997); Mark Fenster, *Conspiracy Theories: Secrecy and Power in American Culture* (Minneapolis: University of Minnesota Press, 1999); Patrick O'Donnell, *Latent Destinies: Cultural Paranoia and Contemporary U.S. Narrative* (Durham, N.C.: Duke University Press, 2000); Chip Berlet and Matthew N. Lyons, *Right-Wing Populism in America: Too Close for Comfort* (New York: Guilford Press, 2000); and Daniel Pipes, *Conspiracy: How the Paranoid Style Flourishes and Where It Comes From* (New York: Free Press, 1997).

2. Fenster, *Conspiracy Theories*, 67.

3. Ibid.

4. Louis Althusser, *Lenin and Philosophy* (London: New Left Books, 1971).

5. Stanley Hauerwas, "Why Abortion Is a Religious Issue," in *The Ethics of Abortion: Pro-Life vs. Pro-Choice*, ed. Robert M. Baird and Stuart E. Rosenbaum (Buffalo, N.Y.: Prometheus Books, 1993), 163.

6. Ibid.

7. Ibid., 162.

8. Barbara Duden, *Disembodying Women: Perspectives on Pregnancy and the Unborn* (Cambridge: Harvard University Press, 1993), 104.

9. Daniel Callahan, "The Sanctity of Life," in *Updating Life and Death: Essays in Ethics and Medicine*, ed. Donald R. Cutler (Boston: Beacon Press, 1969), 208.

10. Ibid.

11. Ibid., 199.

12. Ibid., 197.

13. As quoted ibid., 186.

14. Michael Bray, *A Time to Kill* (Portland, Ore.: Advocates for Life Publications, 1994), 69.

15. James Risen and Judy L. Thomas, *Wrath of Angels: The American Abortion War* (New York: Basic Books, 1998), 88, 84.

16. Bray, *Time to Kill*, 172.

17. Ibid., 69.

18. Risen and Thomas, *Wrath of Angels*, 96.

19. Barbara Duden makes this claim: "The substantive use of the notion life in Western society has unacknowledged Christian roots. Its semantic field barely coincides with the Hindu and Buddhist cognates and constitutes a specific development beyond the Hebrew and Koranic usages of the corresponding expressions" (*Disembodying Women*, 102). Joseph Boyle suggests that "The relatively recent language of sanctity of life originally developed, at least within the Catholic tradition, within the normative framework that emphasized the divine dominion of human life" ("The Sanctity of Life and Its Implications: Reflections on James Keenan's Essay," in *Choosing Life: A Dialogue on* Evangelium Vitae, ed. Kevin Wm. Wildes, S.J., and Alan C. Mitchell, 71–76 [Washington, D.C.: Georgetown University Press, 1997], 71).

20. James F. Keenan, "The Moral Argumentation of *Evangelium Vitae*," in Wildes and Mitchell, *Choosing Life: A Dialogue on* Evangelium Vitae, 55.

21. Ibid., 56.

22. Alan C. Mitchell, "The Use of Scripture in Evangelium Vitae: A Response to James Keenan," in Wildes and Mitchell, *Choosing Life: A Dialogue on* Evangelium Vitae, 63.

23. Keenan, "Moral Argumentation of *Evangelium Vitae*," 53.

24. Ibid., 56.

25. Boyle, "Sanctity of Life and Its Implications," 72.

26. Mitchell, "Use of Scripture in Evangelium Vitae," 68.

27. John Conley, "Narrative, Act, Structure: John Paul II's Method of Moral Analysis," in Wildes and Mitchell, *Choosing Life: A Dialogue on* Evangelium Vitae, 4.

28. *Evangelium Vitae*, Encyclical Letter addressed by the Supreme Pontiff John Paul II to the Bishops, Priests, and Deacons, Men and Women Religious, Lay Faithful, and All People of Good Will on the Value and Inviolability of Human Life (Vatican City, 1995), sec. 17. Additional citations, referring to the numbered sections of the encyclical, are given within parentheses in the text.

29. James F. Childress, "Moral Rhetoric and Moral Reasoning: Some Reflections on *Evangelium Vitae*," in Wildes and Mitchell, *Choosing Life: A Dialogue on* Evangelium Vitae, 31.

30. Priests for Life is an organization that also bridges the gap to Protestant millennialists. The group's leader, Father Frank Pavone, is sanctioned both by the National Right to Life Committee and the Vatican and "brings into play active collaboration with militant direct action movements in the U.S., in particular Joseph Scheidler's Pro-Life Action League." See the briefing paper *Priests for Life: A New Era in Antiabortion Activism* (New York: Institute for Democracy Studies, 2001), 1. Priests for Life also employs some tactics described by Life Dynamics, as is evidenced in a full-page advertisement that appeals to

those who are worried about the "exploitation of women," ostensibly by way of abortion injuries and murderous doctors. The ad appeared in *USA Today*, June 13, 2001, 7D.

31. Duden, *Disembodying Women*, 103.

32. Sara Diamond, *Spiritual Warfare* (Boston: South End Press, 1989), 176.

33. Fenster, *Conspiracy Theories*, 67.

34. Paul Marx is quoted in Caryle Murphy, "Family Values Feud," *Washington Post*, April 8, 2000. Marx's books include *The Death Peddlers* (Collegeville, Minn.: Saint John's University Press, 1971) and *Confessions of a Pro-Life Missionary* (Gaithersburg, Md.: Human Life International, 1988).

35. Marx, *Confessions of a Pro-Life Missionary*, 268.

36. Marx, *Death Peddlers*, 185.

37. Murphy, "Family Values Feud."

38. Linda Kintz, *Between Jesus and the Market: The Emotions That Matter in Right-Wing America* (Durham, N.C., and London: Duke University Press, 1997), 15.

39. Ibid., 260.

40. Mary Guiden, "Abortion's Guerrilla War," *The Nation*, June 26, 2000, 6.

41. Ibid., 7.

42. Ibid.

43. Ibid.

44. Tom Burghardt, *Dialectics of Terror: A National Directory of the Direct Action Anti-Abortion Movement and Their Allies* (San Francisco: Bay Area Coalition for Our Reproductive Rights, 1995).

45. Hillary Frey and Miranda Kennedy, "Abortion on Trial," *The Nation*, June 18, 2001, 12–16.

46. Tracie Stein is quoted ibid., 14.

47. Charlene Carres, attorney and lobbyist, is quoted in Theresa M. McGovern, *Building Broader Women's Health/Reproductive Health Care Coalitions in the States: A Look at Idaho, Texas, and Florida* (New York: Open Society Institute, 2000), 28–29.

48. Frey and Kennedy, "Abortion on Trial," 14.

49. Surina Khan, *Calculated Compassion: How the Ex-Gay Movement Serves the Right's Attack on Democracy* (Somerville, Mass.: Political Research Associates, 1998), 19.

50. Khan explains that the leader of the National Association for the Research and Therapy of Homosexuality, Dr. Joseph Nicolosi, reports a 33-percent success rate: "Nicolosi states that one third of patients experience no change, one third experience some change, and one third are cured. But by 'cure' he doesn't mean that people don't experience homosexual feelings, but rather 'the intensity of the attractions diminish to the point of being insignificant.' . . . In other words, reparative therapists attempt to teach gay men and

lesbians to repress their sexual identity, yet have a dismal failure rate of 67% in trying to reach this goal, even by their own questionable standards" (ibid., 9).

51. Ibid., 21.

52. Andrew Sullivan, "Going Down Screaming," *New York Times Magazine*, October 11, 1998, 49.

53. Khan, *Calculated Compassion*, 1.

54. Laurie Goodstein, "Woman Behind Anti-Gay Ads Sees Christians as Victims," *New York Times*, August 13, 1998.

55. For a more specific discussion of how writing splits what it doubles, see Jacques Derrida, *Of Grammatology* (Baltimore: Johns Hopkins University Press, 1974), 36.

56. Kintz, *Between Jesus and the Market*, 269–70.

57. For a frank discussion of unethical providers from a pro-choice perspective, read K. Kaufmann, *The Abortion Resource Handbook* (New York: Simon and Schuster, 1997), esp. chap. 1, "Finding a Pro-Choice Clinic and Avoiding Fakes," 12–13.

58. The standard pro-choice history of legalized abortion begins with the inception of the American Medical Association and the consequential outlawing of abortion in the 1860s, the innovations of Margaret Sanger as the founder of the birth control movement during the 1910s, the fears of thalidomide and German measles as exemplified in the Sherrie Finkbine case in the 1960s, and the botched, illegal abortions that resulted in the deaths of many women throughout the first half of the twentieth century. This history tends to omit any indictment of Sanger's eugenics and a larger critique of the first wave of feminism as based on social Darwinism, nation building, and the bodily integrity of white women; to ignore the grassroots efforts of Pat Maginnis, Lana Phelan, and Rowena Gurner who founded the Society for Humane Abortion and to feature instead Sarah Weddington, the young Texas lawyer who argued *Roe v. Wade;* and to see *Roe* and constitutional rights as the pinnacle of reproductive freedom rather than a compromise of the efforts to repeal laws that regulated reproductive matters such as abortion. On first-wave feminism, see Louise Michele Newman, *White Women's Rights: The Racial Origins of Feminism in the United States* (New York: Oxford University Press, 1999); and Stephanie Athey, "Eugenic Feminisms in Late Nineteenth-Century America," *Genders* 31 (2000). On the Society for Humane Abortion, see Ninia Baehr, *Abortion without Apology: A Radical History for the 1990s* (Boston: South End Press, 1990).

59. Norma McCorvey, *I Am Roe* (New York: HarperCollins, 1994); idem, *Won by Love* (Nashville: Thomas Nelson Publishers, 1997); all page references to these volumes are given in the text in parentheses.

60. Fenster, *Conspiracy Theories*, 167.

61. Debbie Nathan, "The Death of Jane Roe," *Village Voice*, April 30, 1996, 38.

62. Ibid., 39.

63. Mike Doughney and Lauren Sabina Kneisly, "Norma McCorvey's Strange Bedfellows," Biblical America Resistance Front home page (http://www.barf.org). Last updated November 13, 1999.

Conclusion

1. "Stem Cell Research: Analysis of George W. Bush's Embryonic Stem Cell Decision" was posted at the American Life League website no later than a day after Bush's decision. It provides the entire text of the president's speech with point-by-point commentary. Available at (http://www.all.org/issues/scanalyz.htm).

2. Laurie Goodstein, "Abortion Foes Split Over Plan on Stem Cells," *New York Times*, August 12, 2001, 26.

3. Denise Renfrow, Deva Gatica, and Cody Shaw, "Speech and Video at Club Meeting Declared Offensive by Protesters," *The Advocate* 8 (November 11, 2001), a student newspaper of Mount Hood Community College in Oregon, not to be confused with de Parrie's magazine, *Life Advocate*. Available at (http://www.advocate-online.net/archives/fall01/110901/guestcolumn.html).

4. "Falwell Apologizes to Gays, Feminists, Lesbians," Cable News Network, September 14, 2001. Available at (http://www.cnn.com/2001/US/09/14/Falwell.apology/index.html).

5. Horsley made this comment in the film *Soldiers in the Army of God*, Home Box Office, 2001.

6. *Morning Edition*, November 8, 2001, National Public Radio. Andy Bowers's comments are taken from a transcript of the broadcast, supplied by Burrelle's Information Services.

7. Renfrow, Gatica, and Shaw, "Speech and Video at Club Meeting Declared Offensive."

8. "United States of America vs. James Charles Kopp: A Conclusion in Search of Its Evidence," posted at the Life Dynamics website (http://www.ldi.org/kopp.htm).

9. Gore Vidal, "The Meaning of Timothy McVeigh," *Vanity Fair*, September 2001, 347–53, 409–15.

10. Robyn R. Warhol, "Guilty Cravings: What Feminist Narratology Can Do for Cultural Studies," in *Narratologies*, ed. David Herman (Columbus: Ohio State University Press), 343.

11. "Vaginally defeated" is a phrase used by Neal Horsley in the film *Soldiers in the Army of God*.

12. Michael Bray, *A Time to Kill* (Portland, Ore.: Advocates for Life Publications, 1994), 156.

13. Mildred Jefferson, a founder of National Right to Life Committee, is

known for her apocalyptic stance against abortion and was featured in the movie *Whatever Happened to the Human Race*. Alan Keyes, a 1996 Republican presidential candidate and former ambassador to the United Nations Economic and Social Council, has increasingly adopted apocalyptic rhetoric to discuss abortion and has defined violating innocent human life as the common denominator of terrorism and abortion. See "Keyes Declares Abortion as Another Form of Terrorism," *Dominion Post*, November 2, 2001, available at (http:/www.dominionpost.com/a/news/2001/110/02/ae); also, Keyes, "A Conservative's View: Restoring America after September 11," transcript of an address given by Keyes at Hobart and William Smith Colleges, November 29, 2001. When I asked him publicly whether abortion was an eschatological sign of the end times, Keyes ultimately said, "So in that sense I guess I would say I have a kind of urgent view. I wouldn't call it apocalyptic, but I do think that it's an urgent sense of the fateful significance of the whole constellation of issues that we're faced with here—that have implications, by the way, that actually even go beyond our own survival, because some of the evil seeds we plant, this cloning thing, I was talking about a few minutes ago." And finally, he said, "so yeah, so I have a sense that we're in very fateful times, and I just hope we'll take our responsibility here seriously." The exchange is available at (http://www.hws.edu/news/speakers/transcripts/keyespresforum.asp).

14. According to Mark Currie, Jacques "Derrida makes it quite clear that the common denominator that links histories together into a general, metaphysical concept of history more than another is linearity, the implication that one thing leads to another, which supports 'an entire system of implications (teleology, eschatology, elevating and interiorising accumulation of meaning, a certain type of traditionality, a certain concept of continuity, of truth, etc.).' " See Currie, *Postmodern Narrative Theory* (New York: St. Martin's Press, 1998), 79.

15. For a discussion of the dream life of political violence, see Arthur Redding, *Raids on Human Consciousness: Writing, Anarchism, and Violence* (Columbia: University of South Carolina Press, 1998), 30–70.

16. Currie, *Postmodern Narrative Theory*, 90.

17. The text of President Bush's August 9, 2001, address is available at the American Life League website (http://www.all.org/issues/scanalyz.htm).

18. Ibid. See also, George W. Bush, "Stem Cell Science and the Preservation of Life," *New York Times*, August 12, 2001, 13.

Selected Bibliography

Primary Sources

In addition to the publications listed below, pro-life periodicals were a rich source of information. In particular, I read many issues of *Celebrate Life*, *Human Life Review*, *Life Advocate*, *National Right to Life News*, and *Triumph*. The library at Political Research Associates in Somerville, Massachusetts, was a major source for these items. I also frequented pro-life websites, including those of Life Dynamics, Operation Save America, Missionaries to the Unborn, Life Enterprises, Priests for Life, and American Life League.

Army of God. Revised and expanded. Obtained from Political Research Associates, Somerville, Mass., n.d.

Bozell, L. Brent. "The Confessional Tribe." *Triumph*, July 1970, 11–15.

——. *Mustard Seeds: A Conservative Becomes a Catholic*. Manassas, Va.: Trinity Communications, 1986.

Bray, Michael. *A Time to Kill: A Study Concerning the Use of Force and Abortion*. Portland, Ore.: Advocates for Life Publications, 1994.

Brennan, William. *Abortion Holocaust: Today's Final Solution*. St. Louis, Mo.: Landmark Press, 1983.

Colson, Charles. *Born Again*. Old Tappan, N.J.: Chosen Books, 1976.

Colson, Charles, and Ellen Santili Vaughn. *Kingdoms in Conflict*. Grand Rapids, Mich.: Zondervan, 1987.

Colson, Charles, and Ellen Vaughn. *Gideon's Torch: A Novel*. Dallas, Tex.: Word Publishers, 1995.

Crutcher, Mark. *Firestorm: A Guerrilla Strategy for a Pro-Life America*. Denton, Tex.: Life Dynamics, Incorporated, 1992.

De Marco, Donald, with a foreword by Marshall McLuhan. *Abortion in Perspective: The Rose Palace or the Fiery Dragon*. Cincinnati, Ohio: Hiltz and Hayes Publishing, 1974.

de Parrie, Paul. *Haunt of Jackals: A Novel*. Wheaton, Ill.: Crossway Books, 1991.

Farris, Michael. *Guilt by Association: A Novel*. Nashville, Tenn.: Broadman and Holman Publishers, 1997.

Hilgers, Thomas W., Dennis J. Horan, and David Mall. *New Perspectives on Human Abortion*. Frederick, Md.: University Publications of America, 1981.

Koop, C. Everett. "Postabortion Syndrome: Myth or Reality?" *Health Matrix* 7, 2 (summer 1989): 42–44.

——. *The Right to Live; The Right to Die*. Wheaton, Ill.: Tyndale House Publishers, 1976.

Marx, Paul. *Confessions of a Pro-Life Missionary*. Gaithersburg, Md.: Human Life International, 1988.

——. *The Death Peddlers: War on the Unborn*. Collegeville, Minn.: Saint John's University Press, 1971.

McCorvey, Norma, with Gary Thomas. *Won by Love: Norma McCorvey, Jane Roe of Roe v. Wade, Speaks Out for the Unborn as She Shares Her New Conviction for Life*. Nashville, Tenn.: Thomas Nelson Publishers, 1997.

Nathanson, Bernard M., with Richard N. Ostling. *Aborting America*. Garden City, N.J.: Doubleday, 1979.

National Right to Life Committee. "When Does Life Begin? Abortion and Human Rights." Pamphlet. 1993.

Reagan, Ronald. *Abortion and the Conscience of the Nation*. Nashville, Tenn.: Thomas Nelson Publishers, 1984.

Rice, Charles. "Can the Killing of Abortionists Be Justified?" *Wanderer*, September 1, 1994. Reprinted on the Internet at (http://www.trosch.org).

——. "The Death Penalty Dilemma." *New American*, April 4, 1994, 23–24.

Schaeffer, Francis A. *A Christian Manifesto*. Westchester, Ill.: Crossway Books, 1981.

Schaeffer, Francis, and C. Everett Koop. *Whatever Happened to the Human Race?* Old Tappan, N.J.: Fleming H. Revell Co., 1979.

Scheidler, Joseph. *Closed: 99 Ways to Stop Abortion*. Toronto and Lewiston, N.Y.: Life Cycle Books, 1985.

Terry, Randall. *Accessory to Murder*. Brentwood, Tenn.: Wolgemuth and Hyatt, 1990.

Willke, Dr. and Mrs. J. C. *Abortion: Questions and Answers*. Cincinnati, Ohio: Hayes Publishing, 1985.

Williams, George H., Collection, bMS 438 and bMS 404. Andover-Harvard Theological Library, Harvard Divinity School.

Secondary Sources

In addition to the following items, I also relied on the now defunct pro-choice periodical *The Body Politic*.

Adams, Alice. *Reproducing the Womb: Images of Childbirth in Science, Feminist Theory, and Literature*. Ithaca, N.Y.: Cornell University Press, 1994.

Allitt, Patrick. *Catholic Intellectuals and Conservative Politics in America, 1950–1985*. Ithaca, N.Y.: Cornell University Press, 1993.

Baehr, Ninia. *Abortion without Apology: A Radical History for the 1990s*. Boston: South End Press, 1990.

Baird-Windle, Patricia, and Eleanor J. Bader. *Targets of Hatred: Anti-Abortion Terrorism*. New York: Palgrave, 2001.

Berlet, Chip, and Matthew N. Lyons. *Right-Wing Populism in America: Too Close for Comfort*. New York: Guilford Press, 2000.

Blanchard, Dallas. *The Anti-Abortion Movement and the Rise of the Religious Right: From Polite to Fiery Protest*. New York: Twayne Publishers, 1994.

Blanchard, Dallas, and Terry J. Prewitt. *Religious Violence and Abortion: The Gideon Project*. Gainesville: University Press of Florida, 1993.

Blee, Kathleen. *Women of the Klan: Racism and Gender in the 1920s*. Berkeley: University of California Press, 1991.

Boyer, Paul. *When Time Shall Be No More: Prophecy Belief in Modern American Culture*. Cambridge: Harvard University Press, 1992.

Burghardt, Tom. *Dialectics of Terror: A National Directory of the Direct Action Anti-Abortion Movement and Their Allies*. San Francisco: Bay Area Coalition for Our Reproductive Rights, 1995.

——. "Neo-Nazis Salute the Anti-Abortion Zealots." *Covert Action Quarterly* 52 (spring 1995): 26–33.

——. "State Citizenship: Patriot Ties to White Supremacists and Neo-Nazis." *Body Politic*, June/July 1995, 12–18.

Clarkson, Frederick. *Eternal Hostility: The Struggle between Theocracy and Democracy*. Monroe, Me.: Common Courage Press, 1997.

Cuneo, Michael W. "Life Battles: The Rise of Catholic Militancy within the American Pro-Life Movement." In *Being Right: Conservative Catholics in America*, ed. Mary Jo Weaver and R. Scott Appleby. Bloomington: Indiana University Press, 1995.

——. *The Smoke of Satan: Conservative and Traditionalist Dissent in Contemporary Catholicism*. New York: Oxford University Press, 1997.

Dees, Morris. *Gathering Storm: America's Militia Threat*. New York: Harper Perennial, 1997.

Diamond, Sara. *Not by Politics Alone*. New York: Guilford Press, 1998.

——. *Roads to Dominion: Right-Wing Movements and Political Power in the United States*. New York: Guilford Press, 1995.

——. *Spiritual Warfare: The Politics of the Christian Right*. Boston: South End Press, 1989.

DuBowski, Sandi. "Storming Wombs and Waco: How the Anti-Abortion and Militia Movements Converge." *Front Lines Research* 2, 2 (October 1996).

Duden, Barbara. *Disembodying Women: Perspectives on Pregnancy and the Unborn*. Cambridge: Harvard University Press, 1993.

Evangelium Vitae. Addressed by the Supreme Pontiff John Paul II to the Bishops, Priests, and Deacons, Men and Women Religious, Lay Faithful, and All People of Good Will on the Value and Inviolability of Human Life. Encyclical letter. Vatican City, 1995.

Fried, Marlene Gerber, ed. *From Abortion to Reproductive Freedom: Transforming a Movement*. Boston: South End Press, 1990.

Gibson, James William. *Warrior Dreams: Paramilitary Culture in Post-Vietnam America*. New York: Hill and Wang, 1994.

Ginsburg, Faye D. *Contested Lives: The Abortion Debate in an American Community*. Berkeley: University of California Press, 1989.

——. "Rescuing the Nation: Operation Rescue and the Rise of Anti-Abortion Militance." In *Abortion Wars: A Half Century of Struggle, 1950–2000*, ed. Rickie Solinger. Berkeley: University of California Press, 1998.

Ginsburg, Faye D., and Rayna Rapp, eds. *Conceiving the New World Order: The Global Politics of Reproduction*. Berkeley: University of California Press, 1995.

Godzich, Wlad. *The Culture of Literacy*. Cambridge: Harvard University Press, 1994.

Goldberg, Robert Alan. *Barry Goldwater*. New Haven: Yale University Press, 1995.

Hardisty, Jean. *Mobilizing Resentment: Conservative Resurgence from the John Birch Society to the Promise Keepers*. Boston: Beacon Press, 1999.

Hixson, William B., Jr. *Search for the American Right Wing: An Analysis of the Social Science Record, 1955–1987*. Princeton, N.J.: Princeton University Press, 1992.

Kaplan, Jeffrey. "Absolute Rescue: Absolutism, Defensive Action and the Resort to Force." In *Millennialism and Violence*, ed. Michael Barkun. London and Portland, Ore.: Frank Cass, 1996.

——. "America's Last Prophetic Witness: The Literature of the Rescue Movement." *Terrorism and Political Violence* 5, 3 (autumn 1993): 58–77.

Kaufmann, K. *The Abortion Resource Handbook*. New York: Simon and Schuster, 1997.

Keenan, James F. "The Moral Argumentation of *Evangelium Vitae*." In *Choosing*

Life: A Dialogue on Evangelium Vitae, ed. Kevin Wm. Wildes, S.J., and Alan C. Mitchell, 46–62. Washington, D.C.: Georgetown University Press, 1997.

Keller, Catherine. *Apocalypse Now and Then.* Boston: Beacon Press, 1996.

Khan, Surina. *Calculated Compassion: How the Ex-Gay Movement Serves the Right's Attack on Democracy.* Somerville, Mass.: Political Research Associates, 1998.

Kintz, Linda. *Between Jesus and the Market: The Emotions That Matter in Right-Wing America.* Durham, N.C., and London: Duke University Press, 1997.

Luker, Kristen. *Abortion and the Politics of Motherhood.* Berkeley: University of California Press, 1984.

Mason, Carol. "Terminating Bodies: Toward a Cyborg History of Abortion." In *Posthuman Bodies*, ed. Judith Halberstam and Ira Livingston. Bloomington: Indiana University Press, 1995. Revised as "Terminating Cyborgs: Options for Feminism," in Carol Mason, "Fundamental Opposition: Feminism, Narrative and the Abortion Debate." Ph.D. dissertation, University of Minnesota, 1996.

Merton, Andrew. *Enemies of Choice.* Boston: Beacon Press, 1981.

Mitchell, Alan C. "The Use of Scripture in *Evangelium Vitae:* A Response to James Keenan." In *Choosing Life: A Dialogue on* Evangelium Vitae, ed. Kevin Wm. Wildes, S.J., and Alan C. Mitchell, 63–69. Washington, D.C.: Georgetown University Press, 1997.

Morgan, Lynn M., and Meredith W. Michaels, eds. *Fetal Subjects, Feminist Positions.* Philadelphia: University of Pennsylvania Press, 1999.

Newman, Karen. *Fetal Positions: Individualism, Science, Visuality.* Stanford, Calif.: Stanford University Press, 1996.

Paige, Connie. *The Right-to-Lifers: Who They Are, How They Operate, Where They Get Their Money.* New York: Summit Books, 1983.

Petchesky, Rosalind. *Abortion and Woman's Choice: The State, Sexuality, and Reproductive Freedom.* Boston: Northeastern University Press, 1984.

Quinby, Lee. *Anti-Apocalypse: Exercises in Genealogical Criticism.* Minneapolis: University of Minnesota Press, 1994.

Reiter, Jerry. *Live from the Gates of Hell: An Insider's Look at the Antiabortion Underground.* Amherst, N.Y.: Prometheus Books, 2000.

Ridgeway, James. *Blood in the Face: The Ku Klux Klan, Aryan Nations, Nazi Skinheads, and the Rise of a New White Culture.* New York: Thunder's Mouth Press, 1990.

Risen, James, and Judy L. Thomas. *Wrath of Angels: The American Abortion War.* New York: Basic Books, 1998.

Roberts, Dorothy. *Killing the Black Body: Race, Reproduction, and the Meaning of Liberty.* New York: Pantheon Books, 1997.

Roediger, David R. *The Wages of Whiteness: Race and the Making of the American Working Class.* London: Verso, 1991.

Schulder, Diane, and Florynce Kennedy. *Abortion Rap: Testimony by Women Who Have Suffered the Consequences of Restrictive Abortion Laws.* New York: McGraw-Hill, 1971.

Sernett, Milton C. "Black Religion and the Question of Evangelical Identity." In

The Variety of American Evangelicalism, ed. Donald W. Dayton and Robert K. Johnson. Knoxville: University of Tennessee Press, 1991.

——. "The Efficacy of Religious Participation in the National Debates over Abolitionism and Abortion." *Journal of Religion* 64, 2 (April 1984): 205–20.

——. "The Rights of Personhood: The Dred Scott Case and the Question of Abortion." *Religion in Life* 49 (winter 1980): 461–76.

Solinger, Rickie, ed. *Abortion Wars: A Half Century of Struggle, 1950–2000*. Berkeley: University of California Press, 1998.

Stern, Kenneth. *A Force upon the Plain: The American Militia Movement and the Politics of Hate*. New York: Simon and Schuster, 1996.

Stock, Catherine McNicol. *Rural Radicals: Righteous Rage in the American Grain*. Ithaca, N.Y.: Cornell University Press, 1996.

Strozier, Charles, and Michael Flynn, eds. *The Year 2000: Essays on the End*. New York: New York University Press, 1997.

Theweleit, Klaus. *Male Fantasies*. Vol. 1. *Women, Floods, Bodies, History*. Trans. by Stephen Conway. Minneapolis: University of Minnesota Press, 1987.

Weber, Timothy. "Premillennialism and the Branches of Evangelicalism." In *The Variety of American Evangelicalism*, ed. Donald W. Dayton and Robert K. Johnson. Knoxville: University of Tennessee Press, 1991.

Index

media, print
Los Angeles Times, 82, 182
New York Times, 64, 137–38, 140–41, 187–88
Rolling Stone, 93
Star, 140, 145
Time, 100
Vanity Fair, 189
Village Voice, 183
Washington Post, 145
Wichita Eagle, 89
media, television
Boot Camp, 11
"Cracking Down," 93
Life Talk, 173–74
Millennium, 74
Nightline, 185
The 700 Club, 136, 188–89
"Signs of the Times: A Special Programming Report," 136–37
60 Minutes, 93
Soldiers in the Army of God, 1
20/20, 174
The X-Files, 74
Medical Board of California, 60–61
Midnight Call Ministries, 103
militias
and Christian Identity, 32
links with pro-life groups, 23
as manifestation of New War culture, 11
referenced by J. D. Alder, 35–36
and Eric Robert Rudolph, 27–28
and tax evasion, 23
and John Salvi III, 70
millennialism
and anti-Semitism, 103–5
and apocalypse, 75, 130–31
and L. Brent Bozell, 149–51
and George W. Bush, 191–93
as calendar for violence, 103
and Catholic political activism, 151–54
and crack babies, 73, 91, 95, 97–98
defined, 73
and Evangelium Vitae, 168–71
and Gallup survey, 74
in Gideon's Torch, 108, 129
as guiding principle of pro-life activism, 72–73, 97–98, 130–31

and the interpellation of enemies, 160–61, 172–74, 185–86
and narrative time, 133–36, 147–48
and the New Warrior, 87–88
as political fundraising tool, 137–38
and Reconstructionism, 77
and televangelists, 136–37
and Whatever Happened to the Human Race? 115–18
and white slavery, 123
and white supremacy, 78
See also postmillennialism; premillennialism
Millennium, 74
Millerites, 132, 133
Missionaries to the Pre-Born, 24, 78
Mitchell, Alan C., 167–68
modernism, 134
Molnar, Thomas, 143, 151
Moral Majority, 15, 114, 153, 171. See also Falwell, Jerry; New Right
The Morality of Political Action: Biblical Foundations, 156
Mount Hood Community College, 188

narrative
as articulation versus description, 7, 134, 191
as distinct from rhetoric, 6
and history, 134–35, 144, 193
and kairos, 134, 146–48, 161
and materiality, 8, 191, 193
and political mobilization, 133, 135–38
as productive versus repressive, 4, 191
narrative time
and L. Brent Bozell, 7, 144
and kairos, 147
and millennialists, 134–35
and political action, 137–38
narratologists, 134, 190
Nathanson, Bernard, 20
National Abortion Federation, 50
National Association for the Advancement of White People, 96
National Association to Repeal Abortion Laws (NARAL), 20
National Black Lesbian and Gay Leadership Forum, 177
National Lifesource, 48

projection, 26
pro-life legislation, 48–49, 62–65, 81–82
Pro-Life Non-Violent Action Project, 165
pro-life violence
    and guerrilla legislation, 48–49
    justification for, 47
    and the KKK, 36–37
    and natural law, 68–69
    shift in strategy, 49–53
    See also Army of God; clinic violence
Promise Keepers, 43–44, 105
Prophecy, 74

Quack the Ripper, 61, 175

racial suicide, 33–36, 79–80, 177–78
racism
    accusations of, 93, 113
    and castration anxiety, 36–37
    and David Duke, 44
    and the ex-gay campaign, 177
    in *Gideon's Torch*, 119–20, 122–23, 126
    and Norma McCorvey, 182–84,
        184–85
    and militias, 30–32
    and pro-life protests, 36
    and Promise Keepers, 43
    in *Whatever Happened to the Human
        Race?* 115, 117–18
Rambo: First Blood, 11, 12, 14, 28
Ramsey, Paul, 165
rapture, 132
Reagan, Ronald, 15, 109, 120, 138–39
*The Real Holocaust: The Attack on Unborn
    Children and Life Itself*, 39–40, 172
Reconstructionism, 77
Reed, Ralph, 178
Refuse and Resist's Reproductive Free-
    dom Task Force, 101–2
regeneration centers, 111, 123–24
Reiter, Jerry, 70–71, 75–78
Reno, Janet, 28
reproductive freedom, 8, 62
Republican National Coalition for Life,
    187
Republican National Convention, 76
retribution, 69–70, 72
Rice, Charles, 68–70, 142
Roberts, Dorothy, 91–92

Robertson, Pat, 136. See also *The 700 Club*
Robinson, Courtland, 81–82
*Rockefeller Commission Report on
    Population*, 142
Roe v. Wade
    and AUL, 140–41
    and the definition of life, 165
    and Norma McCorvey, 179
    and the Partial-Birth Abortion Ban
        Act, 81
    and Ronald Reagan, 120
    and *Dred Scott*, 120–22
Roediger, David, 122–23
Rolling Stone, 93
Ruby Ridge, Idaho, 28
Rudolph, Daniel, 29–30
Rudolph, Eric Robert, 27–28, 30–31, 78,
    87
Rushdoony, R. J., 77

sacred history, 107–8
Salvi, John, III, 66–68, 70, 88, 159
Sanderson, Robert, 27
Satanism, 141
Schaeffer, Francis, 109, 110, 114–15,
    117–18
Scheidler, Joseph, 57, 76
Schell City, Missouri, 31
Scott, Dred, v. Sandford, 120–21
secular humanism, 118
Seeds of Anarchy, 151
Sernett, Milton, 121–22
The 700 Club, 136, 188–89
Shannon, Rachelle ("Shelley"), 70, 190
"Signs of the Times: A Special Program-
    ming Report," 136–37
The Silent Scream, 20
Silver Shirts, 78
60 Minutes, 93
Slepian, Barnett, 49, 102–3, 172, 189
Society for a Christian Commonwealth
    (SCC), 68, 140–41
Soldiers in the Army of God, 1
Solemn Assembly, 106–8
Sons of Thunder, 144–45
Southen Poverty Law Center, 22, 23
Spectator, 103
Spring of Life, 102, 103
Star, 140, 145